Framers' Construction/ Beardian Deconstruction

Major Concepts in Politics and Political Theory

Garrett Ward Sheldon
General Editor

Vol. 18

PETER LANG
New York • Washington, D.C./Baltimore • Boston • Bern
Frankfurt am Main • Berlin • Brussels • Vienna • Oxford

S. Slonim

Framers' Construction/ Beardian Deconstruction

Essays on the Constitutional Design of 1787

PETER LANG
New York • Washington, D.C./Baltimore • Boston • Bern
Frankfurt am Main • Berlin • Brussels • Vienna • Oxford

Library of Congress Cataloging-in-Publication Data

Slonim, Shlomo.
Framers' construction/Beardian deconstruction: essays
on the constitutional design of 1787 / S. Slonim.
p. cm. — (Major concepts in politics and political theory; vol. 18)
Includes bibliographical references and index.
1. Constitutional history—United States. I. Title. II. Series.
KF4541 .S57 342.73'029—dc21 00-064767
ISBN 0-8204-4891-5
ISSN 1059-3535

Die Deutsche Bibliothek-CIP-Einheitsaufnahme

Slonim, Shlomo:
Framers' construction/Beardian deconstruction: essays
on the constitutional design of 1787 / S. Slonim.
–New York; Washington, D.C./Baltimore; Boston; Bern;
Frankfurt am Main; Berlin; Brussels; Vienna; Oxford: Lang.
(Major concepts in politics and political theory; 18)
ISBN 0-8204-4891-5

The paper in this book meets the guidelines for permanence and durability
of the Committee on Production Guidelines for Book Longevity
of the Council of Library Resources.

Printed in the United States of America

To Avigail, David

and family

Table of Contents

Acknowledgments

Each of the chapters in this volume first appeared as a separate article in a journal or volume as follows:

Chap. 1: *Journal of American History*, vol. 73 (1986), pp. 35-58.

Chap. 2: *Perspectives in American History*, (Charles Warren Center, Harvard University), New Series, vol. 3 (1987), pp. 173-206.

Chap. 3: *Law and History Review* (American Society for Legal History), vol.16 (1998), pp. 527-52, 563-66.

Chap. 4: *Connecticut Bar Journal*, vol. 49 (1975), pp. 391-410.

Chap. 5: *International Lawyer* (International Law Section of American Bar Association), vol. 9 (1975), pp. 117-20.

Chap. 6: *Columbia Journal of Transnational Law*, vol. 14 (1975), pp. 434-50.

Chap. 7: *Mid-America: An Historical Review*, vol. 81 (1999), pp. 125-146.

Chap. 8: *Studies in American Civilization* (Magnes Press for Hebrew University), Scripta Hierosolymitana, vol. 32 (1987), pp. 48-62.

Chap. 9: *Studies in American Political Development* (Cambridge University Press), vol. 14 (2000), pp. 1-19.

I am grateful to the publishers of the aforementioned journals and volumes for their kind permission to reprint in the present collection. Likewise, I wish to express my deep appreciation to

Professor Gordon S. Wood for permitting me to reproduce his response in *Law and History Review* (pp. 553-62), to my article in the same issue. The chart attached to chapter 1, on the origins of the Electoral College, first appeared in a reprint of that article by Garland Publishing Inc. (New American Nation series, vol. 5, pp. 323-25), and their consent to include the chart herein is much appreciated.

I also wish to thank the Awards Committee and the Annenberg Fund, both of the Hebrew University of Jerusalem, for generous grants to facilitate the appearance of the volume. Ms. Yehudit Avraham, of the Faculty of Humanities, and Professor Emily Budick, Chair of the Department of American Studies, were especially helpful in this matter. Ms. Naomi Landau of the Bloomfield Library at the Mt. Scopus campus of the University expeditiously provided me with bibliographic information on various occasions, and I gratefully acknowledge her help.

Mr. Don David Finkel of Leshon Limudim Ltd. worked assiduously to prepare this volume for publication, and his careful and devoted attention to every detail in the production process is greatly appreciated.

Abbreviations

AHR	*American Historical Review*
AJIL	*American Journal of International Law*
APSR	*American Political Science Review*
Beard, *Economic Interpretation*	Charles Beard, *An Economic Interpretation of the Constitution of the United States* (N.Y.: Macmillan, 1913, 1935)
Elliot, *State Debates*	Jonathan Elliot, ed., *The Debates in the Several State Conventions on the Adoption of the Federal Constitution*, 5 vols. (Philadelphia: Lippincott, 1881)
Farrand, *Records*	Max Farrand, ed., *The Records of the Constitutional Convention of 1787*, 4. vols., rev. ed. (New Haven: Yale University Press, 1937)
Farrand, *Framing of Constitution*	Max Farrand, *The Framing of the Constitution of the United States* (New Haven: Yale University Press, 1913)
JAH	*Journal of American History*
Madison, *Papers*	Robert Rutland et al., eds., *The Papers of James Madison*, 17 vols. (Chicago: University of Chicago Press, 1975-)

Poore, *State Constitutions*	Benjamin Poore, ed., *The Federal and State Constitutions, Colonial Charters and other Organic Laws of the United States*, 2 vols. (Washington, D.C.: Government Printing Office, 1870)
PSQ	*Political Science Quarterly*
Warren, *Supreme Court*	Charles Warren, *The Supreme Court in United States History*, 2 vols., rev. ed. (Boston: Little Brown, 1926)
Warren, *Making of Constitution*	Charles Warren, *The Making of the Constitution* (Boston: Little Brown, 1928)
WMQ	*William and Mary Quarterly*
Wood, *Creation*	Gordon S. Wood, *The Creation of the American Republic, 1776-1787* (Chapel Hill: University of North Carolina Press, 1969)

INTRODUCTION

It would be difficult to exaggerate the importance of the 1787 Constitutional Convention for the subsequent history of the United States. While the Declaration of Independence effectively severed the colonial tie with Britain, it did not guarantee that the thirteen emergent states would survive as a single national entity destined to expand across an entire continent and operate under a consistent democratic system of government for over two hundred years. Meeting at Philadelphia in the summer of 1787, the Founding Fathers were keenly and presciently aware of the fateful nature of their enterprise. In their eyes it represented a last-ditch attempt to forestall dismemberment of the Union. Repeatedly, in their pre-Convention correspondence and Constitutional Hall debates, they gave voice to the belief that failure at Philadelphia would spell chaos and anarchy and the inevitable disintegration of the Confederation into three or more units.

For a long time, this was the generally accepted interpretation of the seminal events of 1787. However, at the beginning of the twentieth century, Progressive historians presented a new version of the historical record. They contended that there was neither any real crisis nor any genuine fear of disintegration of the United States. A crisis atmosphere, they alleged, was artificially contrived in order to launch the Federalist revolution – to institute a new and powerful central government committed to safeguarding the economic interests of the propertied class in American society.

This revisionist thesis was enunciated as early as 1907 by J. Allen Smith in his classic study, *The Spirit of American Government*.[1] But

1 J. Allen Smith, *The Spirit of American Government* (N.Y.: Macmillan, 1907).

the foremost exponent of the revisionist school was Charles A. Beard, whose 1913 volume, *An Economic Interpretation of the Constitution of the United States,*[2] ushered in an entirely new era in the historiography of the Constitution. His study had an aura of scientific authority which helped "confirm" certain key facts with regard to the Philadelphia Convention. Unlike Smith and the other Progressive historians, Beard did not limit himself to mere assertion that the Framers were motivated by base considerations. He purported to have the hard evidence to "convict" them of deliberately drafting the provisions of the Constitution to serve economic ends. According to Beard, the Treasury records of the period revealed that the property holdings of the Convention delegates were concentrated essentially in "personalty": public securities, manufactures, trade and shipping. And these specific and distinctive forms of property allegedly reflected the Founders' particular class interest, leading them to draft a Constitution which would operate as a brake on the egalitarian demands of the lower classes. Thus, by extrapolation, the financial holdings of the Framers stamped their constitutional framework with an economic purpose. The Constitution was designed not to promote democracy but rather to frustrate expression of the popular will; it derived not from the Framers' altruistic concern for the fate of their country but from selfish concern for the fate of their economic holdings. In his sixth chapter, Beard identified and analyzed the basic features of the machinery of government established at Philadelphia that, on his reading, stamped the Constitution as an economic document. Moreover, he depicted the campaign for and against adoption of the Constitution as a typical class struggle in which the revolutionary element, the propertied commercial class, prevailed over the more passive element, the agrarian and small artisan classes.

The appearance of Beard's book in 1913 created a sensation in the United States. Americans were not conditioned to thinking of their Founding Fathers as ordinary mortals inspired by ulterior and selfish motives. If they were not the demigods of Thomas Jefferson's

2 Charles A. Beard, *An Economic Interpretation of the Constitution of the United States* (N.Y.: Macmillan, 1913, 1935).

description, they were at least true patriots dedicated to the security, welfare and unity of their country and to the adoption of a constitution "adequate to the exigencies of Government & the preservation of the Union."[3] An effort to depict them as mere selfish entrepreneurs who organized a constitutional "putsch" to secure their personal financial interests seemed too conspiratorial and too damning to be taken seriously. Only with the passage of time did the Beardian thesis seep into the American historical psyche, as textbook writers and historians began to endow the thesis with legitimacy.

Before too long, Beard's version of events became the new orthodoxy. By the 1940's, no serious scholar of American constitutional history could afford to overlook Beard's explanation of the Constitutional Convention and of the origins and operation of American government, and, especially, of the role granted to the court. Whether one accepted Beard's thesis in its entirety or in part, it was now the yardstick by which all analysis of the Founding was measured. To describe the U.S. Constitution, post-Beard, as "the most remarkable work . . . in modern times to have been produced by the human intellect, at a single stroke (so to speak) in its application to political affairs."[4] — the rapturous terms employed earlier by William Gladstone — was to risk being seen as hopelessly naive and simplistic.

A reaction was soon to set in. Starting in the latter part of the 1940's, Beard's findings were re-examined and found to be less scientific and reliable than earlier assumed. Thus, if Beard's revelations dominated discussions in the first half of the century, the second half was largely focused on assailing the tenability of the Beardian thesis. Well before the end of the century the thesis was in tatters, having been steadily and systematically discredited from a variety of angles.

The first to probe the premises of Beard's thesis was Douglass Adair, editor of the prestigious journal, *The William and Mary*

3 Resolution adopted by the United States in Congress Assembled, Feb. 21, 1787 in Charles C. Tansill (ed.) *Documents Illustrative of the Formation of the Union of the American States* (Washington D.C.: Gov't Printing Office, 1927), p. 46.

4 Letter to the committee in charge of the celebration of the Centennial Anniversary of the American Constitution, July 20, 1887; cited in John Bartlett, *Familiar Quotations*, 13th ed. (Boston: Little Brown, 1955), p. 534a.

Quarterly. In an article in that journal entitled "The Tenth Federalist Revisited,"[5] Adair challenged Beard's claim that Madison had enunciated an economic determinist interpretation of history in Federalist No. 10. Madison, intent on finding a means of overcoming the evil of factionalism, suggested that widening the perimeter of the unit of governance would yield a greater number of factions, allowing them to cancel out one another and thereby attenuating their influence. In the course of presenting this argument, Madison had stated that the primary cause for factions in society is the unequal distribution of property. Beard, seizing upon this comment, declared that he had discovered Marx in Madison. Madison had forthrightly revealed the fundamental economic considerations which underlay the promotion of the Constitution. That document was undisguisedly and indisputably a product of the now dominant class in American society and would serve their economic interests by securing property from the assaults of the propertyless masses. Rejecting this claim, Adair observed that while Madison attributed divisions within society to the unequal distribution of property, he nowhere portrayed the class struggle as the basic condition of all societies or suggested that laws and constitutions reflect the aims and desires of the dominant class in society. To attribute to Madison an economic determinist interpretation of American history was, in Adair's view, sheer fantasy. Adair's article knocked out one of the key props sustaining Beard's analysis; but the challenge, turning as it did on the interpretation of one number of the Federalist Papers, was not fatal to the Beard thesis.

While Adair had focussed on Beard's misinterpretation of Madison's political theory, Cecilia M. Kenyon found cause to query Beard's implicit hypothesis that the Antifederalists were more liberal and democratic than the pro-Constitution Federalists. Since, according to Beard, the Constitution was deliberately drafted as "a foil against the attacks of levelling democracy," the opponents of ratification, presumably, were those who were committed to

5 Douglass Adair, "The Tenth Federalist Revisited," *WMQ*, 3d ser., vol. 8 (1951), pp. 48-67.

democratic government and the widest participation of the citizenry therein. In an incisive article entitled "Men of Little Faith: The Anti-Federalists on the Nature of Representative Government,"[6] Kenyon, a member of the Department of Government at Smith College, effectively refuted the foregoing assumption by demonstrating that the Antifederalists were even less democratic and liberal than their Federalist opponents. The Antifederalists railed against undue reliance on elected officials and called for a stricter form of checks and balances and hence for a tighter pattern of the separation of powers. They did not object to the notion of judicial review, which the Constitution implied, and they found no fault in the restrictions imposed on the states under Article 1, Section 10 of the Constitution in relation to such matters as paper money and the sanctity of contracts. Essentially, Kenyon contended, the Antifederalists were localists who feared that the transfer of any authority from the states to the central government placed the liberties of Americans in jeopardy and set the stage for tyrannous rule.

In 1956, Beard's economic thesis was analyzed in great detail for the first time and subjected to withering criticism. Robert E. Brown, in his book *Charles Beard and the Constitution: A Critical Analysis of an Economic Interpretation of the Constitution,*[7] sought to refute, chapter by chapter, Beard's premises, evidence, and conclusions. Highlighting the internal inconsistencies in Beard's work, Brown emphasized the democratic thrust of the Constitution's draftsmen, the non-exclusivity of their concern with property, and their greater link with "realty" than with "personalty." After this "obsessive" critique, as Richard Hofstadter observed, the Beardian view "could never again enjoy an unchallenged position."[8] Though mightily challenged, however, the thesis did survive Brown's broadside, at least for a further two years.

6 Cecelia M. Kenyon, "Men of Little Faith: The Anti-Federalists on the Nature of Representative Government," *ibid.*, vol. 12 (1955), pp. 3-43.

7 Robert E. Brown, *Charles Beard and the Constitution: A Critical Analysis of an Economic Interpretation of the Constitution* (Princeton: Princeton Univ. Press, 1956).

8 Richard Hofstadter, *The Progressive Historians: Turner, Beard, Parrington* (N.Y.: Knopf, 1968), p. 223.

Forrest McDonald's 1958 magnum opus, *We the People: The Economic Origins of the Constitution*,[9] effectively refuted the "scientific" foundation stones upon which Beard had erected his analytical structure. As noted earlier, Treasury records had been utilized by Beard as principal evidence of the dominance of "personalty" interests – finance, shipping, public securities and manufactures – among the 55 participants of the Constitutional Convention. Beard had proceeded to argue, on the basis of this evidence, that the division over ratification of the Constitution was "between substantial personalty interests on the one hand and the small farming and debtor interests on the other." Nevertheless, he conceded that full substantiation of his thesis would require examination of the economic holdings of as many as possible of the one thousand and seven hundred delegates who voted in the state ratifying conventions. This is precisely what McDonald set out to do. Taking up the gauntlet thrown down by Beard, McDonald completed the research which Beard had left undone, and discovered that the economic distinction between the groups arrayed for and against the Constitution was "negligible." The residue of the Beardian thesis was now seriously compromised.

In 1961, Stanley Elkins and Eric McKitrick summarized much of the scholarly criticism of Beard's thesis in their article "The Founding Fathers: Young Men of the Revolution."[10] They too rejected the thesis, and concluded that the Constitutional Convention did not represent a Thermidorian reaction to the Revolution, the difference between the two events being more a factor of age than of ideology.

By the 1960's, then, Beard's interpretation of the adoption of the Constitution was largely discredited, and few scholars were prepared to accept the claim that the Founders were motivated by crude economic considerations or that the division between proponents and opponents of the Constitution revolved essentially around economic interests. However, various scholars continued to

9 Forrest McDonald, *We the People: The Economic Origins of the Constitution* (Chicago: Univ. of Chicago Press, 1958).

10 *PSQ*, vol. 76 (1961), pp. 181-216.

maintain that Beard's piercing questions were focused in the right direction, though his obsession with economic factors may have led him to overplay his hand. According to these historians, the Constitution nevertheless did represent a conservative reaction to the spirit of liberty released by the Revolution. The concerns which suffused the deliberations at the Philadelphia conclave of 1787 were not of a purely economic nature; they were linked to the social conditions in the states, to the problems of maintaining law and order. These were the considerations that induced the Framers to devise a powerfully centralized instrument of government of a type that would not have been dreamt of in 1776. This theme, which might be labelled neo-Beardianism, was taken up by such writers as Merrill Jensen,[11] Jackson Turner Main,[12] and, in particular, Gordon Wood.[13] Their works endowed the Progressive school of historical criticism with a new lease on life.[14]

Curiously, neither supporters nor detractors of Beard's thesis addressed its substance and essential conclusions. While Beard's methodology was assessed from a variety of angles, the gist of his claim – that the provisions of the Constitution manifestly reflected an economic purpose – remained strangely unchallenged, unexplored, indeed ignored. In his sixth chapter, "The Constitution as an Economic Document," Beard contended that the economic character and design were reflected in the machinery of government established under the Constitution. Key features of the American system of government – the separation of powers, checks and balances, staggered elections for different offices, indirect election of President and Senate, a complicated amendment process, and

11 Merrill Jensen, *The New Nation: A History of the United States During the Confederation, 1781-1789* (N.Y.: Knopf, 1950).

12 Jackson Turner Main, *The Antifederalist: Critics of the Constitution, 1781-1788* (Chapel Hill: Univ. of North Carolina Press, 1961).

13 Gordon Wood, *The Creation of the American Republic, 1776-1787* (Chapel Hill: Univ. of North Carolina Press, 1969).

14 Even Leonard W. Levy, no neo-Beardian, stated in the introduction to his edited anthology, *Essays on the Making of the Constitution* (N.Y.: Oxford Univ. Press, 1969), p. xxii: "Since the *Economic Interpretation*, historians have engaged in a prolonged debate, which probably defies settlement, on questions raised by Beard either directly or indirectly."

judicial review – were all devised, according to Beard, "to break the force of majority rule and prevent invasions of the property rights of minorities." Furthermore, Beard alleged, "the records of the proceedings in the Philadelphia Convention reveal the successive steps in the building of the framework of the government under the pressure of economic interests."[15]

This statement, I discovered to my great surprise, was totally unsupported by any evidence. Beard's discussions of the provisions of the Constitution were bereft of any reference to the debates at Philadelphia. Astonishingly, the thesis attributing an economic design to provisions of the Constitution had been postulated without any attempt to trace the evolution of the provisions at the Constitutional Convention, as revealed in the minutes of that assembly. Yet Beard himself acknowledged that the minutes of the Convention, as recorded by Madison and others, furnished the most important source for identifying the motives of the Founding Fathers. As he wrote:

> Doubtless, the most illuminating of these sources on the economic character of the Constitution are the records of the debates in the Convention, which have come down to us in fragmentary form; and a thorough treatment of material forces reflected in the several clauses of the instrument of government created by the grave assembly at Philadelphia would require a rewriting of the history of the proceedings in the light of the great interests represented there.[16]

This, of course, is exactly what Beard did not do,[17] and it led me to scrutinize the Records, as so conveniently edited by Max Farrand, in an effort to determine how far Beard's claim that economic considerations underlay the drafting of the various provisions of the Constitution accorded with the written record of the debates. My conclusions were incorporated in two articles which form the first two entries in this series.

15 Beard, *An Economic Interpretation*, pp. 152-53.
16 *Ibid.*, p. 153.
17 Remarkably enough, John Patrick Diggins seems to endorse a comment by Max Lerner to the effect that Beard "drew his citations from the Founders themselves." "Power and Authority in American History: The Case of Charles A. Beard and His Critics," *AHR*, vol. 86 (1981), p. 702.

The first deals with the origins of the Electoral College and reveals that antimajoritarianism did not lie at the heart of the College; rather, the Electoral College was an ingenious system for allaying the objections of the smaller and slave states to moving the selection of a President out of the Congress, where these two groups of states had respectively gained increments in voting. Thus, the Electoral College was deliberately, and not haphazardly adopted, and its purpose was not, as Beard would have it, to insulate the choice of the executive from popular influence, but to ensure that the President would be elected by a procedure that mirror-imaged the federal Congress.

The second essay focuses on the extent to which major provisions of the Constitution were derived from, and modeled after, the pre-existing state constitutions; and it underscores the Marxist roots of Beard's thesis.

The third entry in the series challenges the neo-Beardian thesis presented by Gordon Wood and seeks to demonstrate that his social analysis of the Constitutional Convention is no more tenable than Beard's economic interpretation. The primary aim of the Framers was not, as Wood asserts, to arrest democratic turbulence in the states but to establish an effective national government. Wood's response and my rejoinder are appended to my original contribution.

In addition, the final chapter in this volume ("Securing States' Interests at Philadelphia: A Reassessment"), drawing, as it does, on several of the other articles in this collection, provides further refutation of Beard's thesis. In this essay, I explore the manner in which the large state-small state dispute permeated the entire course of the debate at Philadelphia and was not limited to settling the single issue of the composition of the upper house of the national legislature. An examination of various contentious issues at the Convention leads to the conclusion that those intent on preserving state sovereignty and autonomy had considerable influence on the formulation of key provisions of the Constitution and confirmed the federal character of the document. Beard's claim that the large state-small state contest at Philadelphia was overshadowed by economic determinants is seen to be unsubstantiated.

The second part of this collection is devoted to an analysis of several important (though occasionally little-noticed) provisions of the Constitution in terms of their drafting, significance, and subsequent evolution. It deals with the framers' construction at Philadelphia, without reference to subsequent Beardian attempts at deconstruction.

"Extrajudicial Activities and the Principle of the Separation of Powers" demonstrates that neither the Constitution nor the historical record bars a judge from performing executively-assigned non-judicial tasks. Objections to such extra-judicial activities may justly arise from ethical, but not constitutional, considerations.

"The U.S. Constitution and Anticipatory Self-Defense under Article 51 of the UN Charter" shows the relevance of a little-noticed Constitutional provision to the contemporary international legal debate on the right of anticipatory self-defense.

"Congressional-Executive Agreements" deals with the question whether an executive agreement approved by simple majority of both houses of Congress is as constitutionally valid as a treaty which receives the constitutionally mandated advice and consent of two thirds of the Senate.

The final entry in this section relates to recent attempts by foreign governments to gain influence in the U.S. government by contributing to the campaign chest of political parties, and highlights the action of the Framers to forestall venal foreign influence through their careful formulation of different provisions of the Constitution.

In the concluding section of this volume, attention is focussed on the pervasive federal impulse at Philadelphia, the less noticed features which reflected this impulse, and those who at Philadelphia gave it voice.

"The Philosophy of a Dissenting Father" examines the impressive credentials of George Mason as a liberal and Founding Father, despite his refusal to sign the final document. And the final article ("Securing States' Interests at the 1787 Constitutional Convention: A Reassessment"), as noted earlier, draws on earlier chapters, and reassesses the federal as against the national component in the final constitutional structure.

PART ONE

Beardian and Neo-Beardian Theses

1

The Electoral College at Philadelphia: The Evolution of an Ad Hoc Congress for the Selection of a President

With the approach of the bicentennial of the adoption of the Constitution, attention is once again focused on the drafting of that remarkable instrument of government. Among the provisions of the Constitution assured of closer examination is the one dealing with the Electoral College, the system devised by the Founding Fathers for the election of a chief executive.[1] No other constitutional provision gave them so much difficulty in its formulation. The subject of the method of electing a president was brought up in the Constitutional Convention on twenty-one different days and occasioned over thirty distinct votes on various phases of the subject. Over the years no other provision has drawn so much criticism or provoked so many constitutional amendments as has the Electoral College clause. Close to seven hundred proposals to amend the Electoral College scheme have been introduced into Congress since the Constitution was inaugurated in 1789. The most recent effort to revise the system for electing a president was undertaken in 1979, when a constitutional amendment, moved by Sen. Birch E. Bayh, Jr., of Indiana and endorsed by President Jimmy Carter, to institute popular election of the president, was soundly defeated.[2]

1 Constitution of the United States, Article 2, Sec. 1.

2 Farrand, *Records*, vol. 2, p. 501, vol. 3, pp. 166, 329, 458, 459. According to Max Farrand, "Whatever difficulties might have been encountered in other directions, they paled into insignificance in comparison with the problem before the convention of determining a satisfactory method of electing the

Two main interpretations have been put forward to explain the adoption of the Electoral College provision. On the one hand, the Progressive school, represented by such writers as J. Allen Smith and Charles Beard, maintained that the complicated, indirect method instituted for selecting a chief executive was a reflection of the Founding Fathers' deep distrust of democracy. The Framers, according to that view, deliberately precluded popular choice of the president to ensure that the leveling force of the masses would not threaten the rights of the propertied minority. That economic-determinist thesis has, in turn, been vigorously challenged by John P. Roche, who asserts that the Electoral College was but a last-minute compromise designed to allow the Constitutional Convention to wind up its business. It was, he writes, merely a "jerry-rigged improvisation . . . subsequently . . . endowed with a high theoretical content. . . . No one seemed to think well of the College as an institution. . . . The future was left to cope with the problem of what to do with this Rube Goldberg mechanism."[3]

---

executive." Farrand, *Framing of Constitution*, p. 160. See also Max Farrand, "Compromises of the Constitution," *AHR*, vol. 9 (1904), p. 486; Herman V. Ames, *The Proposed Amendments to the Constitution of the United States during the First Century of Its History* (Washington, D.C.: American Historical Association, 1897), pp. 75-76; Sen. Doc. No. 93, 69 Cong., 1 sess. (1926); Sen. Doc. No. 163, 87 Cong., 2 sess. (1963); Sen. Doc. No. 38, 91 Cong., 1 sess. (1969); Richard A. David, Congressional Research Service of Library of Congress, Report No. 85,36 Gov.; *Congress and the Nation, vol. 5, 1977-1980* (Washington, D.C.: 1981), pp. 941-43; U.S. Congress, Senate, Committee of the Judiciary, *Direct Popular Election of the President and Vice President of the United States*, 96 Cong., April 9, 1979; and *Public Papers of the President of the United States, Jimmy Carter 1977*, bk. 1, March 22, 1977 (Washington D.C.: Govt. Printing Office, 1980), pp. 481-85.

3 J. Allen Smith, *The Spirit of American Government; A Study of the Constitution; Its Origin, Influence and Relation to Democracy* (N.Y.: Macmillan, 1907), pp. 135-36, 165; Beard, *Economic Interpretation*, pp. 161-62; John P. Roche. "The Founding Fathers: A Reform Caucus in Action." *APSR*, vol. 55 (1961), pp. 799-816, esp. 810-811. Roche was not the first to highlight the compromise nature of the Electoral College. See Farrand, "Compromises of the Constitution." pp. 479-89; Farrand, *Framing of Constitution*, pp. 166-67; and Warren, *Making of Constitution*, pp. 621-23, Neither of the latter writers have accepted the assertion that in the eyes of the Framers the Electoral College was "a jerry-rigged improvisation." See the comments of Gouverneur Morris and James Madison in Farrand, *Records*, vol. 3, pp. 405, 458, 464.

Roche's antideterminist interpretation clearly denies an overall design to the Electoral College; it was in the nature of a makeshift contraption. That is not, however, the way contemporaries viewed the Electoral College. According to Abraham Baldwin, delegate for Georgia (as reported by John Pickering), "late in their session the present complex mode of electing the President and Vice-President was proposed; that the mode was perfectly novel, and therefore occasioned a pause; but when explained and fully considered was universally admired, and viewed as the most pleasing feature in the Constitution." And Alexander Hamilton, in Federalist No. 68, wrote: "The mode of appointment of the Chief Magistrate of the United States is almost the only part of the system, of any consequence, which has escaped without severe censure, or which has received the slightest mark of approbation from its opponents. . . . I venture somewhat further, and hesitate not to affirm that if the manner of it be not perfect, it is at least excellent." Max Farrand, in his succinct work, *The Framing of the Constitution of the United States,* sums up the attitude of the Framers toward the Electoral College: "For of all things done in the convention the members seemed to have been prouder of that than of any other, and they seemed to regard it as having solved the problem for any country of how to choose a chief magistrate."[4]

The true rationale and purpose of the Electoral College scheme can best be unraveled by a close examination of the Constitutional Convention debates. By following the tortuous course the Framers took during the summer months of 1787, we can gain insight into the influences that led them to institute such a complex procedure for selecting a president. The records of the convention debates also shed light on the extent to which the Founding Fathers were consciously guided by such factors as prevailing political theories and past republican practices- ancient or modern. In particular, how prominently did the state constitutional precedents figure in the

4 Farrand, *Records,* vol. 3, pp. 132, 403; E. M. Earle, ed., *The Federalist* (N.Y.: Modern Library, n.d.), p. 441; Farrand, *Framing of Constitution,* p. 175.

deliberations at Philadelphia? Did the other well-known clashes at the convention — large states versus small states, federalists versus nationalists, slaveholders versus non slaveholders — inform the Electoral College debates? A detailed analysis of the 1787 discussions should also help to explain why the Electoral College scheme encountered so little criticism in the state ratifying conventions.[5]

Both the Virginia Plan and the New Jersey Plan, the foundation documents of the Constitution, called for election of the executive by the legislature, as was the practice in all but three of the states. In two of the three states where the choice was by popular election, in the event that no candidate received a clear majority, the choice would fall on the legislature. During the debates the delegates frequently referred to this pattern of state practice.[6]

That both the Virginia and the New Jersey plans endorsed selection by the legislature did not mean that they were at one on

5 See the statements of James Wilson and Rufus King in Farrand, *Records*, vol. 3, pp. 166, 461. See also that of Madison at the Virginia ratifying convention in Elliot, *State Debates*, vol. 3, p. 494. See also Cecelia M. Kenyon, "Men of Little Faith: The Anti-Federalists on the Nature of Representative Government," *WMQ*, 3d ser., vol. 12 (1955), p. 13.

6 Farrand, *Records*, vol. 1, pp. 20-22, 242-45. In both plans the term of office was left blank while reeligibility was ruled out. Election of the executive by the legislature was provided for under the constitutions of Delaware, Georgia, Maryland, North Carolina, New Jersey, Pennsylvania, South Carolina, and Virginia. (In every instance of a bicameral legislature the executive was chosen by joint ballot. Other officers of government, however, were chosen by regular legislative procedures, allowing each house to exercise a veto on the choice of the other. On occasion that procedure produced deadlock and crisis.) Popular election of the executive was provided for under the constitutions of Massachusetts, New Hampshire, and New York. Under the last a simple plurality was sufficient to be elected, and there was no provision for a contingency choice. But in the former two, in the absence of a popular majority for any one candidate, the lower house chose two out of the top four candidates, and the upper house made the final choice out of the two selected. Poore, *State Constitutions*. Contingency proposals surfaced frequently during the convention debates and, of course, the Electoral College scheme contains such an arrangement.

the mode of election. The legislature, in each case, was a very different body. Whereas the Virginia Plan provided for a popularly elected legislature with the representation of each state proportional to the size of its population, the New Jersey Plan proposed that the legislature remain (as under the Articles of Confederation) the representative body of the states, with each state entitled to one vote. Thus while the Virginia Plan called for a "National Executive" to be chosen by the "National Legislature," the New Jersey Plan envisaged a "federal Executive" to be appointed by "the U. States in Congs." In effect, therefore, at the very outset of the convention, the large and small states were at loggerheads over the method of selecting an executive no less than they were over the composition of the legislature.[7]

When, on June 1, the convention moved to debate the scheme outlined in the Virginia Plan for selection of the executive (the New Jersey Plan was first submitted on June 15), three distinct, but interrelated, issues arose for discussion: (1) the mode of election; (2) the term of office; and (3) the question of reeligibility. The three issues formed a sort of tripod where an imbalance on one side disrupted the balance of the whole. Since the executive was to be elected by the legislature, it was deemed essential that he not be eligible for reelection, for reeligibility would compromise his independence; but if he was to serve only one term, then it ought to be a reasonably lengthy one. The relationship between reeligibility and term of office was stressed throughout the debate. James Wilson favored a three-year term "on the supposition that a reeligibility would be provided for." This was endorsed by Roger

7 During the course of the convention two further plans were presented: The Pinckney Plan (May 29) and the Hamilton Plan (June 18). Under the former the executive would be chosen annually by both houses of the legislature in joint session; under the latter the executive would be selected by electors chosen by the people and would serve during good behavior. Neither plan figured in the convention debates and neither was ever voted on. The Hamilton Plan was not even moved to committee. Farrand. *Records,* vol. 1, p. 292; vol. 2, p. 135; vol. 3, pp. 606, 617.

Sherman who was "agst. the doctrine of [compulsory] rotation as throwing out of the office the men best qualified to execute its duties." George Mason, on the other hand, favored "seven years at least" and a prohibition on re-eligibility "as the best expedient both for preventing the effect of a false complaisance on the side of the Legislature towards unfit characters; and a temptation on the side of the Executive to intrigue with the Legislature for a re-appointment." In short order the convention, by a vote of 8 to 2, endorsed Mason's viewpoint (moved by Charles Pinckney) and decided that the executive should be chosen by the legislature for a seven-year term without right of reelection.[8] This was but the first of many times that the convention would settle for this formula.

In the course of the debate, two diverse, even conflicting challenges were directed at the proposed scheme. Wilson, a delegate from Pennsylvania and a "nationalist of the nationalists," advocated popular election of the executive. That system of electing "the first magistrate," he declared, though "it might appear chimerical," was really "a convenient and successful mode" as the experience of New York and Massachusetts had proven. On the next day, June 2, Wilson submitted a motion to divide the states into districts, the voters in each district to choose electors who in turn, would select the "executive Magistracy." (The intervention of electors did not, apparently, make it any less "an election by the people" in Wilson's eyes.) In supporting his proposal Wilson argued for an "an election without the intervention of the States." His suggestion evoked interest but also considerable skepticism. Thus Mason said he favored the idea but thought it "impracticable." Similarly, Elbridge Gerry of Massachusetts said he "liked the principle" but feared "that it would alarm & give a handle to the

8 *Ibid*,. vol. 1, pp. 68-88; vol. 3. pp. 132, 167; Roche, "Founding Fathers," p. 810; George Bancroft, *History of the Formation of the Constitution of the United States of America* (2 vols., N.Y.: Appleton, 1882), vol. 2, p. 166.

State partizans, as tending to supersede altogether the State authorities."[9]

And, indeed, at that very sitting, one of the convention's foremost "State partizans," John Dickinson of Delaware, moved "that the Executive be made removeable by the National Legislature on the request of a majority of the Legislatures of individual States." "He had no idea of abolishing the State Governments as some gentlemen seemed inclined to do. . . . He hoped that each State would retain an equal voice at least in one branch of the National Legislature." James Madison and Wilson both objected to Dickinson's motion on the ground (inter alia) "that it would leave an equality of agency in the small with the great States."[10]

Neither Wilson's not Dickinson's motion was received with much sympathy. (The votes were 2 to 8 and 1 to 9, respectively.) But these divergent suggestions reflected a contrast of views on the measure of state control to be exercised in the selection of the executive. In the eyes of such a nationalist as Wilson, even election by the legislature detracted from the national independent stature of the executive, whereas for Dickinson the states were not accorded adequate control over the nation's chief executive officer. The two viewpoints, in one shape or another, arose repeatedly during the

9 Charles C. Thach, Jr. , *The Creation of the Presidency, 1775-1789: A Study in Constitutional History* (Baltimore: Johns Hopkins, 1923), p. 85; Farrand, *Records*, vol. 1, pp. 68, 69, 77, 80. This was the first of many times in the debate that the use of electors was proposed. Ultimately, of course, the convention adopted a system of indirect election in the form of the Electoral College. One can speculate on the precedents for the introduction of an intermediate step in the selection of an executive. In the Massachusetts ratifying convention, former Gov. James Bowdoin declared, "This method of choosing was probably taken from the manners of choosing senators under the constitution of Maryland." Elliot, *State Debates*, vol. 2, pp. 127-28. Under that constitution the people chose electors, who, in turn, selected the fifteen members of the state Senate for a five year term. In Federalist No. 63 Madison gave high praise to that feature of the Maryland constitution. See also Ames, *Proposed Amendments*, pp. 75-76. For Elbridge Gerry's role in the convention, see George Athan Billias, *Elbridge Gerry: Founding Father and Republican Statesman* (N.Y.: McGraw-Hill, 1976), pp. 153-205, 331-39.

10 Farrand, *Records*, vol. 1, pp. 78, 85, 86, 87, 244.

numerous discussions the convention was to hold on the mode of electing an executive. Dickinson's comment on the composition of the legislature foreshadowed, at this early stage of the discussions, the growing dissatisfaction of the smaller states, with their diminished role in the organs of government.[11]

On June 15 (some two weeks after Dickinson's address), William Paterson presented the New Jersey Plan to the convention, and the issue of the small states versus the large states was joined. The controversy was not settled until July 7, after three weeks of protracted discussion. The Connecticut Compromise, which emerged, resolved the issue of the composition of the legislature.[12] But had it equally settled the procedure for the election of the executive? At first glance it would appear that it had done so since the convention's earlier decision to provide for election of the executive by the legislature remained intact. Delegates could not but realize, however, that the new legislature was a creature very different from the body previously entrusted with the task of selecting an executive. For one thing, the upper house now represented the states. Furthermore, as a result of the principle of equality of representation in the upper house, the smaller states would exercise willy-nilly an inordinate influence on the selection of a chief executive. It is perhaps not surprising, therefore, that no sooner had the convention adopted the Connecticut Compromise than the issue of the mode of electing the chief executive arose once again.

On July 17 Gouverneur Morris, one of the "leading conservatives" of the convention (and probably its "most brilliant member"), criticized the earlier decision to leave the selection of the nation's

11 *Ibid.*, pp. 77, 78, 81, 87. Delaware, John Dickinson's state, alone favored his proposal. There is evidence that even before a quorum had assembled at the Constitutional Convention, the smaller states were already evincing anxiety about the outcome. See the letter of George Read of Delaware to Dickinson on May 21 in *ibid.*, vol 3, pp. 25-26. Subsequently Dickinson endorsed election of the executive "by the people as the best and purest source." *Ibid.*, vol. 2, p. 114. Clearly, Dickinson's present move was designed to ensure a federal system of government in which the role of the states was not entirely eclipsed.

12 *Ibid.*, vol. 1, pp. 242-45, 549-51.

chief magistrate in the hands of the legislature. He moved to insert, in place of "National Legislature," "citizens of U.S."

> He ought to be elected by the people at large, by the freeholders of the Country. . . . If the people should elect, they will never fail to prefer some man of distinguished character, or services; some man . . . of continental reputation. If the Legislature elect, it will be the work of intrigue, of cabal, and of faction. . . . He will be the mere creature of the Legisl: if appointed and impeachable by that body.[13]

Wilson supported the Morris motion for popular election and dismissed the argument that a majority of the people might be unable to agree on any one candidate. In such event, he said, "the expedient used in Masts." could be employed with the legislature choosing between the leading candidates. "This would restrain the choice to a good nomination at least, and prevent in a great degree intrigue & cabal." In response, Pinckney of South Carolina highlighted the fears of the smaller states.

> [He] did not expect this question would again have been brought forward; An Election by the people being liable to the most obvious & striking objections. They will be led by a few active & designing men. The most populous States by combining in favor of the same individual will be able to carry their points.

Sherman of Connecticut also gave voice to the concern of the small states.

> The sense of the Nation would be better expressed by the Legislature than by the people at large. The latter will never be sufficiently informed of characters, and besides will never give a majority of votes to any one man. They will generally vote for some man in their own State, and the largest State will have the best chance for the appointment.[14]

educ'g't.

The smaller states clearly were concerned that in a straight-out popular election the larger states would overwhelm them. The smaller states had not fought for equality in one branch of the legislature only to see control of the executive go by default.

13 Thach, *Creation of the Presidency*, p. 35; Farrand, *Framing of Constitution*, p. 21; Farrand, *Records.*,vol. 2., pp. 29-30.

14 Farrand, *Records*, vol. 2., pp. 29-30.

Mason of Virginia (a large state) did not share the fears of the small states. Nonetheless, he was sharply critical of the suggestion for nationwide popular election of the executive. He graphically portrayed the inability of the people to select a national figure:

> He conceived it would be as unnatural to refer the choice of a proper character for a Chief Magistrate to the people, as it would, to refer a trial of colours to a blind man. The extent of the country renders it impossible that the people can have the requisite capacity to judge of the respective pretensions of the Candidates.[15]

This passage is frequently cited as evidence of the Framers' lack of faith in democracy. If the words are examined in their context, however, it is evident that Mason was not challenging the *right* of the people to choose but, rather, their *ability* to do so given the size of the electoral district within which they would have to exercise that right. The vast expanse of the United States, the difficulty of communication, and the unfamiliarity of the general populace with national personalities — all militated against an informed choice. In fact, as noted above, Mason had earlier expressed himself in favor of popular election but considered it "impractical," for the reasons, no doubt, he now enumerated by reference to "the extent of the Country." As Cecelia M. Kenyon, in discussing the stand of the anti-Federalists, has written:

> This belief that larger electoral districts would inevitably be to the advantage of the well-to-do partially explains the almost complete lack of criticism of the indirect election of the senate and the President. If the "middling" class could not be expected to compete successfully with the upper class in Congressional elections, still less could they do so in state-wide or nation-wide elections. It was a matter where size was of the essence. True representation . . . could be achieved only where electoral districts were small.

It was in this sense that Mason, for one, found fault with nationwide elections of the executive. Under the circumstances, popular election of the executive would have the trappings of representative democracy but not the essence.[16]

15 *Ibid.*, p. 31.

16 Kenyon, "Men of Little Faith," p. 13. This analysis is reflected in Wilson's argument in the Pennsylvania Ratifying Convention on the method of electing

The final speaker on Gouverneur Morris's proposal for popular election of the executive was Hugh Williamson of North Carolina, who added a new slant to the discussions. He reiterated the point made by the earlier speakers that "the people will be sure to vote for some man in their own State, and the largest State will be sure to succede." He went on to say, "This will not be Virga. however. Her slaves will have no suffrage." Williamson was adverting to a key advantage that the slave states presently enjoyed in the projected lower house, where slaves counted three-fifths for purposes of representation. If a system for direct popular election of the executive were instituted, the slave states stood to lose that advantage because only the enfranchised white population could actually vote, and the increment derived from the slaves would be lost. In effect, adoption of the Connecticut Compromise had forged a natural alliance between the small states and the slave states in reserving decisions for the legislature as currently constituted. The slave states gained an advantage in the lower house, and the smaller states gained one in the Senate (small slave states, such as the Carolinas, had a double advantage). It is hardly surprising, therefore, that Morris's motion for popular election was rejected by a vote of 1 to 9 with only his own state, Pennsylvania, voting in favor. Luther Martin of Maryland then proposed that the executive be chosen by electors appointed by the state legislatures. The proposal was defeated by a vote of 2 to 8. Election of the executive by the legislature was thereupon unanimously reendorsed.[17]

At this point, however, the convention took a peculiar step. As matters stood on July 17, the executive was (1) to be elected by the legislature: (2) to serve for seven years; and (3) to be ineligible for a second term. The latter two provisions were designed to ensure the executive's independence of the legislature. But now William

a president. Farrand, *Records,* vol. 3, p. 167. See also Billias, *Elbridge Gerry,* p. 160. George Mason's record, both before and during the convention, demonstrates that he was a foremost champion of democratic causes. Farrand, *Records,* vol. 1, p. 48, vol. 2, pp. 201-203, 273-74, 370, 637; Alfred H. Kelly and Winfred A. Harbison, *The American Constitution: Its Origins and Development,* 4th ed., (N.Y.: Norton, 1970), p. 120.

17 Farrand, *Records,* vol. 2, pp. 22, 32.

Houston of Georgia moved that the clause on ineligibility be struck out. Morris supported the motion because ineligibility, he argued, "tended to destroy the great motive to good behavior, the hope of being rewarded by a re-appointment. It was saying to him, make hay while the sun shines." The argument apparently impressed the other delegates, who proceeded by a vote of 6 to 4 to strike out the ineligibility clause. Such a move, however, meant that one leg of the tripod was out of balance, since the legislature was now in a position to exert undue influence on the executive, who was beholden to it for reelection. By the same token, because the executive could serve more than once, a term as long as seven years was no longer warranted. Various delegates thus suggested substitution of a shorter term. Others, however, maintained that the only way to ensure the executive's independence was to provide that he serve "during good behavior." The latter proposal was vigorously condemned by Mason, who "considered an Executive during good behavior as a softer name only for an Executive for life. . . . the next would be an easy step to hereditary monarchy." The motion for instituting "good behavior" was defeated by a vote of 6 to 4, and the seven-year term was retained by the same margin. Clearly, the delegates were much troubled by the difficulty of maintaining the harmony of the tripod arrangement. Endowing the legislature with authority to reelect the executive compromised the latter's independence and posed problems in fixing the term of office. All this prompted thoughts that only by removing the selection of the executive from the legislature could the tripod be secured firmly. This idea, among others, surfaced in the full-dress debate on the issue held on July 19.[18]

Martin of Maryland opened the discussion with a proposal that the clause barring a second term be reinserted. He was supported by Edmund Randolph of Virginia, who stressed the need to ensure the executive's independence. "If he ought to be independent, he should not be left under a temptation to court a re-appointment. If he should be re-appointable by the Legislature, he will be no check on it." He warned the smaller states that reeligibility would work to

18 *Ibid.*, pp. 23, 33, 35, 36.

their disadvantage, in particular, since the executive would undoubtedly court the larger states to ensure his reelection.[19]

Gouverneur Morris vigorously challenged the Martin proposal. Once again he advocated popular election of the executive, coupled with a right of reeligibility. "If he is to be the Guardian of the people let him be appointed by the people." In a lengthy address he extolled the virtues of popular election: "The Executive Magistrate should be the guardian of the people, even of the lower classes, agst Legislative tyranny, against the Great & the wealthy who in the course of things will necessarily compose — the Legislative body. . . . The Executive therefore ought to be so constituted as to be the great protector of the Mass of the people." He recommended biennial elections of the executive, and in conclusion noted that popular election would make the plan of the constitution "extremely palatable to the people." Both Rufus King of Massachusetts and Paterson of New Jersey also endorsed popular election but feared that the people might not be able to settle on any one man. To obviate the difficulty they suggested "an appointment by electors chosen by the people for this purpose." At this point Wilson remarked that he "perceived with pleasure that the idea was gaining ground, of an election mediately or immediately by the people." Only Gerry spoke out against popular election, regarding it as "the worst [mode] of all." "The people are uninformed," he declared, "and would be misled be a few designing men." But even Gerry endorsed the notion of electors, except that he would entrust their selection to the state executives rather than to the state legislatures.[20]

Madison inveighed strongly against any role by the legislature in the selection of the executive since such an arrangement would tend to "establish an improper connection between the departments." During the debate of two days earlier, he had argued against reelection by the legislature: "A dependence of the Executive on the Legislature would render it the Executive as well as the maker of laws; & then according to the observation of Montesquieu, tyrannical laws may be made that they may be

19 *Ibid.,* pp. 52, 54-55.
20 *Ibid.,* pp. 52-54, 55-56, 57.

executed in a tyrannical manner." In the current debate Madison expressed doubts whether "an appointment in the 1st. instance [even] with an ineligibility afterwards would not establish an improper connection between the two departments." Inevitably, it would produce "intrigues and contentions." He therefore favored lodging the appointment in some other source. "The people at large was in his opinion the fittest in itself." Madison acknowledged, however, "one difficulty . . . of a serious nature attending an immediate choice by the people":

> The right of suffrage was much more diffusive in the Northern than the Southern States; and the latter could have no influence in the election on the score of the Negroes. The substitution of electors obviated this difficulty and seemed on the whole to be liable to the fewest objections.[21]

Madison's reference to the disparity of eligible voters between the North and the South highlighted, of course, the advantage the latter enjoyed under the three-fifths rule. The use of electors on something less than a directly proportionate scale would help preserve the relative advantage of the South (and of the smaller states). In this spirit Oliver Ellsworth of Connecticut moved that in place of "apptment by the Natl. Legislature" there be inserted "to be chosen by electors appointed by the Legislatures of the States in the following ratio": each state with less than 100,000 population — one vote; between 100,000 and 300,000 — two votes; and above 300,000 — three votes. Since the ratio was 1:3, no southern or small state had cause to feel disadvantaged, and it is not surprising, therefore, that the convention summarily, proceeded to endorse the system of electors by a vote of 6 to 4. For the first time in the course of the deliberations, the legislature had been excluded from the executive-selection process. And with the removal of the legislature, the convention felt free to restore the reeligibility clause. The term of office was fixed at six years, and members of the legislature were forbidden to serve as electors.[22] Now the provision for choosing an executive was, in certain key features, approaching the ultimate form that would emerge from the convention.

21 *Ibid.*, pp. 34, 56-57.
22 *Ibid.*, pp. 50, 57, 58, 59, 60, 61, 63-64, 69.

But barely three days later, on July 23, doubts were expressed with regard to the system of electors just adopted. Houston "urged the extreme inconveniency & the considerable expense, of drawing together men from all the States for the single purpose of electing the Chief Magistrate." Obviously, it was envisaged that the electors under the scheme adopted would assemble in some central location to cast their votes. On the next day, July 24, Houston moved that the system of electors be abandoned in favor of restoring to the legislature the choice of the executive. "He dwelt chiefly on the improbability, that capable men would undertake the service of Electors from the more distant States." Houston was supported by Williamson, who argued that "the proposed Electors would certainly not be men of the 1st. nor even of the 2d. grade in the States. These would all prefer a seat in the Legislature." Interestingly, Gerry dismissed Houston's fears and urged retention of the system of electors. "The best men," he declared, would be honored to be electors, since "the election of the Executive Magistrate will be considered as of vast importance and will excite great earnestness." Nonetheless, Houston's motion was carried by a vote of 7 to 4.[23]

Thereupon Martin and Gerry moved to reinstate the ineligibility clause. Involvement of the legislature in selection of the executive compromised his independence, they maintained. "The longer the duration of his appointment the more will his dependence be diminished," said Gerry. "It will be better then for him to continue 10, 15, or even 20 — years and be ineligible afterwards." Others proposed an eight or eleven-year term of office. King recommended a twenty-year term since "this is the medium life of princes." In a footnote Madison remarked, "This might possibly be meant as a caricature of the previous motions in order to defeat the object of them." Williamson favored a seven-year term without eligibility for reelection, but would not object to a ten- or twelve-year term. "It

23 *Ibid.*, pp. 95, 97, 99, 100, 101. A possible explanation for the sudden change of heart on the scheme of electors may lie in the fact that a move to accord New Hampshire and Georgia two electors each, instead of the one each had been allotted, failed. *Ibid.*, pp. 60-61, 63-64.

was pretty certain he thought that we should at some time or other have a King; but he wished no precaution to be omitted that might postpone the event as long as possible."[24]

Once again the convention was thrown into disarray in its efforts to settle on a system for electing the executive that would not leave him overdependent on the legislature. Balancing the tripod — mode of election, term of office, and reeligibility — was proving to be an extremely difficult task. Gerry summed up the frustration of the delegates when he said, "We seem to be entirely at a loss on this head." He recommended that the problem be referred to the Committee of Detail, which was to be set up. "Perhaps they will be able to hit on something that may unite the various opinions which have been thrown out." Wilson, acknowledging "the difficulties & perplexities into which the House is thrown," proposed a scheme whereby a small group, drawn by lot from the legislature, would retire to make the choice "and not separate until it be made." "By this mode intrigue would be avoided . . . and . . . dependence . . . diminished." Gouverneur Morris warned the convention against denying the executive a right of reelection. "He will be in possession of the sword, a civil war will ensue." Wilson's proposal, he said, was worth considering. "It would be better that chance sd. decide than intrigue." Regardless, the delegates were not inclined to accept Wilson's novel suggestion precisely because it left too much to chance.[25]

On the next day, July 25, Ellsworth moved that the executive be selected by the legislature except where the incumbent stood for reelection. In that case the choice would fall to electors appointed by

24 *Ibid.*, pp. 98-99, 100-101, 102.

25 *Ibid.*, pp. 97, 103, 105, 106. On the difficulties encountered by the delegates at this point, compare the descriptions by Robert A. Dahl and George Bancroft. Dahl observed, "Almost to the end, it [the Convention] would move toward a solution and then, on second thought, reverse itself in favor of some different alternative. . . . The Convention twisted and turned like a man tormented in his sleep by a bad dream as it tried to decide." Robert A. Dahl, *Pluralist Democracy in the United States; Conflict and Consent* (Chicago: Rand McNally, 1967), p. 84. Bancroft wrote, "The convention was now like a pack of hounds in full chase, suddenly losing the trail. It fell into an anarchy of opinion and one crude scheme trod on the heels of another ." Bancroft, *History of the Formation of the Constitution*, vol. 2, p. 170. Some writers have suggested that

the state legislatures. Thereupon Madison delivered a lengthy address on the subject. "There are objections agst. every mode that has been, or perhaps can be proposed. The election must be made either by some existing authority under the Natil. or State Constitutions — or by some special authority derived from the people — or by the people themselves." The legislature, he declared, was "liable to insuperable objections." Besides compromising the independence of the executive, conferring the choice on the legislature would (1) "agitate & divide the legislature"; (2) lead to intrigues between the executive and "the predominant faction" within the legislature; and (3) result in foreign meddling in the election. He was also opposed to entrusting the selection of the national executive to the states, whether the choice devolved on their legislatures or on their executives. In conclusion, said Madison, the choice lay between direct elections and the use of electors. In the latter case, "as the electors would be chosen for the occasion, would meet at once, & proceed immediately to an appointment, there would be very little opportunity for cabal, or corruption. As a further precaution, it might be required that they meet at some place, distinct from the seat of Govt." But since that mode had just been rejected, there was little purpose in proposing it anew. There remained "election by he people or rather by the [qualified part of them] at large. With all its imperfections he liked this best." He recognized, however, that there were two serious difficulties with this method. "The first arose from the disposition in the people to prefer a Citizen of their own State, and the disadvantage this wd. throw on the smaller States." Madison expressed the hope "that some expedient might be hit upon that would obviate" that possibility. "The second difficulty arose from the disproportion of [qualified voters] in the N. & S. States, and the disadvantages which this mode would throw on the latter." The latter handicap, he surmised, would be overcome with the passage of time as the

---

Wilson's notion of a choice by lot was drawn from the example of the Ephori elections in ancient Greece. See John Fiske, *The Critical Period of American History 1783-1789* (Boston: Houghton Miflin, 1899), p. 281; and Richard M. Gummere, *The American Colonial Mind and the Classical Tradition: Essays in Comparative Culture* (Cambridge, Mass.: Harvard Univ. Press, 1963), p. 186.

population of the South increased. In any case, "local considerations must give way to the general interest." Madison declared that as a southerner "he was willing to make the sacrifice."[26]

Madison's remarks served to highlight the underlying causes of the opposition to popular election of the executive — the disadvantage from which both the smaller and the southern states would suffer. The fact was confirmed when, immediately after Madison had concluded his remarks, Ellsworth (one of the authors of the Connecticut Compromise) declared, "The objection drawn from the different sizes of the States, is unanswerable. The Citizens of the largest States would invariably prefer the Candidate within the State; and the largest States wd. invariably have the man." The same theme was taken up by Williamson, who said "an election of the Executive by the Legislature . . . opened a door for foreign influence. The principal objection agst. an election by the people seemed to be, the disadvantage under which it would place the smaller States" He suggested that as a "cure" each person should vote for three candidates, two of which would presumably be from states other than his own "and as probably of a small as a large one."[27]

Both Gouverneur Morris and Madison liked the Williamson idea. Morris suggested that "each man should vote for *two* persons one of whom at least should not be of his own State." Madison endorsed the Morris amendment and said that the effect would be that "the second best man in this case would probably be the first, in fact." He expressed fears, however, that after having voted for his favorite candidate, each citizen would throw away his second vote on some obscure person "in order to ensure the object of his first choice. But it could hardly be supposed that the Citizens of many States would be so sanguine of having their favorite elected, as not to give their second vote with sincerity to the next object of their choice."[28]

Dickinson suggested a means to combine popular election and selection by the legislature. He himself, he declared, "had long

26 Farrand, *Records*, vol. 2, pp. 107-11.

27 *Ibid.*, pp. 111, 113.

28 *Ibid.*, pp. 113-14. [Emphasis added.]

leaned towards an election by the people which he regarded as the best and purest source." The difficulty arose, "from the partiality of the States to their respective Citizens." But could this "partiality not be put to use in the search for an executive magistrate? Let the citizens of each state select their favorite son, and from the thirteen candidates thus nominated let the legislature, or electors appointed by it, make the final choice.[29] Because Dickinson did not submit a formal proposal, his scheme never came to a vote. But it did raise the possibility of dividing the nominating and selection procedure so that the legislature would make the final choice from a list of candidates nominated in the states. The procedure was clearly patterned on the contingency arrangements under the Massachusetts and New Hampshire constitutions in the event that no gubernatorial candidate received a popular majority.

The complexity of the task involved in formulating a mode of election was never better demonstrated than at this stage of the debate, which extended over several days. The convention voted down in seriatim various ideas that had been put forward in the course of the debate. Thus Ellsworth's suggestion that in cases where an incumbent stood for election, the choice be left to state-appointed electors rather than to the national legislature was turned down by a vote of 4 to 7. And Willaimson's popular-election proposal (as amended), whereby each person would vote for two candidates, one of whom would not be a citizen of his own state, was defeated by the narrow margin of 5 to 6. A motion by Pinckney for a system of rotation, so that no person serve as executive for more than six years out of twelve, was defeated by the same close margin.[30] The convention adjourned on July 25 without having decided on either the term of office or the matter of reeligibility. The only element that now stood was the decision to have the legislature make the choice.

On the next day, July 26, Mason delivered a lengthy oration in support of restoring once again the seven-year term coupled with ineligibility. He emphasized "the difficulty of the subject and the

29 *Ibid.*, pp. 114-15.

30 *Ibid.*, pp. 107, 111-12, 115. A rotation requirement in the office of governor was present in eight state constitutions.

diversity of the opinions concerning it [that] have appeared. Nor have any of the modes of constituting that department been satisfactory." Earlier in the debate Pierce Butler of South Carolina and Gerry of Massachusetts had both vigorously challenged the idea of popular election of the executive. "The Govt. should not be made so complex & unwieldy as to disgust the States. This would be the case , if the election shd. be referred to the people." declared Butler. According to Gerry the proposal for "popular election in this case" was "radically vicious. The ignorance of the people would put it in the power of some one set of men dispersed through the Union & acting in Concert to delude them into any appointment. He observed that such a Society of men existed in the Order of the Cincinnati." Mason, in challenging the various proposals that had surfaced, also repeated his earlier opposition to popular election. Such an election meant "that an act which ought to be performed by those who know most of Eminent characters, & qualifications, should be performed by those who know least." He was also unable to support Williamson's suggestion that each person vote for several candidates since he was convinced that it "would throw the appointment into the hands of the Cincinnati," as Gerry had observed. The suggestions that the choice be made by the state legislatures or by special electors had all been found wanting. Nor had the idea of a "lottery" produced "much demand" for its "tickets," said Mason. He concluded, therefore, that "an election by the Ntl. Legislature as originally proposed was the best" (that is, for a single term of seven years). In opposing reelection he declared:

> Having for his primary object, for the pole star of his political conduct, the preservation of the rights of the people, he held it as an essential point, as the very palladium of Civil liberty, that the great officers of State, and particularly the Executive should at fixed periods return to that mass from which they were at first taken, in order that they may feel & respect those rights & interests, which are again to be personally valuable to them.[31]

These remarks prompted a rare comment by Benjamin Franklin:

31 *Ibid.*, pp. 112, 114, 118-20.

> It seems to have been imagined by some that the returning to the mass of the people was degrading the magistrate. This he thought was contrary to republican principles. In free Governments the rulers are the servants, and the people their superiors & sovereigns. For the former therefore to return among the latter was not to *degrade* but to *promote* them — and it would be imposing an unreasonable burden on them, to keep them always in a State of servitude, and not allow them to become again one of the Masters.

In response, Gouverneur Morris said:

> In answer to Docr. Franklin, that a return into the mass of the people would be a promotion, instead of a degradation, he had no doubt that our Executive like most others would have too much patriotism to shrink from the burden of his office, and too much modesty not to be willing to decline the promotion.

At the same time Morris pronounced himself opposed to the whole paragraph on the selection of the executive if reeligibility be denied. Despite that objection, the convention adopted Mason's proposal by a vote of 7-3-1 and reendorsed selection by the legislature, for a seven-year term, without right of reelection. This formula was taken up in late July by the five-member Committee of Detail for incorporation into the draft constitution that it was to prepare.[32]

Although the convention had resolved on election by the legislature, no one had broached the question whether it was to be by joint ballot of both houses (voting together) or by each house acting separately. In the eight states where the legislature chose the executive, the election was by both houses jointly. Other state officials, however, were chosen according to regular legislative procedure, with each house exercising a veto. The latter arrangement for the selection of a president would give the states, especially the smaller states, substantial leverage in the choice of the executive. One document of the Committee of Detail in the Farrand collection hints that the committee experienced considerable difficulty in settling the matter. Randolph, a member of the committee, had originally written that the executive shall be elected "by joint ballot." Subsequently, "joint" had been crossed out, and

32 *Ibid.*, pp. 116, 117, 120-21, 128. [Emphasis in original.]

Randolph had added to an emendation of South Carolina's John Rutledge the words "& in each Ho. Havg a Negative on the other." However, the final report of the Committee of Detail, issued on August 6, reverted to the simple form adopted by the convention plenum, namely, "He shall be elected by ballot by the Legislature." The relevant provision (X) on the election of an executive (for the first time labeled "The President of the United States") read as follows: "He shall be elected by ballot by the Legislature. He shall hold his office during the term of seven years; but shall not be elected a second time."[33]

When the convention on August 7 took up the committee's report, the issue of electing the president arose in discussion of the procedures of the legislature (for the first time called the "Congress"). According to Article III of the draft constitution, each house "shall, in all cases, have a negative on the other." Mason expressed doubts regarding "the propriety of giving each branch a negative on the other 'in all cases.'" He assumed that there were some cases in which no negative was intended, "as in the case of balloting for appointments." Morris moved to insert "legislative acts" in place of "all cases." Sherman objected that such wording would "exclude a mutual negative in the case of ballots." Nathaniel Gorham of Massachusetts supported election by joint ballot and cited the difficulties experienced in his own state in selecting officers because of separate balloting by each house of the state legislature. "If separate ballots should be made for the President, and the two branches should be each attached to a favorite, great delay, contention & confusion may ensue." Wilson also advocated a joint ballot, "particularly in the choice of the President. Disputes between the two Houses, during & concerning the vacancy of the Executive might have dangerous consequences," he declared. Nonetheless, Morris's motion failed to carry by a tie vote, 5 to 5. In the meantime, however, Madison argued that a provision spelling out a negative by one house on the other was in any case unnecessary since the same was implied by the very existence of a

33 *Ibid.*, pp. 145, 185.

bicameral legislature. Madison's motion to strike out the reference to a mutual negative in the legislature carried by a vote of 7 to 3.[34] Since the powers of each house were left unchanged, the vote in effect postponed a decision on the matter of legislative balloting for the office of president.

When on August 24 the convention took up the provision on the election of the executive in the report of the Committee of Detail, the delegates were once again divided on the procedure of balloting by the legislature. The previous week, on August 17, a similar clash had arisen over appointment of the treasurer by the legislature (as envisaged under the report of the Committee of Detail). Gorham had moved to insert "joint" before "ballot." "Mr [Roger] Sherman opposed it as favoring the large States." Nonetheless, Gorham's amendment was upheld by a vote of 7 to 3. Now Rutledge moved to make election of the executive also by "joint" ballot "as the most convenient mode of electing." But, as on the previous occasion, Sherman objected to the motion "as depriving the *States* represented in the *Senate* of the negative intended them in that house." Gorham again responded that "it was wrong to be considering, at every turn whom the Senate would represent. The public good was the true object to be kept in view." His words, in turn, drew the following retort from Jonathan Dayton of New Jersey: "It might be well for those not to consider how the Senate was constituted, whose interest it Was to keep it out of sight. — If the amendment should be agreed to," he declared, " a *joint* ballot would in fact give the appointment to one House. He could never agree to the clause with such an amendment."[35] At this point Daniel Carroll of Maryland, with the support of Wilson, vainly tried to have "election by the people" inserted in place of "by the Legislature." The motion was quickly dismissed by a vote of 2 to 9.

Reverting to the proposal for a joint ballot, David Brearley of New Jersey, in opposing the proposal, reminded the delegates that "the argument that the small States should not put their hands into the pockets of the large ones did not apply in this case." This was a

34 *Ibid.*, pp. 177, 193, 196-97.
35 *Ibid.*, pp. 314-15, 401, 402. [Emphasis in original.]

reference to the demand of the larger states that money bills originate in the House of Representatives and not be subject to amendment in the Senate. That arrangement had formed an essential part of the Connecticut Compromise. In effect, Brearley was arguing that, unlike money bills, which affected the larger and wealthier states more directly and which were, therefore, left to the determination of the lower house, the selection of an executive concerned all states, smaller no less than larger, and was therefore a legitimate subject for Senate control. In contrast, Wilson "urged the reasonableness of giving the larger States a larger share of the appointment and the danger of delay from a disagreement of the two houses." He also pointed out that the Senate had a privileged position in other spheres, "balancing the advantage given by a joint ballot in this case to the other branch of the Legislature." Madison pointed out that even with a joint ballot, the larger states would still not exercise influence commensurate with their size. "The rule of voting will give to the largest State, compared with the smallest, an influence as 4 to 1 only, altho the population is as 10 to 1." This, declared Madison, "cannot be unreasonable as the President is to act for the *people* not for the *States*." But the most telling speech in favor of a joint ballot was delivered by John Langdon of New Hampshire. In his home state, he declared, "the mode of separate votes by the two Houses was productive of great difficulties. . . . He was for inserting 'joint' tho' unfavorable to N. Hampshire as a small State." The proposal for a joint ballot of both houses was accepted by a vote of 7 to 4, with two small states (New Hampshire and Delaware) breaking ranks and voting with the large states. The smaller states did not concede defeat, however. Immediately after the vote, Dayton of New Jersey, seconded by Brearley of the same state, moved to insert after "Legislature" the words "each State having one vote." The motion failed, by the close vote of 5 to 6.[36] (Delaware, in this instance, sided with its natural allies, the smaller states.)

36 *Ibid.*, vol. 1, pp. 524, 526; vol. 2, pp. 397, 402-403. [Emphasis in original.] Although the executive in New Hampshire was elected by popular vote, other officers were selected by the legislature, with each house voting separately.

It was now Gouverneur Morris's turn to express displeasure at the decision of the convention. The executive, he complained, can never be truly independent if he is chosen by the legislature. "Cabal & corruption are attached to that mode of election; so also is ineligibility a second time . . . rivals would be continually intriguing to oust the President from his place." He proposed that as a means of guarding against "all these evils," the president "be chosen by Electors to be chosen by the people of the several States." His motion was defeated by the narrow margin of 5 to 6 in one vote and by a split vote, 4-4-2 (1 absent) on a second try.[37]

But the convention was apparently still not satisfied with the arrangements it had settled on for choosing the president. Although it had confirmed election by the legislature in joint ballot, it was not yet ready to determine with finality the term of office or the reeligibility issue. Those matters were postponed, at the suggestion of the New Jersey delegation, to the next day, August 25.[38] The matter was not broached then, however, and apparently the convention preferred to let the issue ride.

The convention's continuing vacillation and soul-searching on the whole subject was subsequently revealed when on August 31 the delegates took up for consideration Article XXIII of the draft Constitution. That provision described the procedures for instituting the government, including a direction to Congress to "choose the President of the United States." Morris moved to strike those words out of the provision, "this point, of choosing the President not being yet finally determined." The clause was struck out by the rather surprising vote of 9-1-1 (one state divided). Clearly the convention had not yet pronounced the last word on the method of selecting a president. The delegates, even at this late stage, were still groping for a solution free of the serious shortcomings raised against every single method proposed to date. At the conclusion of the day's session, the issue of the election of a president, together with all other pieces of unfinished business, were referred to a committee composed of a representative from each state. Appar-

37 *Ibid.*, vol. 2, pp. 397, 404.
38 *Ibid.*, pp. 397-98, 404.

ently the convention was hoping that the members of the committee, as Gerry had put it, would be able to come up with something that would "unite the various opinions which have been thrown out."[39]

The Brearley Committee on Unfinished Parts (named thus after its chairman) completed its work on procedures for electing an executive in four days and reported back to the Convention on September 4. The result was the Electoral College.[40] It was striking in its innovation and quite remarkable for having combined all the salient features of the numerous plans proposed during the debate while having overcome the deficiencies of each. First and foremost, it removed the choice of president from the Congress and conveyed it to an independent, ad hoc body whose sole function was the selection of a chief executive. The independence of the president was thus assured while cabal and foreign influence were safely excluded, and the president was free to run for reelection without fear that his independence would be compromised. Yet at the same time, and this was the really critical point, in terms of numbers the Electoral College was an exact replica of Congress, since each state was entitled to as many votes in the Electoral College as it had in Congress, with even the smallest state entitled to at least three votes; moreover, the southern states would enjoy the bonus of the three-fifths rule. The smaller and the southern states thus would continue to enjoy the relative advantage they possessed in Congress itself, either in the Senate or in the House of Representatives, or in both. In mathematical terms the advantage in the first Congress (with sixty-five members in the House of Representatives and twenty-six in the Senate) was as follows:

Delaware (smallest state)

$$\frac{1 + 2 = 3}{65 + 26 = 91}$$

Virginia (largest state)

$$\frac{10 + 2 = 12}{65 + 26 = 91}$$

39 *Ibid.*, pp. 103, 472, 473, 480, 481.

40 According to Charles Warren, the reason for the success of the committee is that it consisted of "almost the ablest men from each State." Warren, *Making of Constitution*, p. 621 n. 1. See also Roche, "Founding Fathers," p. 810.

Thus, as a result of the Electoral College, the ratio was 1:4 rather than 1:10 as it would have been had size of population been the sole criterion.[41]

In effect, the Electoral College was simply a special congress elected to choose a president, without the shortcomings of the real Congress. Since the electors would never assemble together at one national site but would meet to vote, "in their respective States" and immediately thereafter disband, there was no danger of corruption, plotting or cabal. As Gouverneur Morris indicated, "The principal advantage aimed at was that of taking away the opportunity for cabal." To prevent the larger states from dominating the selection process, each elector was to vote for two persons, one of whom, at least, was not to be a citizen of his own state. At the same time, since a majority was required for selection of the president, no elector would be prone to throw away his second vote. Thus the outcome would be, not simply the selection of thirteen favorite sons, but a genuine possibility that a national figure would be chosen at the first round. In the event that no candidate received an absolute majority in the electoral College, the Senate would choose the president (from the five highest on the list.) In effect, the smaller states were to get two bites of the cherry under the new plan. First, they retained their numerical advantage in the Electoral College. Second, if no candidate succeeded in obtaining an absolute majority, the choice would devolve on the Senate, where again the smaller states had a built-in advantage. As noted above, this contingency arrangement was derived from the constitutions of Massachusetts and New Hampshire.[42]

41 Constitution of the United States, Article 1 secs. 2, 3. In the 1790 census Delaware had a population of 59,000 while that of Virginia was 692,000. In the 1792 elections Virginia elected nineteen members to the House of Representatives whereas Delaware continued to elect only one. Since the Electoral College total was 132, the resultant ratio was Delaware, 3:132; Virginia, 21:132. Thus the ratio was 1:7 rather than 1:12 as the population figures would warrant. (These figures allow 3 votes for 5 blacks under the census.) U.S. Bureau of the Census, *Historical Statistics of the United States, Colonial Times to 1970*, (Washington, D.C.: Govt. Printing Office, 1975), pt. 1, pp. 24, 36; *ibid.*, pt. 2, pp. 1074, 1085. Representation in the House was apportioned on the basis of 30,000 population per seat. Constitution of the United States, Article 1, sec. 2.

42 Farrand, *Records*, vol. 2, p. 501.

Presentation of the Electoral College scheme to the convention excited considerable surprise. "Mr. Randolph & Mr. Pinkney wished for a particular explanation & discussion of the reasons for changing the mode of electing the Executive." Gouverneur Morris served as the committee's spokesman in explaining the "reasons" for the new proposal: (1) "The danger of intrigue & faction if the apptmt should be made by the Legislature." (2) "The inconveniency of an ineligibility" were the choice to remain with the legislature. (3) "The difficulty of establishing a Court of Impeachments, other than the Senate," which would be an improper body to judge the executive if he were to be chosen by the legislature. (4) "No body had appeared to be satisfied with an appointment by the Legislature." (5) "Many were anxious even for an immediate choice by the people." (6) "The indispensable necessity of making the Executive independent of the Legislature. — As the Electors would vote at the same time throughout the U.S. and at so great a distance from each other, the great evil of cabal was avoided."[43]

In response, Mason expressed his satisfaction that the plan "had removed some capital objections, particularly the danger of cabal and corruption." It was liable, however, "to this strong objection, that nineteen times in twenty the President would be chosen by the Senate, an improper body for the purpose," Randolph "dwelt on the tendency of such an influence in the Senate over the election of the President in addition to its other powers, to convert that body into a real & dangerous Aristocracy." Pinckney and Rutledge also argued that conferring the choice on the Senate, even in the ultimate resort, was likely to compromise the president's independence. Sherman apparently sensed that some delegates were objecting to the Senate because of the influence of small states there. He "reminded the opponents of the new mode . . . that if the Small States had the advantage in the Senate's deciding among the five highest candidates, the Large States would have in fact the nomination of these candidates." Nonetheless, when Mason moved that the choice be made from the top three rather than the

43 *Ibid.*, p. 500.

top five, the smaller states objected. Sherman declared he "would sooner give up the plan." Apparently, the smaller states reasoned that a choice out of five rather than three allowed them some prospect to land a candidate of their own. Other delegates stressed that, in fact, the choice would most likely be made in the Electoral College, and there would be no need to resort to the Senate. "The increasing intercourse among the people of the States." declared Baldwin, "would render important characters less & less unknown; and the Senate would consequently be less & less likely to have the eventual appointment thrown into their hands." Wilson also stressed that "Continental Characters will multiply as we more & more coalesce, so as to enable the electors in every part of the Union to know & judge of them." Gouverneur Morris similarly felt that the matter would be settled by the electors and would never reach the Senate. Madison considered it "a primary object to render an eventual resort to any part of the Legislature improbable." He referred to two features of the plan that made such an eventuality unlikely. First, given the reluctance of the large states to see the choice fall to the Senate, their "concerted effort . . . would be to make the appointment in the first instance conclusive." Second, the fact that the vice-president, unlike the president, could be selected without a majority would deter electors from wasting their second votes and would heighten the chance that the choice would be made in the Electoral College.[44]

The delegates, it appears, were impressed with the Electoral College scheme, which so successfully blended all the necessary elements to ensure a safe and equitable process for electing a

44 *Ibid.*, pp. 500, 501, 507, 511, 512-13, 514, 523; Bancroft, *History of the Formation of the Constitution* vol. 2, p. 177. The remarks by Abraham Baldwin, Wilson, Gouverneur Morris, and Madison demonstrate that a considerable body of opinion at the convention did not share Mason's view that "nineteen times in twenty" the selection would be made in the Senate (House). Roche's claim that "no one seriously disputed [Mason's] point" is thus unsupportable. Moreover, as Madison notes, certain features of the Electoral College scheme were specifically designed to heighten the prospects of a final choice in the College. On this point, see Warren, *Making of the Constitution*, p. 629. But cf. Farrand, *Framing of Constitution*, p. 167; and Farrand, *Records*, vol. 3, p. 405.

president and which reserved considerable influence for the states. They beat back, by large majorities, every attempt to upset the plan and to restore legislative selection of the executive. There was, however, considerable sentiment against leaving the ultimate choice in the hands of the Senate. Mason regarded it as "utterly inadmissable. He would prefer the Government of Prussia to one which will put all power into the hands of seven or eight men, and fix an Aristocracy worse than absolute monarchy." Mason was vigorously supported by Wilson, who complained that too much power was concentrated under the Constitution in the Senate. As a means of avoiding resort to the Senate, Mason proposed that the candidate receiving the highest number of ballots in the Electoral College be pronounced president whether or not the vote constituted a majority. Wilson proposed that the final choice be accorded the whole legislature rather than the Senate alone. The convention, however, rejected both proposals, just as it rejected numerous other proposals that tended to alter the finely tuned instrument that had evolved. The Electoral College constituted a package deal in which diverse interests and safeguards were neatly balanced. Even the slightest change was likely to undermine the entire structure and to make the machinery inoperable. The delegates were not prone to tamper with the delicate compromise. Only in the matter of the Senate as the venue of ultimate resort were the delegates ready to accept change. Sherman, alert to objections that the Senate represented a center of "aristocracy," proposed that the House of Representatives be substituted for the Senate in the ultimate resort, with voting by states, not per capita. Since this proposal, in contrast to the other suggestions, preserved state power, the amendment was readily accepted by a vote of 10 to 1. Another amendment readily accepted (this time unanimously) was a clause barring "a member of the Legislature of the United States or who holds any office of profit or trust under the United States" from serving as an elector. An incidental by-product of the new scheme was the emergence of the office of vice-president, designed to take care of the electors' second vote. Some delegates voiced opposition to creation of the office, and others protested that the vice-president's appointment as ex officio president of the Senate would violate the principle of the separation of powers. But once again the vast majority wished to preserve the Electoral College plan intact, and the office of vice-president and his role in the Senate were overwhelmingly confirmed.[45]

The convention records demonstrate that the protracted discussion over the mode of electing an executive was but a continuation of the struggle that marked the debate on the composition of the legislature. The smaller states were no more prepared to concede to the large states domination of the process of selecting a chief executive than they were prepared to allow them to dominate the legislature. From a truly "nationalist" choice, as envisaged under the Virginia Plan, the United States executive was transformed, in the give and take of the debates at Philadelphia, into a "federal" institution in which the rights and interests of the states, particularly the smaller states, would also be safeguarded.[46] The compromise that marked the creation of the Electoral College is thus revealed as simply a second round of the Connecticut Compromise in settling large state–small state differences.

This second state of the running battle between the large and the small states was distinguished from the first in several ways. The dispute over the mode of electing an executive never assumed the same dimensions of crisis that nearly disrupted the convention with respect to the issue of the composition of the legislature. Of that confrontation Gouverneur Morris said that "the fate of America was suspended by a hair."[47] After having backed down on the issue of

45 Farrand, *Records.*, vol. 2, pp. 507, 511, 512, 513, 514, 515, 517-21, 522-23, 525-29, 532, 536-38. Gouverneur Morris quipped that the vice president "will be the first heir apparent that ever loved his father." *Ibid.*, p. 537.

46 See the subsequent comment of Jonathan Dayton, delegate from New Jersey: "The States, whatever was their relative magnitude, were equal under the old Confederation, and the small States gave up a part of their rights as a compromise for a better form of government and security; but they cautiously preserved their equal rights in the Senate and in the choice of a Chief Magistrate." *Ibid.*, vol. 3, pp. 400-401. See also the remarks of Gouverneur Morris, *ibid.*, p. 405; and of Rufus King, *ibid.*, p. 462.

47 *Ibid.*, p. 391.

the legislature, the large states were neither able nor willing to create a new impasse. Nevertheless, a major and prolonged struggle (down to the wire) ensued over the system to be instituted for choosing an executive.

Second, the small states were not the only ones to feel directly affected by the various schemes proposed. Once the Connecticut Compromise had accorded the smaller states a handsome increment in the Senate, they understandably refused to contemplate removal of the choice from the legislature. But the slave states were no less reluctant to agree to such a move since it would dissipate the advantage they had secured in the lower house through the three-fifths rule. As a result, a natural alliance existed between the two groups — the slave states and the smaller states — in reserving the decision to the national legislature. However, according the legislature such a role would inevitably have compromised the executive's independence, something that tended to violate the principle of the separation of powers, regarded as sacrosanct by the Founding Fathers. To overcome this deficiency, it was decided that the executive's term of office be relatively long (seven years) and that he be ineligible for reelection. Those conditions, however, were found wanting in other respects, so that the delegates kept probing and testing for an alternative to the triangular arrangement — choice by the legislature, long term, ineligibility.

Now it was the turn of the small states to make a valuable concession, which represents a third noteworthy aspect of the Electoral College compromise. Given the equality of both houses in the legislature, the Senate would be free to exercise a veto in the choice of the executive. In the interest of preventing deadlocks, however, several smaller states resolved to endorse a joint ballot of both houses in selecting an executive. Unlike the Connecticut Compromise, in which the concession of the smaller states was limited to granting the lower house the right to initiate money bills, in this instance the concession was significant and meaningful. It paved the way for a transference of the responsibility of choosing the executive from the legislature to some outside body. The most logical outside body was the people, in direct popular elections. Such a step, however, would have canceled the advantages enjoyed by the smaller and the slave states in the legislature. In response, the committee on Unfinished Parts invented the Electoral College — an ingenious means of preserving the built-in advantages of those states while removing the choice from the legislature. The Electoral College represented a congress away from home for the express and limited purpose of choosing the nation's chief magistrate. The institution of the Electoral College represented the first, indeed the primary, compromise in the arrangements for selecting an executive. National and federal elements were neatly balanced therein. But it was only part of the package. In the event that the Electoral College failed to come up with a sufficiently national choice, the Senate (ultimately the House of Representatives) as the constitutive body of the states, would choose. In effect, therefore, in the event that the Electoral College became a mere nominating body under the domination of the large states, the smaller and the slave states would be well placed to exercise a controlling voice over the final election in the Senate (House of Representatives).[48] (Although the three-fifths rule did not operate at this point, the slave states retained influence by virtue of the number of southern states present.)

The convention's records indicate that many delegates favored direct popular election of the executive but, for the reasons noted, were unable to institute such a system. The most prominent advocates of direct elections were those campaigning for a strong executive — Wilson, Gouverneur Morris, and Madison. Their

48 At various times the contingency arrangement, with the House of Representatives voting by states, has been depicted as the key element of compromise in the electoral College scheme. See for instance, Farrand, "Compromises of the Constitution," pp. 487-48; and Farrand, *Records*, vol. 3, pp. 458, 461, 464. However, as noted, this is only part of the package. The first and fundamental element of compromise lay in the composition of the Electoral College. As summed up by Baldwin, "The Constitution in directing *Electors* to be appointed throughout the United States equal to the whole number of the Senators and Representatives in congress . . . had provided for the existence of as respectable a body as Congress, and in whom the constitution on this business has more confidence than in Congress." *Ibid.*, p. 382. See also the remarks of Gouverneur Morris, *ibid.*, p. 405; and of King, *ibid.*, p. 461.

motives possibly were mixed. They were opposed to lodging the choice in the legislature because the executive's independence would be compromised. They were also concerned about the disproportionate influence of the smaller states in that body. As Martin told the Maryland legislature, "Those who wished as far as possible to establish a *national* instead of a *federal* government, made repeated attempts to have the President chosen by the people at large." Democratic doctrine — the belief that the executive should represent the mass of the people — also seems to have been a factor. In the end the proponents of direct elections achieved partial success. Although the election of the president was not to be a direct act of the people, the state legislatures would be free, if they wished, to confer the choice of electors upon the people themselves. Indeed, that seems to have been the expectation of the Framers. For this reason Madison, in one of the last sessions of the convention, described the election of the president as one "by the people."[49]

Only a few delegates — most notably Mason, Gerry, and Butler — were opposed in principle to direct election of the executive. But such opposition reflected, at least in the case of Mason, not mistrust of representative democracy, but a conviction that the extent of the country and the difficulty of communication did not permit informed selection of a national candidate. True representation could work only over a small area where the people could be acquainted firsthand with the candidates. An attempt to apply representative democracy on a national scale was a distortion of the principle and would simply lead to the manipulation of elections by nefarious characters. The ultimate solution of state electors was, from that standpoint, a sound means of giving expression to the popular will, and it was viewed in that light by the antifederalists in the state ratifying conventions

What clearly emerges from the foregoing is that, contrary to the claim of the Progressive historians, antimajoritarianism was by no means the primary motivation behind the creation of the Electoral College. Nor was it, as Roche would have it, simply the product of a

49 *Ibid.*, pp. 217, 330, 422-23; vol. 2, p. 587; vol. 1, p. 50. [Emphasis in original.] See also *Federalist Papers* Nos. 60 and 68.

last-minute accident of history. Design and purpose guided the creation of the Electoral College. At the same time, however, it would be wrong to suggest that the Electoral College was based on some grand concept of political theory. Also, there is no evidence that the convention was inspired in the matter by classical or medieval precedents. Not once did the delegates advert to the procedures that prevailed in ancient Rome or Greece or in republican Venice. (The Federalist Papers, equally, do not mention any such historical forerunners of the Electoral College.) The delegates were confronted with a practical problem arising from the constellation of clashing forces at Philadelphia, and they devised a practical solution — an ad hoc congress reflecting faithfully the pattern of weighted voting that was an integral part of the operation of the real Congress. The precedents guiding their deliberations were all drawn from state practice.[50]

Two alternatives presented themselves. The indirect method of selection by the legislature and the direct method of popular choice (qualified by a contingency procedure entailing a legislative role.) The latter method represented too national a choice for some; the former, while it offered a satisfactory federal solution, clashed with accepted republican principles. Concepts that had come to be viewed by many as essential components of representative government — separation of powers, limited terms of office, reeligibility, rotation in office, and devices for minimizing electoral corruption — were analyzed and weighed in the search for an unassailable solution. Thus if political theory did not inform the creation of the Electoral College, it provided the essential backdrop to the evolution of this new instrument of government. The device of a congress away from home represented, in sum, an adaptation of state experience modified by the need to resolve the central

50 King commented, "The members of the Convention in settling the manner of electing the Executive of the U.S. seem to have been prejudiced in favor of the manner, to which they were accustomed, in the election of the Governor of their respective States." *Ibid.*, vol. 3, p. 459. Also, as indicated earlier, the notion of establishing an electoral college may well have been drawn from the precedent of the Maryland senate. Elliot, *Debates in State Conventions*, vol. 2, pp. 127-28.

dispute at Philadelphia, namely the large state–small state controversy. Concessions to the federal impulse were reflected in the manner in which the composition of the Electoral College was fixed; in the option accorded the state legislatures to appoint the electors; and in the ultimate choice being bestowed upon the House of Representatives, voting by states. These features stamped the compromise nature of the Electoral College and assured its acceptability both within the convention and without. For in the eyes of its admirers, the Electoral College represented a brilliant scheme for successfully blending national and federal elements in the selection of the nation's chief magistrate.

Table 1: The Evolution of the Electoral College at the Constitutional Convention 1787*

Date	*Source of Proposal*	*Proposal*	*Action Taken*	*Idea Reflected in EC Scheme*	*Citation in Farrand's Records of Constitutional Convention*
May 29	Virginia Plan	Election by national legislature without right of reeligibility. Term undefined.	See next entry		Vol. 1, pp. 20-22
June 1	Pinckney (Mason)	Election by legislature for 7 year term without right of reelection.	Adopted June 1. Vote 8:2		Vol. 1, pp. 77, 78, 81, 88
May 29	Pinckney Plan	Annual election by both houses of legislature in joint ballot.	Never voted upon		Vol. 2, p. 135; Vol. 3, p. 606
June 1	Wilson	People choose electors who select executive.	Rejected June 2. Vote 2:8	X	Vol. 1, pp. 77. 81.
June 1	Dickinson	Removal of executive by national legislature upon request of majority of state legislatures.	Rejected June 2. Vote 1:9		Vol. 1, pp. 78, 87.
June 15	New Jersey Plan	Plural executive to be elected by national legislature representing states, without right of reeligibility. Term undefined. Removable by Congress upon request of majority of state executives.	Never voted upon		Vol. 1, pp. 242-45.
June 18	Hamilton Plan	Election by electors chosen by people; to serve during good behavior.	Never taken up for consideration.		Vol. 1 p. 292; but cf. vol. 3, pp. 617-18
July 17	Gouverneur Morris	Election "by the Citizens of the United States."	Rejected July 17. Vote 1:9		Vol. 2, pp. 22, 32.
July 17	Luther Martin	Election by electors appointed by state legislatures.	Rejected July 17. Vote 2:8	X	Vol. 2, pp. 22, 32.

continued on next page

* This table lists each of the proposals on the mode of electing the executive, as well as several crucial amendments; it does not record the action of the convention on every single amendment proposed.

Table 1 (continued)

Date	*Source of Proposal*	*Proposal*	*Action Taken*	*Idea Reflected in EC Scheme*	*Citation in Farrand's Records of Constitutional Convention*
July 17	Wm. Houston	To strike out ineligibility clause.	Adopted July 17. Vote 6:4	X	Vol. 2, pp. 23, 33.
July 19	Oliver Ellsworth	Executive to be chosen by electors appointed by state legislatures in ratio range of 1:3. Term of 6 years; unlimited right of reelection.	Adopted July 19-20. Vote 6:3:1; 8:2	X	Vol. 2, pp. 50, 57-58.
July 24	Wm Houston	Election by legislature.	Adopted July 24. Vote 7:4		Vol. 2, pp. 97, 101.
July 24	James Wilson	Election by group of electors to be drawn by lot from legislature.	Unanimously postponed		Vol. 2, pp. 97, 106.
July 24	Elbridge Gerry	State legislatures elect executive; if no candidate receives a majority, lower house nominates 2 of 4 and upper house makes final choice.	Overwhelmingly rejected.		Vol. 2, pp. 98-99, 101
July 25	Oliver Ellsworth	Election by legislature but where incumbent is standing, selection be made by electors appointed by state legislatures.	Rejected July 25. Vote 4:7.		Vol. 2, pp. 107, 111.
July 25	Pickney	No person serve in executive more than 6 years out of 12.	Rejected July 25. Vote 5:6.		Vol. 2, pp. 107, 115.
July 25	Williamson	Each person votes for 2 candidates one of whom should not be of voter's state.	Rejected July 25, Vote 5:6	X	Vol. 2, pp. 107, 115.
July 26	Mason	Election by legislature for 7 year term without right of reelection.	Adopted July 26. Vote 7:3:1		Vol. 2, pp. 117, 120.
Aug. 24	Rutledge	Election by legislature in joint ballot.	Adopted Aug. 24. Vote 7:4		Vol. 2, pp. 397, 402-3.

Date	*Source of Proposal*	*Proposal*	*Action Taken*	*Idea Reflected in EC Scheme*	*Citation in Farrand's Records of Constitutional Convention*
Aug. 24	Daniel Carroll	Election by the people.	Rejected Aug. 24 Vote 2:9		Vol. 2, pp. 397, 402
Aug. 24	Gouverneur Morris	Election by electors chosen by people.	Rejected Aug 24. Votes 5:6, 4:4:2		Vol. 2, pp. 397, 404.
Aug. 24	Dayton	Election by legislature with each state having one vote.	Rejected Aug. 24. Vote 5:6.	X	Vol. 2, pp. 397, 403.
Sept. 4	Brearley Committee on Unfinished Parts	Election by electors appointed by state legislatures. Number of electors for each state proportionate to representation in Congress. In absence of majority vote in Electoral College, Senate chooses out of top 5 candidates.	Adopted Sept. 6. Vote 9:2	X	Vol. 2, pp. 517-21, 525-29
Sept. 5	Rutledge	Election by legislature in joint ballot. Term of 7 years without right of reeligibility.	Rejected Sept. 5. Vote 2:8:1		Vol. 2, pp. 507, 511.
Sept. 5	Wilson	Contingency selection by legislature rather than Senate.	Rejected Sept. 5. Vote 3:7:1		Vol. 2, pp. 507, 513.
Sept. 6	Sherman	Contingency selection by House of Representatives rather than Senate, with each State delegation in House having one vote.	Adopted Sept. 6. Vote 10:1	X	Vol. 2, pp. 518-19, 527.

2

Beard's Historiography and the Constitutional Convention

In the scholarly discussions which the bicentennial of the 1787 Constitutional Convention will generate, Charles Beard's *Economic Interpretation of the Constitution of the United States* will undoubtedly be the focus of renewed historiographic debate.[1] Although Beard's revolutionary analysis of the events in Philadelphia was severely challenged during the 1950s by such writers as Douglass Adair, Cecelia M. Kenyon, Robert E. Brown, and Forrest McDonald,[2] later

1 Beard, *Economic Interpretation*. For the impact of Beard's study on later generations of scholars, see Maurice Blinkoff, *The Influence of Charles A. Beard upon American Historiography*, University of Buffalo Studies 12, Monographs in History, vol. 4 (1936), chap. 2. See also Max Lerner, *Ideas Are Weapons: The History and Uses of Ideas* (N.Y.: Viking, 1939), pp. 152-69; Robert E. Brown, *Charles Beard and the Constitution: A Critical Analysis of "An Economic Interpretation of the Constitution"* (Princeton: Princeton Univ. Press, 1956), introduction; and Richard Hofstadter, *The Progressive Historians: Turner, Beard, Parrington* (N.Y.: Knopf, 1968), chap. 6.
For excellent and comprehensive reviews of the debate on the struggle surrounding the adoption of the Constitution, see Jack P. Greene, ed., *The Reinterpretation of the American Revolution, 1763-1789* (N.Y.: Harper & Row, 1968), Introduction; and James H. Hutson, "Country, Court, and Constitution: Antifederalism and the Historians," *WMQ*, 3d ser., vol. 38 (1981), pp. 337-68. Greene, incidentally, after surveying the critical literature, acknowledges "how giant a shadow Beard had cast." *Reinterpretation*, p. 66.

2 Douglass Adair, "The Tenth Federalist Revisited," *WMQ*, 3d ser., vol. 8 (1951) pp. 48-67; Cecelia M. Kenyon, "Men of Little Faith: The Anti-Federalists on the Nature of Representative Government," *WMQ*, 3d ser., vol. 12 (1955), pp. 3-43; Cecelia M. Kenyon, ed., *The Antifederalists* (Indianapolis: Bobbs-Merrill, 1966); Brown, *Charles Beard and the Constitution;* Forrest McDonald, *We the People: The Economic Origins of the Constitution* (Chicago: Univ. of Chicago

commentators have given a new spurt of life to Beard's interpretation. The appearance in 1969 of Gordon Wood's *Creation of the American Public, 1776-1787,* heralded a revival of interest in Beard's work on the Constitution.[3]

The Beard thesis, in brief, held that the Founding Fathers were not a dedicated band of statesmen intent on saving the United States from economic chaos and political anarchy but rather a group of conspirators working to protect their own financial interests and the property interests of the class in society to which they belonged. It was wrong to assume that the Constitution reflected democratic principles since, in fact, it was really designed to serve as a barrier against the rising onslaughts of the leveling masses intent on challenging the sanctity of property. The Constitution was not intended to promote majority will but rather to frustrate it. In Beard's words, it was to be "a government endowed with certain positive powers, but so constructed as to break the force of majority rule and prevent invasions of the property rights of minorities."[4] The Constitution was the product of a cabal, a giant conspiracy in the service of personal property to foist upon the American people a scheme of government that would constrain their striving for democracy.

The evolution of the "plot" is described by Beard as follows:

> Personality . . . was . . . the dynamic element in the movement for the new Constitution.[5] . . . Large and important groups of economic interests were adversely affected by the system of government under the Articles of Confederation, namely, those of public securities, shipping and manufacturing, money at interest; in short, capital as opposed to land. . . . [B]y an increasing recognition of the desperate

trade

Press, 1958). See also McDonald's introduction to the 1986 edition of Beard, *Economic Interpretation*.

3 Wood, *Creation*. Further testimony to the continued vitality of Beard's study is provided by the number of textbooks on American history and American government that continue to explain the Constitutional Convention in terms of his thesis on the economic interests of the Founding Fathers.

4 *Economic Interpretation*, p. 154.

5 *Ibid.*, pp. 50-51.

> straights [sic] in which they were placed, a remarkable fusion of interested forces was effected. The wealth, the influence, and a major portion of the educated men of the country were drawn together in a compact group, "informed by a conscious solidarity of interests," as president Wilson has so tersely put it. . . . Having failed to realized their great purposes through the regular means, the leaders in the movement set to work to secure by a circuitous route the assembling of a Convention to "revise" the Articles of Confederation with the hope of obtaining, outside of the existing legal framework, the adoption of a revolutionary programme.[6]

Undoubtedly, the key chapter in Beard's work is the sixth, entitled "The Constitution as an Economic Document," and the key section of that chapter is the first part, devoted to a consideration of *The Federalist* and the structure of government established at Philadelphia.[7] Upon this section Beard's entire argument depends. In his first five chapters Beard analyzes the 1787 movement for the Constitution and the economic interests of the members of the Constitutional Convention. In the last five chapters he analyzes the process of ratification in the states and the extent to which the vote on behalf of the Constitution represented the wishes of the majority of the population. But it is only by exposing "the true inwardness of the Constitution"[8] that Beard purports to prove the existence of a plot. For even if he succeeded in establishing the relationship of the Framers to a certain class in society, his whole case would fail unless he could also demonstrate how that class affiliation was reflected in the drafting of the particular provisions of the Constitution related to the machinery of government. Only by confirming the link between the interests of the drafters and the actual formulation of the provisions on the "structure of government" can Beard establish his case and label the Framers as conspirators. Beard's originality lay not only in revealing to an unsuspecting America that its Founding Fathers were men of clay (and not the "demigods" that Jefferson had called them)[9] but also in demonstrating that the

6 *Ibid.*, pp. 61-63
7 On the lesser relevance of the second and third parts of chap. 6, see text below, p. 73.
8 *Economic Interpretation*, p. 152.
9 Farrand, *Records*, vol. 3, p. 76.

provisions relating to the framework of government were artifices for crippling democracy, "a foil" in the service of personalty to ward off "the attacks of levelling democracy."[10]

Despite the vast literature that Beard's thesis has spawned, his methodology in the crucial section of Chapter 6 on the "economic implications of the structure of the federal government," has not been subjected to close examination.[11] Beard's assertion regarding the rationale that underlies the framework of government warrants particular scrutiny, as does his use of sources. In analyzing the provisions on "the structure of the federal government" (pp. 152-164 of Chapter 6), Beard ignored almost entirely the most reliable source extant — the records of the Constitutional Convention, documents that he used extensively in Chapter 7 to establish the sociopolitical views of the Founders.[12] Finally, while writers have noted Beard's obsession with "personalty," as against property in general, at Philadelphia, none has suggested an explanation for his singling out personalty in this manner.[13] This paper addresses itself to these aspects of the Beardian thesis not previously dealt with in the literature.

The first purpose is to examine those features of the Constitution bearing on the framework of the federal government that, according to Beard, stamp it as an economic document. In particular, this review will ascertain to what extent Beard succeeded in establishing that "the political science of the new system" was informed by an essentially economic motive. If it can be shown that the structural features of which Beard complained were, since the dawn of

10 *Economic Interpretation*, p. 154

11 *Ibid.*, p. 156. Brown, of course, in his chapter-by-chapter refutation of Beard, also challenges Beard's conclusions on the nature of the Constitution. However, his critical study does not present the analysis of Beard's methodology offered here.

12 In the entire thirteen pages devoted to analyzing the structure of the federal government, Beard makes a solitary reference (p. 157) to the *Records*, and that on an issue tangential to the provisions on government structure. He makes no effort to establish the motives of the Founders on any given provision by reference to their remarks at the Constitutional Convention.

13 See, for instance, Hofstadter, *The Progressive Historians*, p. 231; and Brown, *Charles Beard and the Constitution*, pp. 94-96, 111.

independence in 1776 or shortly thereafter, part and parcel of the constitutions of the various states — the repositories of freedom and liberalism — then how relevant is the claim that these features were introduced to protect a propertied minority "adversely affected" under the Articles of Confederation? In short, given the widespread and simultaneous adoption of these features of government in the states, would it not be reasonable to assume that they were introduced into the federal Constitution for the same reason that they had been incorporated in the state constitutions, namely, because they were deemed vital elements of republican representative government?

Beard describes in the following terms "the structure of the government . . . devised at Philadelphia [which] reflects these several interests and makes improbable any danger to the minority from the majority."[14]

> Their leading idea was to break up the attacking forces at the starting point: the source of political authority for the several branches of the government. This disintegration of positive action at the source was further facilitated by the differentiation in the terms given to the respective departments of the government. And the crowning counterweight to "an interested and over-bearing majority," as Madison phrased it, was secured in the peculiar position assigned to the judiciary, and the use of the sanctity and mystery of the law as a foil to democratic attacks. . . . no two of the leading branches of the government are derived from the same source. The House of Representatives springs from the mass of the people whom the states may see fit to enfranchise. The Senate is elected by the legislatures of the states, which were, in 1787, almost uniformly based on property qualifications. . . . The president is to be chosen by electors selected as the legislatures of the states may determine — at all events by an authority one degree removed from the voters at large. The judiciary is to be chosen by the President and the Senate, both removed from direct popular control and holding [office] for longer terms than the House.

14 *Economic Interpretation*, p. 160.

> A sharp differentiation is made in the terms of the several authorities, so that a complete renewal of the government at one stroke is impossible. The House of Representatives is chosen for two years; the Senators for six, but not at one election, for one-third go out every two years. The President is chosen for four years. The judges of the Supreme Court hold [office] for life. Thus "popular distempers," as eighteenth century publicists called them, are not only restrained from working their havoc through direct elections, but they are further checked by the requirement that they must last six years in order to make their effects felt in the political department of the government, providing they can break through the barriers imposed by the indirect election of the Senate and the President. Finally, there is the check of judicial control that can be overcome only through the manipulation of the appointing power which requires time, or through the operation of a cumbersome amending system.
> The keystone of the whole structure is, in fact, the system provided for judicial control — the most unique contribution to the science of government which has been made by American political genius.[15]

Thus according to Beard, the economic antidemocratic character of the Constitution is revealed by the following features:

1. the separation of powers;
2. checks and balances;
3. a cumbersome amendment system;
4. different modes of election for each branch of government;
5. different terms of office for the respective branches of government;
6. indirect election of the Senate and President;
7. judicial control of legislation.

The Separation of Powers

In Beard's view there was a direct link between *Federalist 10,* in which Madison supposedly enunciated "the fundamental theory of political economy" underlying the Constitution, and *Federalist 47, 48, 49,* and *51,* in which he expounded, in Beard's words, "the original American conception of the balance of powers." Citing

15 *Ibid.*, pp. 161-162

Madison's language in the second part of *Federalist 51*, Beard asserted that the doctrine of the separation of powers was also designed "to guard one part of the society against the injustice of the other part." Beard's conclusion was that "by reflecting these contending interests . . . in the very structure of the government itself," there would be assurance "that a majority cannot dominate the minority — which minority is of course composed of those who possess property that may be attacked."[16]

Besides misrepresenting Madison's analysis of the purposes of the principle of the separation of powers (on which, see below), Beard fails to note that the principle was regarded in the States as an "axiom" of free government.[17] The principle of the separation of powers was expressly spelled out in six of the eleven state constitutions adopted between 1776 and 1787, when the Constitutional Convention sat. The clearest expression of the principle of the separation of powers and its purpose was to be found in the Massachusetts Constitution of 1780.

> In the government of this commonwealth, the legislative department shall never exercise the executive and judicial powers, or either of them; the executive shall never exercise the legislative and judicial powers, or either of them, the judicial shall never exercise the

16 Ibid., pp. 159-160. It is interesting to note that according to Beard , Madison was intent on reflecting the conflicting social interests in the structure of government. Wood's analysis leads him to the opposite conclusion. As he says, "The Americans had taken the people out of the government altogether." "Americans had retained the forms of the Aristotelian schemes of government but had eliminated the substance, thus divesting the various parts of the government of their social constituents. Political power was thus disembodied and became essentially homogeneous." "Separation of powers . . . was simply a partitioning of political power. . . . Such a 'repartition' of power was designed to provide for the safety and ease of the people. . . . But it was not a balance of 'any intrinsic or constitutional properties,' of any social elements, but rather only a balance of governmental functionaries without social connections, all monitored by the people who remained outside." Wood, *Creation*, pp. 599, 604.

17 See Madison in *Federalist* 47. The principle of the separation of powers did not, however, as Madison noted, imply *total* separation, either in theory or in the practice of the states.

> legislative and executive powers, or either of them; to the end it may be a government of laws, and not of men.[18]

The principle of the separation of the powers was not stated explicitly in the federal Constitution, but it lay at the base of the whole document. The absence of this principle in the Constitution would have flawed it beyond reprieve. Indeed, the debates in the state ratifying conventions on this subject revolved around the charge of the Antifederalists that the principle was not adequately instituted in the new Constitution — that the division between the three branches of government was not absolute or at least sufficiently categorical. It was Madison's task in the several numbers of *The Federalist* to prove that the concept as applied in the federal Constitution, while it did not institute a watertight division between the branches of government, conformed to the concept as enunciated by "the celebrated Montesquieu," the "oracle" "always consulted and cited" on the subject, and was consistent with state practice.[19]

Checks and Balances

The great fear of the Founding Fathers was that the legislature was becoming an all-powerful institution. "The legislative department is everywhere extending the sphere of its activity, and drawing all power into its impetuous vortex," declared Madison in *Federalist 48*.

18 Article 30 of Part the First of the Massachusetts Constitution. The other state constitutions with an analogous provision were those of Georgia, Maryland, North Carolina, New Hampshire, and Virginia; see appendix. Copies of the state constitutions can be found in Poore, *State Constitutions*.

19 *Federalist 47*. In the course of the state ratifying debates, two states — North Carolina and Virginia — proposed an amendment to the Constitution spelling out the separation of powers. See Charles C. Tansill, ed., *Documents Illustrative of the Formation of the Union of the American States* (Washington, D.C.: Govt. Printing Office, 1927), pp. 1028-1029, 1045. A draft resolution to this effect was adopted by the House of Representatives but barred by the Senate. As a result, no such draft amendment was adopted for inclusion in the Bill of Rights. The Senate journal provides no explanation for the Senate's decision. For discussion, see Louis Fisher, *President and Congress: Power and Policy* (N.Y.: Free Press, 1972), pp. 22-27.

"Legislative usurpations" he warned "by assembling all power in the same hands, must lead to the same tyranny as is threatened by executive usurpations." The experience of the states in the period after the Revolution, Madison claimed, demonstrated the aggrandizing character of the legislatures. "In republican government," said Madison, "the legislative authority necessarily predominates."[20] To overcome this "inconveniency" it was necessary to divide the legislature into different branches; and to render them, by different modes of election and different principles of action, as little connected with each other as the nature of their common functions and their common dependence on the society will admit."[21]

Bicameral legislatures existed in all of the states except two — Pennsylvania and Georgia. At the Constitutional Convention, George Mason, delegate from Virginia, noted the consensus on the necessity of bicameralism in a legislature. The minutes record his views as follows:

> Much has been said of the unsettled state of the mind of the people, he believed the mind of the people of America, as elsewhere, was unsettled as to some points; but settled as to others. In two points he was sure it was well settled. 1. In an attachment to Republican Government. 2. in an attachment to more than one branch in the Legislature. Their constitutions accord so generally in both these circumstances, that they seem almost to have been preconcerted. This must either have been a miracle, or have resulted from the genius of the people.[22]

The debate at Philadelphia on the form of the legislature reflected, of course, the small-state/large-state controversy. The smaller states were content to retain the one-house Congress of the Articles of Confederation in which each state had but one vote. The larger states, intent that the weight of population be reflected in a two-house legislature, opposed the whole notion of representation by states. The Connecticut Compromise, by resolving the small-state/

20 *Federalist* 51.

21 *Ibid.*

22 Farrand, *Records*, vol. 1, p. 339.

large-state controversy, also resolved the dispute over a bicameral legislature.[23]

Bicameralism represented one form of checks and balances; other devices were the veto in the hands of the executive, authority in the legislature to override the veto, the pardoning power, a council of revision, impeachment of officers, and joint appointment of officials by the executive and some part of the legislature. Without exception, each of the state constitutions contained one or more of these forms of checks and balances. Particularly noteworthy were the constitutions of Massachusetts and New York. Besides bicameral legislatures, these two constitutions provided for a veto of legislation by the governor acting alone or as part of a council of revision, a veto that could be overriden by a two-thirds vote of both houses. Both constitutions also provided for legislation to enter into force automatically if, within a certain period, a bill was neither signed nor vetoed.[24] Impeachment of officers (including the governor), a pardoning power, and a role for both the governor and the legislature in the appointment of judges and officers (civil and military) were also provided for.[25] These two constitutions, in

23 "There is a tradition that, on his return from France, Jefferson called Washington to account at the breakfast table for having agreed to a second chamber. 'Why,' asked Washington, 'did you pour that coffee into your saucer?' 'To cool it,' quoth Jefferson. 'Even so,' said Washington, 'we pour legislation into the senatorial saucer to cool it.'" Farrand, *Records*, vol. 3, p. 359. The story is quite apocryphal since Jefferson, no less than Washington who presided at Philadelphia, realized that it was only the adoption of the Connecticut Compromise, with its provision for state representation in the second house, that saved the Convention from complete collapse.

24 See Article 2, Chapter 1, of Part the Second of the 1780 Massachusetts Constitution and Article 3 of the 1777 New York Constitution.

25 For these various provisions, see the New York Constitution: Articles 3, 18, 23, 32, and 33; and the Massachusetts Constitution: Part the Second, Chapter 1, Section 1, Articles 2 and 4, and Chapter 1, Section 3, Article 6, and Chapter 2, Section 1, Articles 8, 9, and 10. At the Constitutional Convention Madison remarked, "The Revisionary check [was formed] on that [model] of N. York." Farrand, *Records*, vol. 2, p. 291. See also on this point *Federalist 69* by Hamilton, who claims that the Massachusetts Constitution which had no council of revision, was actually the model.

particular, served as convenient models for the framing of various checks and balances in the federal Constitution.

A Cumbersome Amendment System

According to Beard, the constitutional requirement for the adoption of amendments — a two-thirds vote of both houses of Congress and ratification by three-fourths of the state legislatures — represented another major obstacle in the path of majority rule. The system was "cumbersome." In making this charge, Beard was overlooking how radical a departure the new amendment system was from what had obtained under the Articles. The extreme difficulty in gaining the adoption of amendments had been a major complaint against the Articles of Confederation.[26] The unanimity requirement, by which every state legislature had to approve an amendment before it could enter into force, raised an insuperable burden. Twice an important amendment on raising revenue had failed because of the opposition of one state.[27] In the new constitution, the novelty lay in the acceptance of an amending procedure that did not require unanimous consent. In the Virginia Plan, Madison had suggested a liberalized procedure for the adoption of amendments.[28] Given the need to placate the states, the ultimate form adopted by the Convention represented a federal solution to the problem — joint action by the national legislature and the state legislatures, where something less than unanimity was required of each party. Far from being a cumbersome and obstructive procedure, the amending process represented a significant liberalization of the procedures hitherto in force.

26 See remarks by Hamilton in Farrand, *Records*, vol. 2, p. 558, and the comment of Charles Pinckney, *ibid.*, vol. 3 , pp. 120-121.

27 See Alfred H. Kelly and Winfred A. Harbison, *The American Constitution: Its Origins and Development*, 4th ed. (N.Y.: Norton, 1970), p. 111.

28 See Farrand, *Records*, vol. 1, p. 22, Art. 13. "Resd. that provision ought to be made for the amendment of the Articles of Union whensoever it shall seem necessary, and that the assent of the National Legislature ought not to be required thereto."

Precedents in the states existed for both easy and difficult methods of adopting amendments. In Delaware, it was sufficient that an amendment receive slightly more than a two-thirds majority in both houses of the legislature to be adopted,[29] and in South Carolina a majority of the legislature could amend the constitution after ninety days' notice.[30] In Maryland, the proposal had to be published at least three months in advance of elections to the lower house and approved by the new legislature.[31] In effect, the election would serve as a referendum on the proposal. But in Pennsylvania only a special convention convened by the Council of Censors could adopt amendments to the constitution.[32] Similarly, in Georgia the state constitution required a special convention that could be convened only upon petitions from a majority of counties, endorsed by a majority of voters in each county in the state.[33]

The federal amendment procedure was neither as simple as that of Delaware nor as burdensome as that of Georgia. It was designed, in the words of Madison, to guard "equally against that extreme facility, which would render the Constitution too mutable; and that extreme difficulty, which might perpetuate its discovered faults."[34] But once again, state practice, which offered the example of an amendment system not subject to a crippling unanimity requirement, had shown the way.

Different Modes of Election for Each Branch of Government

In republican government, declared Madison in *Federalist 51*, since "the legislative authority necessarily predominates," it was necessary to divide the legislature into different branches "and to render them, by different modes of election and different principles

29 Article 30 of the 1776 Delaware Constitution.
30 Article 44 of the 1778 South Carolina Constitution.
31 Article 59 of the 1776 Maryland Constitution, or Form of Government.
32 Section 47 of the 1776 Pennsylvania Constitution.
33 Article 63 of the 1777 Georgia Constitution.
34 *Federalist* 43.

of action, as little connected with each other as the nature of their common functions and their common dependence on the society will admit." This criterion, to a lesser or greater degree, can be found also in the several state constitutions.

Thus, in the Massachusetts Constitution, while both houses were popularly elected (annually), the lower house (the House of Representatives) was composed of delegates from the corporate towns in proportion to population, while the upper house (the Senate) was composed of forty members elected in proportion to the taxes paid by each district.[35] A similar distinction between population districts and tax districts operated in New Hampshire.[36] In New York, the lower house (the Assembly) was composed of members chosen by the counties according to population, and the upper house (the Senate) was made up of twenty-four members representing the "four great districts" into which the state was divided.[37] In North Carolina, while the Senate was composed of one representative chosen by the people of each county, the House of Commons represented the towns as well as the county districts.[38] Under the Virginia Constitution, the people of each county chose two representatives for the House of Delegates, while the twenty-four members of the Senate were to be chosen by the twenty-four districts into which the state was to be divided.[39] And in Maryland, while the citizens of each county selected four members to the House of Delegates, the members of the Senate were chosen indirectly. The people chose electors of the Senate who, in turn, selected the fifteen senators to sit in the upper house.[40] Clearly, the principle of employing different modes of election for different branches of government was widely applied in the states by 1787.

35 Chapter 1, Sections 2 and 3 of Part the Second of the 1780 Massachusetts Constitution.
36 Part 2: The Form of Government of the 1776 New Hampshire Constitution.
37 Articles 4, 10 and 12 of the 1777 New York Constitution.
38 Articles 1-3 of the 1776 North Carolina Constitution, or Form of Government.
39 Constitution of Virginia.
40 Article 2, 14, and 15 of the Maryland Constitution, or Form of Government.

Different Terms of Office for the Respective Branches of Government

In about half of the states, both branches of the legislature were elected annually. But in the remainder, while the first branch was usually elected annually,[41] the second branch had a longer term of office. In Delaware the members of the Council served for three years, with one-third retiring annually after the first set of elections.[42] Similarly, in New York,[43] and Virginia,[44] the members of the Senate were chosen for four years, with one-fourth retiring annually. In contrast, in Maryland, the full Senate was elected for a five-year term with no staggered terms for its members.[45]

The term of office of the state governors in many cases did not extend beyond a year, but there were also precedents for longer terms. In South Carolina, the governor served for two years (matching the terms of both branches of the legislature);[46] in Delaware he held office for three years, equal to the term of office of the members of the upper house of the legislature (one-third of whom retired annually);[47] and in New York the governor served for three years, while the members of the lower house were elected annually and the members of the upper house served for four years.[48]

Indirect Election of the Senate and the President

In all but three of the states, the executive was elected by the state legislature.[49] In some of these states, the choice was made in a joint

41 The one exception was South Carolina, where the members of the lower house were elected for a two-year term. Articles 12 and 13 of the 1778 South Carolina Constitution.
42 Article 4 of the 1776 Delaware Constitution.
43 Article 11 of the 1777 New York Constitution.
44 The 1776 Constitution of Virginia.
45 Articles 14 and 15 of the 1776 Maryland Constitution.
46 Articles 3, 12, and 13 of the 1778 South Carolina Constitution.
47 Articles 7 and 4 of the 1776 Delaware Constitution.
48 Articles 17, 4, and 11 of the 1777 New York Constitution.
49 See the appendix on state Constitutional practice, 1776-1787.

vote of both houses; in others, each house retained a negative on the other. In two of the three states where the choice was made by popular election, if no candidate received a clear majority, the choice fell to the legislature.[50] Only in New York was the legislature denied any role in choosing the executive even on a contingency basis. A plurality of the popular vote was sufficient to select the governor.[51]

There was also a precedent in the states for the indirect election of the upper house. The Senate in Maryland, as noted earlier, was elected for a five-year term by a group of electors chosen by the people.[52] But in contrast to the federal Senate, elections to the Maryland Senate took place only at the end of the five-year term, since no part of the Senate retired in between. Madison duly noted all of this in *Federalist 63* in his discussion of the proposed United States Senate. He concluded; "The Maryland constitution is daily deriving, from the salutary operation of this part of it [an indirectly elected Senate], a reputation in which it will probably not be rivalled by that of any State in the Union."

Judicial Control of Legislation

Beard's analysis contains two elements: first, that the Founding Fathers actually intended to confer the power of judicial review upon the courts;[53] and second, that the system of appointing judges "during good behavior" was meant to operate as an antimajoritarian device. Whether or not either of these charges is supportable, state

50 See Chapter 2, Article 3, Part the Second, of the 1780 Massachusetts Constitution and the section in the New Hampshire Constitution entitled "Executive Power — President." In the absence of a majority, in both cases the lower house nominated two out of the top four, and the upper house made the final choice out of the two nominees.

51 Article 17 of the 1777 New York Constitution.

52 Article 15 of the 1776 Maryland Constitution. At the Convention, Madison stated categorically, "The Senate was formed on the model of that of Maryld." Farrand, *Records*, vol. 2, p. 291. See also vol. 1, pp. 218-219.

53 A year prior to the appearance of his work on the Constitution in 1913, Beard had published a book, *The Supreme Court and the Constitution*, that endeavored to establish that the Framers intended the courts to exercise the power of judicial review. For Beard this resolved the issue. As he says, "In view of the evidence . . . it is incumbent upon those who make this [contrary] assertion to bring forward positive evidence to the effect that judicial control was not a

practice had long before 1787 instituted appointment during good behavior for judges to ensure the independence of the judiciary. Hamilton, of course, in *Federalist 78,* assumed that the federal judiciary would exercise the power of judicial review, but this does not tell us anything conclusive about the intentions of a majority of the Framers at Philadelphia, given the silence of the Constitution itself on the subject of judicial review. And Hamilton, in this same number of *The Federalist*, highlighted the fact that judicial appointment "during good behavior" was a common feature of the state constitutions. In nine out of thirteen states, judges were accorded such tenure.[54] The Massachusetts Constitution well expressed the dominant concern underlying such provisions:

> It is the right of every citizen to be tried by judges as free, impartial, and independent as the lot of humanity will admit. It is therefore, not only the best policy, but for the security of the rights of the people, and of every citizen, that the judges of the supreme court should hold their offices as long as they behave themselves well, and that they

---

part of the Philadelphia programme" (*Economic Interpretation*, pp. 162-163). This, however, has not stilled the debate. See the discussion in the introduction by Alan F. Westin to Beard's *The Supreme Court and the Constitution* (Englewood Cliffs, N.J.: Prentice-Hall, 1962). The absence of any express clause on judicial review in the Constitution places the onus on those asserting that such a power was, in fact, invested in the Supreme Court. As for Beard, it is clear that his two books served as but a two-stage, concerted attack on the economic motives of the Founding Fathers. The economic thesis that Beard was to enunciate in the 1913 work on the Constitution was already foreshadowed in several passages in his 1912 work on the Court. Judicial review was but one of many "devices" that "bear witness to the fact that the underlying purpose of the Constitution was not the establishment of popular government by means of parliamentary majorities" (*The Supreme Court and the Constitution,* p. 96).

Beard's 1915 study, *Economic Origins of Jeffersonian Democracy* (N.Y.: Macmillan, 1915), extended his economic analysis to the emergence of the Federalist and Republican parties after the Constitution went into force. "The men who framed the Constitution and were instrumental in securing its ratification constituted the dominant group in the new government formed under it . . . . The spokesmen of the Federalist and Republican parties, Hamilton and Jefferson, were respectively the spokesmen of capitalistic and agrarian interests" (pp. 465-466). In effect, the work on Jeffersonian democracy constituted the third volume of a trilogy tracing the economic significance of the drafting, adoption, and implementation of the Constitution.

54 See the appendix. Madison in *Federalist* 39 makes the same point.

should have honorable salaries ascertained and established by standing laws.[55]

In borrowing from these various precedents, the Founding Fathers were clearly motivated by a desire to ensure the absolute independence and integrity of the members of the judiciary, free from pressure and undue influence. Security of tenure and salary was a mainstay of judicial freedom and independence — regardless of any concept of judicial review.

State practices in the matter of life tenure for judges — as in the spheres of the separation of powers, checks and balances, the bicameral legislature, separate modes of appointment for the different branches of government, and staggered terms of office — served as clear guidelines and valuable precedents for the Founding Fathers in their drafting of the provisions of the Constitution. These devices had emerged in the states with the birth of American constitutionalism in 1776.[56] Their simultaneous

55 Article 29 of Part the First. See also Article 30 of the Maryland Constitution.

56 Cf. Max Farrand: "Every provision of the Federal constitution can be accounted for in American experience between 1776 and 1787. *Framing of Constitution*, p. 204.

For a discussion of the emergence of the principle of the separation of powers in the Revolutionary era, see Bernard Bailyn, *The Ideological Origins of the American Revolution* (Cambridge, Mass.: Harvard Univ. Press, 1967), pp. 272-301. On the application of the separation of powers and other basic principles of government in the states, see Part Two, "The Constitution of the States," in Wood, *Creation*, pp. 125-255. According to Wood, by the end of the Critical Period the separation of powers was conceived differently from the way it was originally in the state constitutions. But as Wood notes, the change related to the redistribution of powers among the branches of government. It was widely believed that equilibrium, or balance in government, warranted enhancement of executive power at the expense of legislative power. Wood does not suggest that the separation of powers had now been drained of its republican purpose or endowed with an antisocial, antimajoritarian purpose, in the Beardian sense. On the contrary, the principle was now even more firmly entrenched in the minds of Americans as an essential safeguard of representative republican government. As Wood says, "By 1787 the doctrine of separation of powers, as the various debates over reforming the state constitutions revealed, had become something far more important than what it had been in 1776, becoming in fact for many Americans an 'essential precaution in favor of liberty'" (p. 549). See also pp. 604, 608.

acceptance among so many states signified the consensual basis underlying them. Deriving essentially from the works of the political philosophers Aristotle, Locke, Montesquieu, and Hume, these measures were widely viewed as mainstays of sound republican government. They had not been adopted on the state level as antimajoritarian devices; nor was there any apparent reason to attribute such a purpose to them on the federal level — unless, of course, evidence could be produced to prove that the Founders deliberately designed the framework of the federal government to fulfill an essentially economic purpose and to insulate the interests of the propertied minority from the democratic majority. The next section is devoted to examining the strength of Beard's evidence.

The fundamental flaw in attributing an economic motive to the drafting of the Constitution lies in Beard's interpretation, or misinterpretation, of Madison's concept of the separation of powers as enunciated in *The Federalist*. According to Beard, Madison regarded the principle of the separation of powers as a means of controlling social dissent. As Beard explains, "the attacking forces" (representing "levelling democracy") would be broken up and disintegrated "at the starting point" by force of the separation of powers and the other constitutional barriers.[57] But even a superficial glance at Madison's discussion of the separation of powers in *The Federalist*, upon which Beard relies so heavily, reveals that the principle, according to Madison, was designed to prevent tyranny in government and had nothing to do with preventing the tyranny of popular majorities or the socially deprived.[58] As Madison remarks, in words familiar to every political science student:

57 *Economic Interpretation*, pp. 154, 161.

58 Beard was quite well aware of the true purposes of the separation of powers, as his discussion on *ibid.*, pp. 315-316 reveals. Remarkably enough, a host of other scholars have followed Beard in misinterpreting *The Federalist* and in confusing the purposes for which the separation of powers was adopted. Such prominent writers as E. E. Schattschneider in his *Party Government* (N.Y.:

> The accumulation of all powers legislative, executive and judiciary, in the same hands, whether of one, a few, or many, and whether hereditary, self-appointed, or elective, may justly be pronounced the very definition of tyranny . . . [T]he preservation of liberty requires that the three great departments of power should be separate and distinct.[59]
>
> [T]he great security against a gradual concentration of the several powers in the same department, consists in giving those who administer each department the necessary constitutional means and personal motives to resist encroachments of the others. . . . Ambition must be made to counteract ambition. . . . In framing a government which is to be administered by men over men, the great difficulty lies in this: you must first enable the government to control the governed; and in the next place oblige it to control itself.[60]

Rinehart, 1942), pp. 7-9; Robert A. Dahl, *A Preface to Democratic Theory* (Chicago: Univ. of Chicago Press, 1956), p. 31; James MacGregor Burns, *The Deadlock of Democracy* (Englewood Cliffs, N.J.: Prentice-Hall, 1963), chap. 1; and Paul Eidelberg, *The Philosophy of the American Constitution* (N.Y.: Free Press, 1968), p. 153, have all alleged that the separation of powers was instituted so as to check factious majorities. Illustrative is the following extract from the Burns study (pp. 20-21), which echoes Beard even in its choice of terminology:

> In these seven words [ambition must be made to counteract ambition] Madison drove straight to the heart of the whole problem; here he showed his genius as a political scientist. For he was not content with a flimsy separation of power that lunging politicians could smash through like paper. He was calling for barricade after barricade against the thrust of a popular majority — and the ultimate and impassable barricade was a system of checks and balances. . . . It was a stunning solution to the Framers' problem of checking the tyranny of the majority.

For a discussion of the misunderstanding surrounding the purposes of the separation of powers, see George W. Carey, "Separation of Powers and the Madisonian Model: A Reply to the Critics," *APSR*, vol. 72 (1978), pp. 151-164. However, Carey fails to appreciate that Beard was in fact the trailblazer and that all the other scholars were merely following in his footsteps in misinterpreting the function of the separation of powers. Carey, of course, was also unaware of the key factor that led to the Beard error — his juxtaposition of two quite unrelated passages of *The Federalist* (see below). At the same time, however, it should be pointed out that Carey's article fails to take account of what Madison said at the Constitutional Convention on the role of the Senate, which throws a new light on Madison's intentions (see below).

59 *Federalist 47.*

60 *Federalist 51.*

There is not a word here about breaking up majorities or controlling social dissent. Only in the last third of *Federalist 51* does Madison address himself to social strife, and in this section he makes no reference to the separation of powers. Instead, he reverts to the theme which he had first adumbrated in *Federalist 10* on factions, namely, that an expanded republic provides better prospects for conflicting groups in society to cancel one another out. Here is Beard's rendition of Madison's argument juxtaposed against Madison's own words in *Federalist 51*:

Beard

"It is of great importance in a republic not only to guard the society against the oppression of its rulers, but to guard one part of the society against the injustice of the other part. Different interests necessarily exist in different classes of citizens. If a majority be united by a common interest, the rights of the minority will be insecure." There are two ways of obviating this danger: one is by establishing a monarch independent of popular will, *and the other is by reflecting these contending interests* (so far as their representatives may be enfranchised) *in the very structure of the government itself* so that *a majority cannot dominate the minority – which minority is of course*

Madison

It is of great importance in a republic not only to guard the society against the oppression of its rulers [by the operation of the separation of powers discussed in the first half of this number of *The Federalist*], but to guard one part of the society against the injustice of the other part. Different interests necessarily exist in different classes of citizens. If a majority be united by a common interest, the rights of the minority will be insecure. There are but two methods of providing against this evil: the one by creating a will in the community dependent of the majority — that is, of the society itself; the other, by comprehending in the society so many separate descriptions of citizens as will render an unjust combination of a majority of the whole very improbable, if not impracticable. The first method prevails in all governments possessing an hereditary or self-appointed authority. . . . The second method will be exemplified in the federal republic of the United States. Whilst all authority in it will be derived from and dependent on the society, the society itself will be broken into so many parts, interests and classes of citizens, that the rights of individuals, or of the minority, will be in little danger from interested combinations of the majority. In a free government the security for civil rights must be the same as that for religious rights. It consists in the one case in the multiplicity of interests, and in the other in the multiplicity of sects. The degree of security in both cases will depend on the number of interests and sects; and this may be presumed to depend on the extent of country and number of people comprehended under the same government. . . . It can be little doubted that if the State of Rhode Island was separated from the Confederacy and left to itself, the insecurity of rights under the popular form of government within such narrow limits would be

Beard

composed of those who possess property that may be attacked. "Society itself will be broken into so many parts, interests and classes of citizens, that the rights of individuals, or of the minority, will be in little danger from interested combinations of the majority."[61]

Madison

displayed by such reiterated oppressions of factious majorities that some power altogether independent of the people would soon be called for by the voice of the very factions whose misrule had proved the necessity of it. In the extended republic of the United States, and among the great variety of interests, parties and sects which it embraces, a coalition of a majority of the whole society could seldom take place on any other principles that those of justice and the general good; whilst there being thus less danger to a minor from the will of a major party, there must be less pretext, also, to provide for the security of the former, by introducing into the government a will not dependent on the latter, or, in other words, a will independent of the society itself.

Quite clearly, Beard took liberties with Madison's words in *Federalist 51* just as he did with his words in *Federalist 10*, as Douglass Adair has so effectively demonstrated.[62] The italicized phrases in the Beard passage have no basis in Madison's text. Madison made no reference in *The Federalist* to the structure of government as a means of controlling contending groups in society. This task he left to the natural tendency of society to split into countervailing groups that would neutralize one another. Since he listed only two possible solutions for preventing the injustice of one part of society against the other, it appears obvious that Madison did not regard the separation of powers, discussed earlier by him in this number of *The Federalist*, as a solution to this problem. Moreover, Madison clearly enough, was concerned to preserve control of the government by society and to ward off the alternative solution, namely, external control of the reins of government. Nowhere did Madison suggest here the separation of powers as a

61 *Economic Interpretation*, p. 160; emphasis added.

62 Adair, "The Tenth Federalist Revisited," p. 60. On Madison's notion that stability in society emerges from the interaction of divergent groups, see Douglass Adair, "'That Politics May be Reduced to a Science': David Hume, James Madison and the Tenth *Federalist*," *Huntington Library Quarterly*, vol. 20 (1957), pp. 343-60.

safeguard for the minority (of property owners) against threats from the (propertyless) majority.

Obviously, Beard was intent on establishing a socioeconomic basis for the provisions of the Constitution that dealt with the structure of government. Given the absence of any evidence in the text of the Constitution itself, he turned to Madison's *Federalist 51* to establish such a basis, even if it meant integrating two unconnected passages (one on the structure of government and the other on the divisions within society). Beard could find no source in *The Federalist* to support his claim that the separation of powers was instituted as an antisocial, antimajoritarian device.

This leads to a fundamental question about Beard's methodology. While his chapter entitled "the Constitution as an Economic Document" is divided into three parts, it is only the first part that need interest us. The second and third parts were in no way revelatory. They dealt respectively with the economic powers granted the federal government, such as the power to tax, and the prohibitions imposed on the states in such matters as paper money and laws impairing the obligation of contracts. Manifestly, these provisions had an economic character, and students of the Constitution did not need Beard to underscore that fact for them. It is only in the first part of his Chapter 6 (pp. 152-164), in which the elements of the governmental system — the separation of powers, for instance — are branded as economically inspired antimajoritarian devices, that Beard challenges accepted doctrines. Yet remarkably enough, in this section of Chapter 6 Beard relied exclusively on *The Federalist* to convict the Founders of economic bias in formulating the new structure of government. It is legitimate to ask: Can *The Federalist*, written after the event, and moreover, as a propaganda tract, "a piece of special pleading, offered in the rough-and-tumble of partisan politics,"[63] really furnish meaningful evidence about the intentions of the Framers at Philadelphia? Chief Justice Marshall, it is true, regarded *The Federalist* as a valuable guide to the meaning of the clauses of the Constitution.[64]

63 See the introduction by Edward Mead Earle to *The Federalist* (N.Y.: Modern Library), p. xi.

64 *Ibid.*

But this was before the minutes of the Convention, recorded by Madison (and other participants), were published. However, once Madison's notes had appeared, surely they, rather than any other source, could best serve "as a complete commentary on our Constitution" by elucidating the meaning of any given provision and the motives that lay behind its adoption. Reference to *The Federalist* could only be supplementary, at best.

Interestingly enough, Beard himself recognizes the validity of this argument. In the opening words of his chapter entitled "The Constitution as an Economic Document," he says:

> The true inwardness of the Constitution is not revealed by an examination of its provisions as simple propositions of law; but by a long and careful study of the voluminous correspondence of the period, contemporary newspapers and pamphlets, the records of the debates in the Convention at Philadelphia and in the several state conventions, and particularly, *The Federalist*, which was widely circulated during the struggle over ratification . . . .
>
> Doubtless, the most illuminating of these sources on the economic character of the Constitution are the records of the debates in the Convention, which have come down to us in fragmentary form; and a thorough treatment of material forces reflected in the several clauses of the instrument of government created by the grave assembly at Philadelphia would require a rewriting of the history of the proceedings in the light of the great interests represented there. But an entire volume would scarcely suffice to present the results of such a survey, and an undertaking of this character is accordingly impossible here.[65]

65 *Economic Interpretation*, pp. 152-153. This disclaimer, however, did not prevent Beard from asserting in a footnote: "From this point of view, the old conception of the battle at Philadelphia as a contest between small and large states — as political entities — will have to be severely modified" (n. 1). Beard's thesis on the primacy of economic factors in shaping the structure of government led him to discount accepted interpretations of the controversies that marked the debates at Philadelphia, even though he frankly acknowledged he was not prepared to draw on the minutes themselves. A review of the Convention records would seem to establish that the large-state/small-state controversy was, in fact, central to the discussions and affected the drafting of many more provisions than that of the Senate alone. See, in this regard, chap. 9 below.

This explanation is not convincing. It is particularly puzzling that Beard could have found it easier to wade through voluminous quantities of dusty records in the basement of the U.S. Treasury in search of the Framers' motives[66] than to leaf through the actual minutes of the Convention, conveniently published by Farrand only two years earlier in three handy volumes, complete with an index! Moreover, in other parts of his book, Beard refers quite extensively to the Farrand volumes, just as he does in his work on the Supreme Court published a year earlier in 1912. In fact, the chapter entitled "The Political Doctrines of the Members of the Convention" in his book on the Constitution is based almost exclusively on Farrand's *Records*.[67] Indeed, Beard, in the opening of the chapter, highlights the importance of these volumes for revealing the intentions of the Framers.

> Happily for science, the proceedings at Philadelphia during the drafting of the Constitution were secret, and they were able to discuss with utmost frankness the actual politico-economic results which they desired to reach. Fortunately, also, fragmentary reports of these proceedings have come down to us, and have been put in a definitive form by Professor Farrand.[68]

It is strange, therefore, that Beard should have eschewed using the Records to establish his case on the design of the government instituted under the Constitution and should instead have relied on the far inferior source, namely, the polemics of *The Federalist*. It is submitted, however, that Beard in fact deliberately declined to use the original source, the actual Records of the Convention, since these did not support the particular thesis that he was presenting regarding the role of personalty in instituting a constitution that would serve as a "foil against the attacks of levelling democracy."[69] Concern over property was clearly in evidence during the

66 Beard writes that he was able to use some of the records "only after a vacuum cleaner had been brought in to excavate the ruins" (*Economic Interpretation*, p. 22, n. 1).

67 Beard cites Farrand no less than sixty-eight times in this chapter alone.

68 *Economic Interpretation*, p. 190.

69 *Ibid.*, p. 154.

constitutional debates at Philadelphia,[70] and the delegates were not slow or timid in imposing categorical restrictions on the states in such spheres as the regulation of legal tender and laws impairing the validity of contracts.[71] But Beard's thesis regarding the centrality of property, and most especially personalty, at Philadelphia went beyond the restrictions on the states. He claimed that the very structure of the federal government — separation of powers, checks and balances, etc. — had an essentially economic motive. Beard insisted that "the framework of government" was formed "under the pressure of economic interests."[72] But in the Convention's discussions on the organs of government, concern over property, while clearly in evidence, was far from being central in the debate; and when such concern did surface, as in the discussion on the formation of the Senate, it related to real property rather than to personalty. All this emerges quite clearly from Madison's remarks at the Convention on the subject of a suitable term of office for members of the Senate, quoted here at length, in both his own version and in that of Yates:

> In order to judge of the form to be given to this institution, it will be proper to take a view of the ends to be served by it. These were first to protect the people agst. their rulers: secondly to protect [the people] agst. the transient impressions into which they themselves might be led. A people deliberating in a temperate moment, and with the experience of other nations before them, on the plan of Govt. most likely to secure their happiness, would first be aware, that those charged with the public happiness, might betray their trust. An obvious precaution agst. this danger wd. be to divide the trust

70 See the listings under the heading "Property" in the index of the Farrand volumes.

71 Article 1, Section 10 of the Constitution.

72 *An Economic Interpretation*, p. 153. In Beard's words, the constitutional system "consisted of two fundamental parts — one positive, the other negative: I. A government endowed with certain positive powers, but so constructed as to break the force of majority rule and prevent invasions of the property rights of minorities. II. Restrictions on the state legislatures which had been so vigorous in their attacks on capital." (p. 154.)

between different bodies of men, who might watch & check each other. In this they wd. be governed by the same prudence which has prevailed in organizing the subordinate departments of Govt. where all business liable to abuses is made to pass thro' separate hands, the one being a check on the other. It wd. next occur to such a people, that they themselves were liable to temporary errors, thro' want of information as to their true interest, and that men chosen for a short term, & employed but a small portion of that in public affairs, might err from the same cause. This reflection wd. naturally suggest that the Govt. be so constituted, as that one of its branches might have an oppy. of acquiring a competent knowledge of the public interests. Another reflection equally becoming a people on such an occasion, wd. be that they themselves, as well as a numerous body of Representatives, were liable to err also, from fickleness and passion. A necessary fence agst. this danger would be to select a portion of enlightened citizens, whose limited number, and firmness might seasonably interpose agst. impetuous counsels. It ought finally to occur to a people deliberating on a Govt. for themselves, that as different interests necessarily result from the liberty meant to be secured, the major interest might under sudden impulses be tempted to commit injustice on the minority. In all civilized Countries the people fall into different classes havg. a real or supposed difference of interests. There will be creditors & debtors, farmers, merchts. & manufacturers. There will be particularly the distinction of rich & poor. It was true as had been observd. (by Mr. Pinkney) we had not among us those hereditary distinctions, of rank which were a great source of the contests in the ancient Govts. as well as the modern States of Europe, nor those extremes of wealth or poverty which characterize the latter. We cannot be regarded even at this time, as one homogeneous mass, in which every thing that affects a part will affect in the same manner the whole. *In framing a system which we wish to last for ages, we shd. not lose sight of the changes which ages will produce. An increase of population will of necessity increase the proportion of those who will labour under all the hardships of life, & secretly sigh for a more equal distribution of its blessings. These may in time outnumber those who are placed above the feelings of indigence. According to the equal laws of suffrage, the power will slide into the hands of the former No agrarian attempts have yet been made in this Country, but symptoms of a leveling spirit, as we have understood, have sufficiently appeared in a certain quarters* [sic] *to give notice of the future danger. How is this danger to be guarded agst. on republican principles? How is the danger in all cases of interested coalitions to oppress the minority to be guarded against? Among other means by the establishment of a body in the Govt. sufficiently respectable for its wisdom & virtue, to aid on such emergencies, the preponderance of justice by throwing its weight into that scale. Such being the objects of the second*

> *branch in the proposed Govt. he thought a considerable duration ought to be given to it.*[73]

In Yates's minutes Madison's comments are recorded as follows:

> Mr. Madison. We are now to determine whether the republican form shall be the basis of our government — I admit there is weight in the objection of the gentleman from South Carolina [Pinckney]; but no plan can steer clear of objections. That great powers are to be given, there is no doubt; and that those powers may be abused is equally true. It is also probable that members may lose their attachments to the states which sent them — Yet the first branch will control them in many of their abuses. But we are now forming a body on whose wisdom we mean to rely, and their permanency in office secures a proper field in which they may exert their firmness and knowledge. Democratic communities may be unsteady, and be led to action by the impulse of the moment. — Like individuals they may be sensible of their own weakness, and may desire the counsels and checks of friends to guard them against the turbulency and weakness of unruly passions. Such are the various pursuits of this life, that in all civilized countries, the interest of a community will be divided. There will be debtors and creditors, and an unequal possession of property, and hence arises different views and different objects in government. This indeed is the ground-work of aristocracy; and we find it blended in every government, both ancient and modern. Even where titles have survived property, we discover the noble beggar haughty and assuming.
>
> The man who is possessed of wealth, who lolls on his sofa or rolls in his carriage, cannot judge of the wants or feelings of the day laborer. *The government we mean to erect is intended to last for ages. The landed interest,*

73 Farrand, *Records*, vol. 1, pp. 421-423 (emphasis added). On another occasion Madison said: "The three principle [sic] classes into which our citizens were divisible, were the landed the commercial, & the manufacturing. The 2d. & 3rd. class [sic], bear as yet a small proportion to the first. The proportion however will daily increase. We see in the populous Countries in Europe now, what we shall be hereafter." (*Ibid.*, vol. 2, p. 124).
Charles Pinckney, delegate from South Carolina, divided the people of the United States into three different classes: (1) professional men, (2) commercial men, and (3) "The landed interest, the owners and cultivators of the soil, who are and ought ever to be the governing spring in the system." Of the commercial class Pinckney said: "If that commercial policy is pursued which I conceive to be the true one, the merchants of this Country will not or ought not for a considerable time to have much weight in the political scale." Farrand, *Records*, vol. 1, pp. 402, 411. See also, on the primacy of the "landed class," Hamilton in *Federalist 60*.

at present, is prevalent; but in process of time, when we approximate to the states and kingdoms of Europe; when the number of landholders shall be comparatively small, through the various means of trade and manufactures, will not the landed interest be overbalanced in future elections, and unless wisely provided against, what will become of your government? In England, at this day, if elections were open to all classes of people, the property of the landed proprietors would be insecure. An agrarian law would soon take place. If these observations be just, our government ought to secure the permanent interests of the country against innovation. Landholders ought to have a share in the government to support these invaluable interests and to balance and check the other. They ought to be so constituted as to protect the minority of the opulent against the majority. The senate, therefore, ought to be this body; and to answer these purposes, they ought to have permanency and stability. Various have been the propositions; but my opinion is, the longer they continue in office, the better will these views be answered.[74]

74 Farrand, *Records*, vol. 1, pp. 430-431 (emphasis added). The delegates frequently referred to the Senate as the "aristocratic " body in the legislature, designed to restrain or balance the turbulent lower or "democratic" house. Since the Senate was meant to represent and protect "wealth," there was even a suggestion that membership therein be conditional on the ownership of considerable property. The proposal was rejected , as was a suggestion that senators not be paid a salary, to encourage only the wealthy to submit their candidacies. *Ibid.*, pp. 424-27, 433-34, 512-14, 517-18, 562.
Designation of the lower house as the "democratic" one and the upper house as the "aristocratic" body accorded with the widely accepted notion, popularly espoused by John Adams, that the only sound government was a balanced one reflecting the three elements — democracy, aristocracy, and monarchy (the executive). Confirmation of the measure of influence which Adams' theory of government exercised at the Convention can be gleaned from the following letter sent by Benjamin Rush to Richard Price in the first week of the deliberations: "Mr. Adam's book [Defense of the Constitutions of Government of the United States of America] has diffused such excellent principles among us, that there is little doubt of our adopting a vigorous and compounded federal legislature. Our illustrious minister in this gift to his country has done us more service than if he had obtained alliances for us with all the nations of Europe." (Farrand, *Records*, vol. 3, p. 33.)
For further discussion of this topic, see Wood, *Creation*, chap. 14: "The Relevance and Irrelevance of John Adams." On the subject of the Yates notes, see Arnold A. Rogow, "The Federal Convention: Madison and Yates," *AHR*, vol. 60 (1954-55), pp. 323-35. Questions have been raised recently regarding the reliability of the published version of Yates's notes. See James H. Hutson, "Robert Yates' Notes on the Constitutional Convention of 1787: Citizen Genet's Edition," *Quarterly Journal of the Library of Congress*, vol. 35 (1978), pp. 173-82. However, where states' rights issues are not involved, as in the present instance, there is no reason to doubt the accuracy of Yates's minutes.

In contrast to his discussion in *The Federalist,* Madison here clearly postulates also a sociopolitical function for the Senate. Bicameralism and the format of the Senate are intended to preclude not only governmental tyranny but also the tyranny of the dispossessed. In short, they serve a class purpose and not strictly a constitutional purpose. Given those remarks by Madison, the question arises: Why did Beard not make use of them? Why did he prefer to revise Madison's comments on the subject of the separation of powers in *The Federalist* rather than refer to the one true source of incriminating evidence, the Convention records? Could it be that Beard was unaware of this material in Farrand? This seems hardly credible, given his extensive use of the Farrand volumes in this and other studies, as noted above. In fact, Beard on p. 192 cites, in a different connection, the very page in Farrand (I, 421) where Madison's remarks are excerpted.

Beard abjured citing as evidence the most relevant remarks of Madison at the Convention because these remarks did not fit in, and in fact collided with the thesis that Beard was presenting. For one thing, Madison seems to have been more concerned with agrarian laws than with debtor laws,[75] although if he and his colleagues represented "personalty," the latter should have been the subject of their prime concern. Second, Madison provides a string of "governmental" considerations for a strong and stable Senate, and only at the end does he list an economic factor. This hardly demonstrates the primacy of economic considerations in the Convention's deliberations. Third, why was Madison only concerned with the long-range economic consequences which the "ages" would effect? If, indeed, Madison was acting as the representative of "personalty" interests "adversely affected under the Articles of Confederation," that is over the past decade, then why was he referring to some "future danger"? Should he not have waxed strong on the "current danger" that was threatening "property interests . . . immediately at stake"?[76] And should he

75 An agrarian law in Madison's terms clearly means a law for "the equal division of land," which is, of course, to be distinguished from a debtor law.

76 Beard, *Economic Interpretation*, p. 188. Cf. Brown, *Charles Beard and the Constitution*, pp. 94-95, who also makes this point.

not have urged the necessity of a strong Senate to ward off the *immediate* threat? Finally, and most crucially, Madison's words (certainly in the Yates version) are directed to protecting the *landed interest*. Madison seeks to protect that interest not only from the landless element but from the challenge of *personalty* ("trade and manufactures"). This is precisely the opposite of Beard's thesis, according to which personalty was the driving force behind the adoption of the Constitution. Instead of campaigning *on behalf* of personalty against realty, Madison is bent on preserving the influence and status of realty. Little wonder that Beard found it inopportune to advert to the records of the Philadelphia convention. Madison's comments at Philadelphia on the subject of property not only fail to corroborate Beard's interpretation; they contradict it. As a result, they could not be cited.

But why, indeed, was Beard so insistent on interpreting the struggle for the Constitution as one of personalty versus realty, "capital as opposed to land"?[77] Would it not have been sufficient for him to assert that the Convention was committed to protecting property, without seeking to distinguish between one species of property and another? For, as Richard Hofstadter has commented, both radicals and conservatives were then in agreement that government should protect property,[78] and few would have taken issue with Beard on this point. Why was the dichotomy of personalty versus realty of such fundamental importance for Beard's thesis? The answer, it is suggested, lies in an appreciation of Beard's real aim.

Numerous writers, and particularly Max Lerner, Morton White, Douglass Adair, and Richard Hofstadter, have noted Beard's debt to Marxist thought.[79] Interestingly enough, Beard does not refer to Marx or to Marxist writings, even in a footnote. Only in his introduction to the 1935 edition, in the course of denying that his

77 Beard, *Economic Interpretation*, pp. 63, 325.

78 Hofstadter, *The Progressive Historians*, p. 231. See also Brown, *Charles Beard and the Constitution*, pp. 94-96, 111.

79 Lerner, *Ideas Are Weapons. The History and Uses of Ideas*, p. 165; Morton G. White, *Social Thought in America: The Revolt Against Formalism* (N.Y.: Viking, 1949), chap. 8; Adair, "The Tenth Federalist Revisited," pp. 60-62; Hofstadter, *The Progressive Historians*, pp. 196-200.

work was derived from "Marxian theories," does Beard acknowledge that when he wrote his book on the Constitution he was "in common with all students . . . in modern history conversant with the theories and writings of Marx."[80] Given the nature of his study — an analysis of the Constitution based on concepts of economic determinism — it is odd, to say the least, that Beard found not a single occasion to refer to Marx. However, in propounding his thesis of economic determinism (as reflected in Madison's *Federalist 10*), Beard relies heavily[81] on a book by Edwin Seligman, *The Economic Interpretation of History*.[82] The Seligman work, in turn, is based essentially on Marx's philosophy of history; and in fact, the passage cited by Beard, is, as noted by Morton White and Douglass Adair, nearly a verbatim quotation from one of Engels's studies.[83] Beard obviously could not have been unaware of the heavy debt that he owed Marx and Engels at second hand. As Morton White notes, Seligman's work "was the most forthright academic defense of Marx's theory of history available in America at the time."[84]

Even more significant is Beard's understanding of the economic factor in history. He professes to have found the theory of economic determinism in Madison's *Federalist 10*.[85] After quoting extensively from this number, to the effect that "the most common and durable source of factions has been the various and unequal distribution of property," Beard presents his own summary of Madison's views:

> Different degrees and kinds of property inevitably exist in modern society; party doctrines and "principles" originate in the sentiments and views which the possession of various kinds of property creates in the minds of the possessors; class and group divisions based on

80 *An Economic Interpretation*, 1935 edition, p. xiii.

81 See references *ibid.*, p. 6, n. 2 and p. 15 n. 1.

82 Edwin Seligman, *The Economic Interpretation of History* (N.Y.: Columbia Univ. Press, 1902).

83 White, *Social Thought in America*, p. 120; Adair, "Tenth Federalist Revisited," pp. 60-61, and n. 25. See also Hofstadter, *The Progressive Historians*, pp. 198-99.

84 White, *Social Thought in America*, p. 120. In this connection, however, it is important to bear in mind the caveat of Douglass Adair: "It should be noted . . . that the connotations of the term 'Marxist,' are different in 1913 and 1951." (The Tenth Federalist Revisited," p. 61, n. 26.)

85 *An Economic Interpretation*, pp. 14-16.

> property lie at the basis of modern government; and politics and constitutional law are inevitably a reflex of these contending interests.

This leads Beard to declare:

> Those who are inclined to repudiate the hypothesis of economic determinism as a European importation [that is, from Marx] must, therefore, revise their views, on learning that one of the earliest, and certainly one of the clearest, statements of it came from a profound student of politics who sat in the Convention that framed our fundamental law.[86]

But whatever this "profound student of politics" would say of Beard's summary of his views on economic determinism, it is clear that Beard goes far beyond Madison when he makes the following assertion: "The whole theory of the economic interpretation of history rests upon the concept that social progress in general is the result of contending interests in society — some favorable, others opposed, to change."[87]

There is not a word about "social progress" in Madison or that such progress is the result of contending interests in society, that is, the class struggle. In contrast, Beard posited a dynamic interaction between the divisions in society as an essential condition for producing "social progress." This concept is, of course, in the classical Marxist tradition. While it is alien to Madison's theories (he, in fact, deplored the existence of factions), it is intrinsic to those of Marx.[88] It is drawn from the dialectic interpretation of history as

86 *Ibid.*, pp. 15-16. It is curious that Beard could obliquely refer to Marx in this passage on economic determinism and yet not find it necessary to cite his name here or at any other point in his study.

87 *Ibid.*, p. 19.

88 As noted by Morton White, Marx acknowledged: "No credit is due to me for discovering the existence of classes in modern society nor yet the struggle between them. Long before me bourgeois historians had described the intellectual development of this class struggle . . . What I did that was new was to prove . . . that the *existence of classes* is only bound up with *particular, historic, phases in the development of production*." Emphasis in original. *Karl Marx and Friedrich Engels: Correspondence, 1846-1895*, ed. and trans. Dona Torr (N.Y., 1936), p. 57; cited in *Social Thought in America*, p. 124, n. 27.
Hofstadter points out that the notion of "progress" as a product of the economic interpretation of history is fundamental in Seligman, upon whom Beard relied so heavily. (*The Progressive Historians*, p. 200).

reflected, for instance, in the opening words of *The Communist Manifesto*: "The history of all hitherto existing society is the history of class struggles."[89] And, in the words of Engels:

> In every historical epoch, the prevailing mode of economic production and exchange, and the social organisation necessarily following from it, form the basis upon which is built up, and from which alone can be explained, the political and intellectual history of that epoch; that consequently the whole history of mankind . . . has been a history of class struggles, contests between exploiting and exploited, ruling and oppressed classes; that the history of these class struggles forms a series of evolution."[90]

If Beard found Marx (on economic determinism) in Madison, it is likewise easy enough to find Marx (on the dialectical interpretation of history) in Beard. History is an unfolding of progressive stages in the social development of mankind resulting from the class struggle which manifests itself in each age. Given this perspective on Beard's thinking, it is not difficult to understand his particular appreciation of the Constitutional Convention in the dialectical time chart of history and his obsession with personalty as against realty. The word "personalty" is a euphemism for the bourgeoisie, for, as he says, it was composed of these four groups: money, public securities, trade and shipping, and manufacturing.[91] Beard was, in fact, portraying the Constitutional Convention as one of the revolutionary stages in the dialectic of history: the revolt of the bourgeoisie against the landed aristocracy — the "landed proprietors," as Beard labeled them.[92] Had Beard resorted to Marxist terminology, his thesis would have been discounted from the start.

89 Karl Marx and Friedrich Engels, *Manifesto of the Communist Party* (N.Y.: International Publishers, 1948), p. 9.

90 *Ibid.*, preface by Engels, p. 6.

91 *An Economic Interpretation*, pp. 16-17, 31-51, 63, 324. *The Communist Manifesto* refers to the bourgeoisie as "the manufacturing middle class" involved in "commerce," "navigation" and "industry" (p. 10).

92 Beard, *An Economic Interpretation*, p. 28. Note that in discussing the funding of the public securities by the new government after adoption of the Constitution, Beard refers to this act as "the first really great achievement of *nascent capitalism* in the United States" (p. 21, emphasis added). In his work *Economic Origins of Jefersonian Democracy*, Beard was quite candid in depicting

It was only by "wrapping himself in the American flag" and revealing Marx in Madison under a more neutral terminology that he was able to promote the radical thesis he was enunciating on the purpose of the Constitution "as an instrument of class exploitation."[93] The secret of Beard's success was his ability to portray his economic thesis as a distinctively American contribution to political science. But, at base, Beard's economic interpretation was a classical Marxist interpretation —personalty (bourgeoisie) as against realty (gentry).[94] For Beard, the Constitutional Convention was simply a stage in the "social progress" effected by the dialectic of history.

---

the Constitution as "the product of a conflict between capitalistic and agrarian interests. . . . The capitalistic interests whose rights were especially safeguarded by the Constitution had been harried almost to death, during the few years preceding the adoption of the Constitution. . . . In the contest for the Constitution, they formed the aggressive party, and though a minority of the nation, they were able to wring from the reluctant voters a ratification of the new instrument of government" (pp. 464-65).

It should also be noted that in his conclusions (*Economic Interpretation*, p. 325), Beard omits any reference to the landed aristocracy. The struggle for and against the Constitution becomes one purely of "substantial personalty interests on the one hand and the small farming and debtor interests on the other." This is not sufficient to cancel the lines of analysis presented in the body of his study and summed up in his terse phrase: "In short, [it was] capital as opposed to land" (p. 63).

93 Adair, "Tenth Federalist Revisited," p. 61. As Adair says, "Beard's study . . . [of] Madison's 'master theory' merely revealed him [Madison] as a writer who was indiscreet enough to reveal in the Tenth *Federalist* the grinning death's head of economic exploitation concealed behind the decorous and misleading phrases of the Constitution" (*ibid.*, p. 62).

94 In saying that Beard's economic interpretation of the Constitution is *at base* Marxist, of course, it is not suggested that his interpretation was completely Marxist. As Max Lerner (*Ideas Are Weapons*, pp. 160-62) and Morton White (*Social Thought in America*, pp. 121-25) have pointed out, Beard, while presenting a Marxist line of argument, nevertheless diverged in several crucial ways from orthodox Marxist theory. What is suggested here is that in stressing personalty above all other property as the driving force behind the Constitution (an issue which, as noted, some of the foregoing writers adverted to but never sought to explain), Beard is attempting to place the Convention in the dialectic time chart of history as the American counterpart of the rise of the bourgeoisie. In this respect, Beard's approach was clearly Marxist and not Madisonian.

Conclusions

Beard's thesis on the economic significance of the Constitution is composed, essentially, of two parts. The first part is devoted to establishing the economic interest of the Framers and to demonstrating that they represented a distinct economic group in society: personalty. The second part relates to the manner in which this economic interest was translated into the drafting of the

---

An interesting paradox in Beard's writing was highlighted by Robert E. Thomas, in "A Reappraisal of Charles A. Beard's *An Economic Interpretation of the Constitution of the United States,*" *AHR*, vol. 57 (1951-52), pp. 370-75, and Pope McCorkle, in "The Historian as Intellectual: Charles Beard and the Constitution Reconsidered," *American Journal of Legal History*, vol. 28 (1984), pp. 314-63. On one hand, Beard alleged that the Constitution was foisted on the American people by property-minded individuals representing personalty who were bent on frustrating, rather than promoting, majority will. On the other hand, Beard contemporaneously praised profusely the handiwork of the Founding Fathers and warmly endorsed the Hamiltonian economic system which was made possible by the adoption of the Constitution. Beard charged that the Framers had instituted judicial review in order to provide a bulwark against leveling tendencies and at the same time hailed the role of the court as a brilliant contribution to the science of government. To resolve this paradox, Thomas maintains that Beard was a Hamiltonian who, nonetheless, wished to discredit "the juristic theory of the origin and nature of the Constitution." Beard, Thomas concludes, was in no way intent on disparaging either "the Court, the Fathers or the Constitution" (p. 374). McCorkle contends that Beard was a Progressive reformer who saw in the Federalist Hamiltonian system, with its emphasis on a strong central government armed with wide-ranging powers, the answer to the social needs of the industrial state which the United States had become at the beginning of the twentieth century. According to McCorkle, Beard was a Tory Radical and his views were heterodox. McCorkle dismisses as inadequate the attempts by historians Richard Hofstadter, Richard B. Morris, and Leonard Levy to explain Beard's heterodoxy and the dichotomies in his ideology by reference to an "intellectual split personality." At the same time, McCorkle is reduced to suggesting that "a psychological analysis may help illuminate the reasons for Beard's heterodox stance" (pp. 341-42 and n. 159).

The interpretation presented here, it is submitted, renders such a request unnecessary. Beard was consistent throughout. The Constitutional Convention, according to Beard, represented the rise to power of the capitalist class which desired a charter of government that would both defend and promote its economic interests, essentially personalty. In accordance with his dialectical materialistic approach to history, Beard, while analyzing the provisions of the Constitution. The result was an instrument of government so structured as to shatter the electoral demands of the masses. Various writers, most notably McDonald and Brown, have challenged Beard's conclusions regarding the economic interests of the Founding Fathers and of those who opposed them in the debate on the adoption of the Constitution. Likewise, Cecilia Kenyon disputed Beard's claim that the Anti-Federalists were more democratic than the Federalists.[95] The present paper focuses on the second part of the Beardian thesis by questioning the economic nature of the structure of the Constitution through an examination of its antecedents. According to Beard, the assembly that gathered at Philadelphia in 1787 was engaged in a giant conspiracy to foist onto the American people a constitution that would secure the property interest of the conspirators. To this end, they produced a series of devices in government, such as the separation of powers, and checks and balances to break the force of majority demands.

Upon examination however, it becomes clear that every feature of the federal Constitution that Beard lists as an antimajoritarian device already existed in the state constitutions in one form or

manner in which an economically conscious minority engineered a constitutional revolution, hailed the ascendance of the Federalists (at Philadelphia and in the new government) as the driving force behind the emergence of a capitalist America. There was no contradiction between Beard's interpretation of the significance of the Constitutional Convention and his endorsement of the Hamiltonian system. The adoption of the Constitution and the implementation of the Federalist program were but consecutive chapters in the rise of the capitalist class to power in the United States. By the same token, Beard could only decry Republican efforts in 1800 to set the clock back and cause the United States to revert to an agrarian republic. However, as Beard makes clear, Jefferson's entry into office that year effected no essential change in the capitalist course upon which America had embarked in 1787. "Jeffersonian Democracy . . . did not involve any fundamental alterations in the national Constitution which the Federalists had designed as a foil to the levelling propensities of the masses," Beard concluded in his *Economic Origins of Jeffersonian Democracy* (p. 467). Given Beard's view of the role that the Constitutional Convention and the Federalist programs fulfilled in the dialectic of history, there was a measure of inevitability in the powerlessness of the Jeffersonians to alter the capitalist course of America's development.

95 See above, note 2.

another. The federal Constitution, in fact, represented a composite of various practices instituted in the states for securing representative republican government. Drawing their inspiration from the writings of political philosophers, the Framers designed these measures, as Madison made clear in *The Federalist*, to forestall tyranny in government. The onus was clearly on Beard to demonstrate that the Founders, in introducing these various features into the federal system of government, intended to "break the force of majority rule and prevent invasions of the property rights of minorities." This he failed to do. Instead, he adopted an a priori argument based on the economic interests of the delegates to the Philadelphia Convention. The economic interests of the Framers were never persuasively linked with the provisions of the Constitution on the framework of government. Rather, Beard assumed what he had undertaken to prove.

But Beard's analysis of the provisions of the Constitution on the structure of government is open to challenge on a yet more fundamental basis. He omitted to utilize the one unimpeachable source that could establish the clear motives of the Framers: the records of the Constitutional Convention. In lieu of this, he sought to extract from *The Federalist* the evidence he needed to convict the Founding fathers of economic bias in the drafting of the provisions of the Constitution on the structure of government. First, he cited Madison's *Federalist 10*, which discusses the causes for divisions within society, primarily economic. He then adduced *Federalist 51*, which ostensibly provides a blueprint of government for controlling those diverse elements to protect property interests of the minority. But this is a distortion of Madison's thesis, since nowhere in *Federalist 51* does Madison assign a role to the instruments of government for checking fractious majorities. This task he left to the expanse of territory and the multiplicity of contending groups that it would produce, groups that would tend to neutralize one another. Had Beard turned to Farrand, he would have found clear-cut evidence of a socioeconomic motive, at least on the part of Madison, in the formulation of the Senate. Beard does not cite this source, since it does not support his thesis regarding the centrality of personalty at Philadelphia. Indeed, it contradicts his thesis.

Rather than evidencing concern over the fate of personalty, Madison was at pains to preserve the influence of realty in the face of the challenge from personalty. At all events, personalty was certainly not at the center of the deliberations at the Constitutional Convention. This raises the question of why Beard was so obsessed with the role of personalty, as opposed to property generally, in the adoption of the Constitution. For there is no doubt that the protection of property seriously exercised the delegates to the Convention.

The explanation lies in the Marxist roots of Beard's thesis. He saw in the work of the Constitutional Convention the hand of dialectical materialism. It was a distinct stage in the progressive march of history. If America did not need to cast off the shackles of feudalism, it nonetheless had to proceed through the stages of economic development. In accordance with the Marxist principle of economic determinism, the growing commercial and industrial classes were supposed to seize the reins of power from the landed proprietors and formulate an instrument of government to serve their needs. What Beard labeled *personalty* was nothing other than the bourgeoisie. If in Europe the contest pitted the bourgeoisie against the aristocracy, in America it was a case of personalty as distinguished from realty, or "capital as opposed to land."[96] Beard was intent on establishing a thesis according to which the

96 *An Economic Interpretation*, p. 63. Cf. the following comment made by Beard in 1916 in a series of lectures at Amherst College. "In the United States where there was no clerical estate or established nobility to be represented in the government, the existence of the two fundamental property groups — the owners of realty and the owners of personalty — was taken into account either in positive constitutional law or in the check and balance system provided by the separation of powers." In a footnote appended at this point Beard says: "Much ingenuity has been spent by American lawyers in elaborating the theoretical fictions of Montesquieu. The real significance of the separation of powers and its relation to the balance of class interests in society was appreciated by eighteenth century writers." (*The Economic Basis of Politics* [London: Allen & Unwin, 1935], pp. 69-70.) This comment on the nature of the American constitutional system and the reference to "the theoretical fictions of Montesquieu" sum up Beard's assessment of the Framer's purposes in establishing a system of government based on the separation of powers.

constitutional revolution was engineered by personalty. He sought to establish his case by the circumstantial evidence derived from the economic holdings of the Framers rather than by drawing on their actual words at the Convention, which did not coincide with, and indeed contradicted his thesis. Beard resorted to *The Federalist*, even at the cost of adjusting Madison's arguments; and for this reason he abjured drawing on the constitutional records themselves.

In all the extended debate that has ensued since Beard's study on the Constitutional Convention first appeared, the flaws in his methodology noted above somehow escaped the attention of even his severest critics. Any attempt in this bicentennial season to resuscitate the Beardian analysis of the structure of government adopted at Philadelphia must address itself to the question of whether Beard's views were not stamped with an ideological bias that led to selective and tendentious use of the evidence upon which his thesis was purportedly based. No one doubts that the movement for drafting a new constitution at Philadelphia was informed by, among other factors, concern over the state of the national economy and by a desire also to secure property interests — objectives as eagerly sought by the leading Antifederalists as by the Federalists. But it is one thing to recognize the Founders' desire to ensure the rights of property under the Constitution, in common with other rights, and it is another thing to attribute the very structure of government to a desire to serve a particular form of property by hamstringing popular rule. Beard, it must be recognized, never did succeed in establishing that the primary impulse which engendered the American system of government was antidemocratic and antimajoritarian.

Table 2: State Constitutional Practice, 1776-1787

					Mode of Election & Term of Legislature		
	Year of Adoption of Constituion	*Form of Adoption of Constitution*	*Separation of Powers Clause*	*Bicameralism*	*Lower House*	*Upper House*	*Staggered Elections*
Delaware	1776	Convention	no	yes	popular; 1	popular; 3	Upper House
Georgia	1777	Convention	yes; Art. I	no	popular; 1		no
Maryland	1776	Convention	yes; Art. VI	yes	popular; 1	Indirect elections for Senate via electors; 5	no
Massachusetts	1780	Convention & ratification by people	yes; Art XXX, Part the First	yes	popular; 1	popular; 1	no
New Hampshire	1784	Convention & ratification by people	yes; Art. XXXVII	yes	popular; 1	popular; 1	no
New Jersey	1776	Convention	no	yes	popular; 1	popular; 1	no
New York	1777	Convention	no	yes	popular; 1	popular; 4	Upper House
North Carolina	1776	Convention	yes; Art. IV	yes	popular; 1	popular; 1	no
Pennsylvania	1776	Convention	no	no		popular; 1	no
South Carolina	1776	Provincial congress of state	no	yes	popular; 2	Legislative Council elected by lower house; 2	no
South Carolina	1778	Act of legislature	no	yes	popular; 2	popular; 2	Privy Council
Virginia	1776	Convention	yes; Sec. 5	yes	popular; 1	popular; 4	Upper House

continued on next page

Table 2 (continued)

	Year of Adoption of Constitution	*Mode of Election of Governor*	*Term of Office of Governor*	*Rotation of Governor's Office*	*Governor's Veto*	*Mode of Appointing Judges*	*Term of Judges*	*Money Bills*	*Ammendment Procedure*
Delaware	1776	Joint ballot of legislature	3 yrs.	yes		Governor and legislature	Good behavior	Originate in lower house, ammendments in upper house	5/7 majority of lower jouse, 7/8 of upper house
Georgia	1777	Legislature	1 yr.	yes					By special convention upon petition of majority voters in majority of counties
Maryland	1776	Joint ballot of legislature	1 yr.	yes		Governor with advice of council	Good behavior	Originate in lower house	Proposal by one legislature to be confirmed by succeeding legislature
Massachussets	1780	Popular; if no majority by Senate from top 2 nominated by House of Representatives	1 yr.	no	yes; 2/3 legislature override	Governor with advice of council	Good behavior but removable	Originate in lower house, ammendments in Senate	Convention to be convened in 1795 if requested by 2/3 of voters
New Hampshire	1784	Popular; if no majority by Senate from top 2 nominated by House of Representatives	1 yr.	no		President (gov.) and council	Good behavior but removable	Originate in lower house, ammendments in Senate	

	Year of Adoption of Constitution	*Mode of Election of Governor*	*Term of Office of Governor*	*Rotation of Governor's Office*	*Governor's Veto*	*Mode of Appointing Judges*	*Term of Judges*	*Money Bills*	*Ammendment Procedure*
New Jersey	1776	Joint session of legislature	1 yr.	no		Joint ballot of legislature	7 yrs.	Cannot be ammended by upper house	Act of legislature
New York	1777	Popular	3 yrs.	no	Governor in council but 2/3 legislature override	Appointments council of legislature with governor presiding	Good behavior but retirement at 60		
North Carolina	1776	Joint session of legislature	1 yr.	yes		Joint ballot of legislature	Good behavior		
Pennsylvania	1776	Joint ballot of legislature and council	1 yr.	yes		President and council	7 yrs.		Special convention after publication of proposal by council of censors
South Carolina	1776	Joint ballot of legislature	2 yrs.	no	Absolute	Joint ballot of legislature	Good behavior but removable	Can only be accepted or rejected by upper house	By legislature
South Carolina	1778	Joint ballot of legislature	2 yrs.	yes	None	Joint ballot of legislature	Good behavior but removable	Can only be accepted or rejected by upper house	By legislature after 90 days' notice
Virginia	1776	Joint ballot of legislature	1 yr.	yes		Joint ballot of legislature	Good behavior	All bills originate in lower house; money bills accepted or rejected by upper house, no possibility of ammendments	

3

Motives at Philadelphia, 1787: Gordon Wood's Neo-Beardian Thesis Reexamined

Ever since Charles Beard published his seminal work, *An Economic Interpretation of the Constitution of the United States*, in 1913,[1] a vigorous debate has ensued among historians over the purpose and design of the Constitutional Convention.[2] Was it, as Beard claimed, a Thermidorean counterrevolution, a reaction to the leveling propensities unleashed by the Revolution, or was it a conclave of patriots dedicated to the preservation of the Union and intent on strengthening the federal government so as to overcome the centrifugal forces tearing the confederation apart? For about forty years after its appearance, Beard's interpretation reigned supreme. It became the accepted wisdom that the Founders had acted out of selfish class interests in fashioning a constitution that would serve to protect the forms of property with which they were particularly associated.[3] Subsequently, however, during the 1950s, Beard's analysis was subjected to more exacting scrutiny and found wanting. Vigorous challenges against his methodology and conclusions were raised by such writers as Douglass Adair, Cecelia M. Kenyon, Robert E. Brown, and Forrest McDonald.[4] In the wake of their analyses very little of Beard's thesis was left intact.

More recently, Beard's social approach to the events of the Founding received a new lease of life with the appearance of fresh

1 Beard, *An Economic Interpretation*.
2 See references cited above, chap. 2, p. 52 n. 1.
3 *Ibid*.
4 *Ibid*., n. 2.

revisionist writing. The publication of works by Merrill Jensen, Jackson Turner Main, and, in particular, Gordon Wood heralded a new appreciation of Beard's analysis.[5] Thus, while Wood dismisses Beard's interpretation as too narrow, he credits him with asking the right questions and being on the right track in his quest for answers:

> It seems obvious by now that Beard's notion that men's property holdings, particularly personalty holdings, determined their ideas and their behavior was so crude that no further time should be spent on it. Yet while Beard's interpretation of the origins of the Constitution in a narrow sense is undeniably dead, the general interpretation of the Progressive generation of historians — that the Constitution was in some sense an aristocratic document designed to curb the democratic excesses of the Revolution — still seems to me to be the most helpful framework for understanding the politics and ideology surrounding the Constitution.[6]

Wood's social approach to the Founding is, of course, also reflected in his most recent work, *The Radicalism of the American Revolution,* published in 1992. But his distinctive ideological interpretation of the Constitutional Convention receives its clearest exposition in his earlier study, *The Creation of the American Republic, 1776-1787,* and in his article, "Interests and Disinterestedness in the Making of the Constitution."[7] While Beard regarded the Federalists as a modernizing, forward-looking force, Wood sees them as members of a retrograde element who failed in the task they had set for themselves at the Constitutional Convention. In Wood's eyes, the Antifederalists were the progressive, modernizing component in the debate that arose over the adoption of the Constitution, and they

5 Merrill Jensen, *The New Nation: A History of the United States, 1781-1789* (N.Y.: Knopf, 1950); Jackson Turner Main, *The Antifederalists: Critics of the Constitution, 1781-1788* (Chapel Hill, N.C.: Univ. of North Carolina Press, 1961); Wood, *Creation.*

6 Wood, *Creation,* p. 626. See also, in the same vein, Joyce Appleby, "The American Heritage: The Heirs and the Disinherited," *JAH,* vol. 74 (1987), pp. 810-11.

7 In Richard Beeman, Stephen Botein, and Edward C. Carter II, eds., *Beyond Confederation: Origins of the Constitution and American National Identity* (Chapel Hill, N.C.: Univ. of North Carolina Press, 1987), pp. 69-109. See also *The Radicalism of the American Revolution* (N.Y.: Knopf, 1992).

were the ones who really shaped the face of America as we know it today. In effect, Wood's explanation of the significance of the Constitutional Convention for the development of the American republic is an obverse version of the Beard thesis. This article examines the manner in which Wood's thesis differs from Beard's; the strength of the evidentiary material adduced in support; whether the new variation is any more tenable than the original Beard thesis; and whether an alternative interpretation of the motives of the Founders is more plausible.[8]

From Beard to Wood

According to Beard, the Federalist drive to draft a new constitution for the United States was a product of the severe frustration felt by the entrepreneurial class engaged in trade and commerce, who, because of the absence of an effective national government, suffered most from the chaotic economic conditions that plagued the country in the 1780s. With each state independently imposing taxes and

8 In 1987, the *WMQ* invited twelve prominent historians to engage in a reassessment of Wood, *The Creation of the American Republic,* nearly twenty years after its appearance. Their comments, together with the author's reply, were published under the heading "Forum," *WMQ,* 3d ser., vol. 44 (1987) pp. 549-640 (hereinafter cited as "Forum"). The contributors uniformly praised the book while highlighting certain features that could have been handled differently or might have been expanded upon. (See, for example, the laudatory comments of Jack Rakove, who noted certain areas of research left undone by Wood, pp. 617-22. In his recent monumental study, *Original Meanings: Politics and Ideas in the Making of the Constitution* [N.Y.: Knopf, 1996], Rakove likewise extols *The Creation of the American Republic* without any serious criticism.) Several of the commentators take issue with Wood's discussion, in the last third of his book, of the Critical Period and the Constitutional Convention. (See, in particular, Ralph Ketcham, pp. 576-82; Pauline Maier, pp. 587-88; and Peter S. Onuf, pp. 615-16.) These writers dispute the claim that the Constitution represented a counterrevolutionary step that radically departed from the ideals that underlay the Revolution. My article seeks to take this analysis a step further by questioning Wood's assertion that the Constitutional Convention was designed primarily to overcome the social turmoil besetting the states.

customs and regulating commerce in accordance with its own interests, the national economy was in complete disarray.

Beard depicts the evolution of the "plot" that underlay the convening of the Constitutional Convention as follows: "Having failed to realize their great purposes through the regular means, the leaders in the movement set to work to secure by a circuitous route the assembling of a Convention to 'revise' the Articles of Confederation with the hope of obtaining, outside of the existing legal framework, the adoption of a revolutionary program."[9]

The class character of the contest surrounding the drafting and adoption of the Constitution is summed up by Beard in his work on Jeffersonian democracy: "The Constitution of the United States was the product of a conflict between capitalistic and agrarian interests."[10] Thus, in Beard's view, the Federalists were the dynamic, innovative element that set the United States on the broad path of capitalist development and promoted the transformation of the country into a giant industrial power. Beard was clearly unsympathetic to the Antifederalists whom he deemed hidebound, bent on preserving the agrarian character of the country and on thwarting the entry of the United States into the industrial age.[11]

While Wood accepts Beard's basic premise that the Constitutional Convention was conspiratorial in nature and designed to fulfill a social purpose,[12] he differs from Beard over the purpose involved and, more particularly, about the focus of the reforms contemplated. According to Beard, the Federalists were manifestly

9 *Economic Interpretation*, pp. 61-63.

10 Charles Beard, *The Economic Origins of Jeffersonian Democracy* (N.Y.: Macmillan, 1915), p. 464. Taking his analysis beyond the Constitutional Convention, Beard asserts: "The spokesmen of the Federalist and Republican parties, Hamilton and Jefferson, were respectively the spokesmen of capitalistic and agrarian interests." *Ibid.*, pp. 465-66.

11 Thus, according to one writer, Beard "identified with the Hamiltonian-Federalist tradition and had nothing good to say about Jefferson or the Anti-Federalist opponents of the Constitution." Pope McCorkle, "The Historian as Intellectual: Charles Beard and the Constitution Reconsidered," *American Journal of Legal History*, vol. 28 (1984) p. 318.

12 See, in this regard, the comments of Ruth H. Bloch, John Patrick Diggins, and John M. Murrin, "Forum," pp. 551, 564 and 599.

concerned with revising the Articles of Confederation and with correcting the deficiencies of the federal government that prevented it from coping with the national problems plaguing the Union. This goal, Wood thinks, was quite incidental, since the primary aim of the Federalists was to redress the chaotic social situation in the states and to restore virtuous government there. In short, they differ over whether the Constitutional Convention was convened primarily to rectify matters on the national or on the state level. Flowing from this disagreement comes a further clash of opinion, namely, whether the Federalists succeeded in what they set out to achieve and whether America, in its modern manifestation, reflects more accurately the societal image of the Federalists or that of the Antifederalists.

According to Wood, the Federalists were convinced that "only by shifting the arena of reform to the federal level . . . could the evils of American politics be finally remedied."[13] These evils were present at the state level, but they could only be corrected on the federal plane. "In the end it was not pressure from above, from the manifest debility of the Confederation, that provided the main impulse for the Federalist movement of 1787; it was rather pressure from below, from the problems of politics within the separate states themselves, that eventually made constitutional reform of the central government possible."[14]

From this viewpoint, "the new national government was not . . . meant merely to save the Union, for strengthening the Confederation along the lines of the New Jersey plan could have done that."[15] The Federalists aimed for something far more ambitious and grandiose. They were interested in instituting a reform that would revamp the entire gamut of republican government in the United States. "Their focus was not so much on the politics of the Congress as it was on the politics of the states. To the Federalists the move for the new central government became the ultimate act of the entire Revolutionary era; it was both a progressive attempt to salvage the

13 *Creation*, p. 463.
14 *Ibid.*, p. 465.
15 *Ibid.*, pp. 474-75.

Revolution in the face of its imminent failure and a reactionary effort to restrain its excesses."[16] The bane of the Federalists was the rampant spirit of democracy that the Revolution had spawned and that permeated state politics. "The supporters of the new federal Constitution thus aimed to succeed where the states, not the Confederation, had failed, in protecting, in John Dickinson's phrase, 'the worthy against the licentious.'"[17] The Federalists looked at American society during the critical period and attributed most of its woes — "the atmosphere of mistrust, the breakdown of authority, the increase of debt, the depravity of manners, and the decline of virtue — ... to a fundamental problem of social disarrangement ... More than anything else the Federalists' obsession with disorder in American society and politics accounts for the revolutionary nature of the nationalist proposals offered by men like Madison in 1787 and for the resultant Federalist Constitution."[18]

It is only by taking account of "the Federalists' social perspective, their fears and anxieties about the disarray in American society," that one can appreciate "how they conceived of the Constitution as a political device designed to control the social forces the Revolution had released."[19] From this standpoint, "the move for a stronger national government thus became something more than a response to the obvious weaknesses of the Articles of Confederation. It became as well an answer to the problems of the state governments."[20]

The struggle over the ratification of the Constitution, Wood maintains, can also be best understood as a fundamental debate over social designs. "Both the proponents and opponents of the Constitution focused throughout the debates on an essential point of political sociology that ultimately must be used to distinguish a

16 *Ibid.*, p. 475.
17 *Ibid.*
18 *Ibid.*, p. 476.
19 *Ibid.*
20 *Ibid.*, p. 467.

Federalist from an Antifederalist. The quarrel was fundamentally one between aristocracy and democracy."[21]

This sums up Wood's thesis on the Constitutional Convention as presented in *The Creation of the American Republic.* In "Interests and Disinterestedness in the Making of the Constitution," written in commemoration of the bicentennial of the Constitution, Wood takes his thesis a step further and posits that the Federalists failed in the goal they strove to attain. Moreover, the Federalists should not be thought of as modernists; this title should be reserved for the Antifederalists. It is wrong, Wood says, to consider the Founders as "masters of events, realistic pragmatists . . . farsighted, economically advanced, modern men in step with the movement of history," and the Antifederalists as "very tame and timid, narrow-minded and parochial men of no imagination and little faith, caught up in the ideological rigidities of the past — inflexible, suspicious men unable to look ahead and see where the United States was going."[22] The reverse was true. "The Federalists were not men of the future after all . . . It was the Antifederalists who really saw best and farthest . . . If either side in the conflict over the Constitution stood for modernity, perhaps it was the Antifederalists. They, and not the Federalists, may have been the real harbingers of the moral and political world we know — the liberal, democratic, commercially advanced world of individual pursuits of happiness." The Framers, Wood concludes, "failed, and failed miserably, in what they wanted it [the Constitution] to do."[23]

Wood notes the significance of the Virginia Plan to the final document. The Federalists acted out of a sense of "crisis in the society." But what crisis? "Certainly it was not the defects of the Articles of Confederation that were causing this sense of crisis. These defects of the Confederation were remediable and were scarcely capable of eliciting horror and despair," says Wood. Reform of the Articles in some way or other — "particularly by granting the Congress a limited authority to tax and the power to

21 *Ibid.*, pp. 484-85.
22 "Interests and Disinterestedness," p. 69.
23 *Ibid.*, p. 70.

regulate commerce" — could have been attended to within the existing system.

> The nationalists' aims and the Virginia Plan went way beyond what the weaknesses of the Articles demanded. Granting Congress the authority to raise revenue, to regulate trade, to pay off its debts, and to deal effectively in international affairs did not require the total scrapping of the Articles and the creation of an extraordinarily powerful and distant government, the like of which was virtually inconceivable to Americans a decade earlier. The Virginia Plan was the remedy for more than the obvious impotence of the Confederation; it was a remedy — and an aristocratic remedy — for what were often referred to as the excesses of American democracy. It was these excesses of democracy . . . popular politics, especially as practiced in the state legislatures, that lay behind the founders' sense of crisis. . . . The weaknesses of the Articles of Confederation were not the most important reasons for the making of the Constitution.[24]. . . Many of the delegates to the Philadelphia Convention were so ready to accept Madison's radical Virginia Plan and its proposed national authority to veto all state laws precisely because they shared his deep disgust with the localist and interest-ridden politics of the state legislatures.[25]

The frenzied pursuit of wealth by the masses was what really disturbed the Federalists and prompted them to institute a powerful new central government that would help contain the headlong rush for wealth and luxury. "Not the defects of the Articles of Confederation, but . . . promotion of entrepreneurial interests by ordinary people — their endless buying and selling, their bottomless passion for luxurious consumption — was what really frightened the Federalists."[26] "They designed the Constitution in order to save American republicanism from the deadly effects of these private pursuits of happiness.[27] . . . The Constitution thus looked backward as much as it looked forward."[28]

Before examining Wood's evidence, one might question, at the outset, a major assumption of his thesis: "that it was not the defects of the Articles of Confederation that were causing this sense of

24 *Ibid.*, pp. 72-73.
25 *Ibid.*, p. 76.
26 *Ibid.*, pp. 80-81.
27 *Ibid.*, p. 81.
28 *Ibid.*, p. 92.

crisis," since these defects were "remediable" by granting Congress "a limited authority to tax and the power to regulate commerce." This is a remarkable statement, since Wood is certainly aware of the numerous efforts undertaken to amend the Articles that invariably ended in defeat, very often by the action of a single state. Every attempt to obtain approval for an impost was rejected. Members of the Congress were maddeningly frustrated at the impossible requirement of obtaining the unanimous ratification of the states before an amendment could enter into force.[29] Little wonder that the Articles of Confederation were never amended. And as for the despair that the Articles induced, one need only cite Madison's letter of February 24, 1787, to Edmund Pendleton:

> In general I find men of reflection much less sanguine as to a new than despondent as to the present System. Indeed the present System neither has nor deserves advocates; and if some very strong props are not applied will quickly tumble to the ground. No money is paid into the public treasury; no respect is paid to the federal authority. Not a single State complies with the requisitions, several pass them over in silence, and some positively reject them. The payments ever since the peace have been decreasing, and of late fall short even of the pittance necessary for the Civil list of the Confederacy. It is not possible that a Government can last long under these circumstances. If the appro[a]ching Convention should not agree on some remedy, I am persuaded that some very different arrangement will ensue.[30]

Innumerable similar quotations abound demonstrating how utterly exasperated the Founders were in their attempt to solve the nation's problems within the framework of the Articles of Confederation. It is difficult to understand, therefore, what Wood means when he suggests that a new constitution was unnecessary and that the

29 In this regard, it is worth recalling Madison's observations, in *Federalist*, No. 40, on the unanimity requirement. He spoke there of "the absurdity of subjecting the fate of 12 States to the perverseness or corruption of a thirteenth"; and of "the example of inflexible opposition given by *a majority* of 1-60th of the people of America to a measure approved and called for by the voice of twelve States, comprising 59-60ths of the people." This example, he said, was "still fresh in the memory and indignation of every citizen who has felt for the wounded honor and prosperity of his country." (Emphasis in original.)

30 Madison, *Papers*, vol. 9, pp. 294-95.

matter could have been readily resolved by attaching a few amendments to the Articles. Even more formidable are the difficulties that his evidentiary material presents.

Wood's Evidence

The first thing to note about Wood's evidence is that it is remarkably sparse in relation to the one source that would provide the strongest indication of the motives of the Founders: quotations from Convention participants delineating the considerations that underlay the convening of the forum at Philadelphia or the purposes that the Constitution was meant to fulfill. In this category, Wood presents three citations in all: a letter by George Washington and two quotations from James Madison. (Notably absent are any references to the Convention debates themselves.)[31]

George Washington's letter of May 18, 1786, to John Jay

Wood writes: "It was popular politics, especially as practiced in the state legislatures, that lay behind the founders' sense of crisis. The legislatures were unwilling to do 'justice,' and this, said Washington, is 'the origin of the evils we now feel.'"[32]

Yet the passage cited by Wood nowhere mentions the situation in the states or the state legislatures. Washington writes:

> I think often of our situation and view it with concern. From the high ground we stood upon, from the plain path which invited our footsteps, to be so fallen! so lost! it is really mortifying; but virtue, I fear has, in a great degree, taken its departure from us; and the want of disposition to do justice is the source of the national embarrassments; for whatever guise or colorings are given to them, this I apprehend is the origin of the evils we now feel, and probably shall labour under for some time yet.[33]

31 See below, pp. 119-23.

32 "Interests and Disinterestedness," p. 73. However, the correct citation from the *Writings of Washington* is, as the next note indicates, from vol. 28, not 18.

33 John C. Fitzpatrick, ed., *The Writings of George Washington* (Washington, D.C.: Govt. Printing Office, 1938), vol. 28, pp. 431-32.

Moreover, Wood, regrettably, does not quote Washington's letter more extensively, since Washington clearly concurs with Jay in attributing the crisis plaguing the Confederacy to the federal arrangements requiring reform:

> I coincide perfectly in sentiment with you, . . . that there are errors in our national Government which call for correction. . . . I scarcely know what opinion to entertain of a general Convention. That it is necessary to revise and amend the articles of confederation, I entertain *no* doubt; but what may be the consequences of such an attempt is doubtful. Yet something must be done, or the fabrick must fall, for it certainly is tottering.[34]

Wood might also have quoted from a second letter by Washington to Jay, written shortly thereafter, on August 1, 1786, that delineates most vividly Washington's view of the nature of the crisis.

> Your sentiments, that our affairs are drawing rapidly to a crisis, accord with my own. . . . I do not conceive we can exist long as a nation without having lodged somewhere a power which will pervade the whole union in as energetic a manner, as the authority of the State Governments extends over the several States. To be fearful of investing Congress, constituted as that body is, with ample authorities for national purposes, appears to me the very climax of popular absurdity & madness. . . . Requisitions are a perfect nihility, where thirteen sovereign, independent disunited States are in the habit of discussing & refusing compliance with them at their option. Requisitions are actually little better than a jest & a bye word throughout the land. If you tell the Legislatures they have violated the Treaty of Peace, & invaded the prerogatives of the confederacy they will laugh in your face — What then is to be done? Things cannot go on in the same train forever . . . . Would . . . that wise measures may be taken in time to avert the consequences we have but too much reason to apprehend.[35]

34 *Ibid.*, p. 431 (emphasis in original).

35 *Ibid.*, pp. 502-3. An extract from a letter written by Washington in 1785 illustrates the chaotic state of the varied values of the dollar. The following instructions were given by Washington to a messenger whom he sent to Boston harbor to collect a gift of two jackasses that had arrived from the Spanish government: "Keep an exact account of your expenses from the time you leave home until you return to it again; remembering that dollars in the States of Maryland, Delaware, Pennsylvania & part of New Jersey, pass at 7/6; bordering on New York, & in that State for 8/ — and in all the New England Governments at 6/ as in Virginia — all other silver, & gold, in that proportion." *Ibid.*, p. 299.

Madison on the "Vices of the Political System of the United States"

Wood writes:[36]

> Throughout the whole period of crisis, Madison, the father of the Constitution if there ever was one, never had any doubt where the main source of the troubles lay. In his working paper drafted in the late winter of 1787 entitled "Vices of the Political System of the United States," Madison spent very little time on the impotence of the Confederation. What was really on his mind was the deficiencies of the state governments: he devoted more than half his paper to the "multiplicity," "mutability," and "injustice" of the laws passed by the states.[37]

A review of the document, however, does not sustain Wood's interpretation.

The memorandum entitled "Vices of the Political system of the U. States" was prepared in April-June 1787 and listed some twelve "Vices."[38] Of these, eight, or fully two-thirds, related to the deficiencies of the national government and its inability to prevent state derelictions and infringement of federal authority. Only the last four of the twelve vices referred exclusively to internal state affairs. A commentary was appended by Madison to each vice listed, except the last. As tabulated by Madison, the vices were:

1. Failure of the States to comply with the Constitutional requisitions.
2. Encroachments by the States on the federal authority.
3. Violations of the law of nations and of treaties.
4. Trespasses of the States on the rights of each other.
5. Want of concert in matters where common interest requires it.
6. Want of Guaranty to the States of their Constitutions & laws against internal violence.
7. Want of sanction to the laws, and of coercion in the Government of the Confederacy.
8. Want of ratification by the people of the articles of Confederation.
9. Multiplicity of laws in the several States.

36 This is actually the second of Wood's two references to Madison, but chronologically it comes first, and therefore it is dealt with first here.

37 "Interests and Disinterestedness," p. 73.

38 Madison, *Papers*, vol. 9, pp. 348-58; and see editor's comment, pp. 345-48.

10. Mutability of the laws of the States.
11. Injustice of the laws of States.
12. Impotence of the laws of the States.

Given this enumeration by Madison, Wood's assertion that "the impotence of the Confederation" concerned Madison "very little" is curious. The title of the Memorandum ("Vices of the Political system of the U. States"), the dominance of the "federal" vices in the list, and the sequence in which they appear — all confirm that Madison was concerned chiefly with the impotence of the national government and only secondarily, and somewhat incidentally, with the domestic situation in the states. Significantly, in presenting the last four vices, on the internal situation in the states, Madison appends an apologetic note:

> 9. In developing the evils which viciate the political system of the U.S. it is proper to include those which are found within the States individually, as well as those which directly affect the States collectively, since the former class have an indirect influence on the general malady and must not be overlooked in forming a compleat remedy.[39]

This is a far cry from any notion that the focal weakness of the United States lay in the condition of the state governments. That condition represents, for Madison, only a subordinate problem that, because of its "indirect influence" on the "general malady," "must not be overlooked."[40]

39 *Ibid.*, p. 353.

40 Apparently, Wood, and others before him, were misled by the size of the commentary on the last four vices, dealing with purely state derelictions, which equaled in length the commentary on the preceding eight vices. (See the editorial comment in Madison, *Papers*, vol. 9, p. 346, citing Edward S. Corwin.) However, in this case, the length of the commentary is not an accurate gauge for judging the importance of the proposed reform. The first eight vices were deemed so patently fatal to the system as not to require much elaboration. Above all, Madison's own comment clearly assigns predominant weight to the "federal" vices.
It might also be noted that Madison attached fistnotes to several of the federal vices listed, indicating their relative importance in his eyes. He attached no fistnotes to the last four vices dealing purely with state derelictions. See notes, *ibid.*, p. 358.

The heart of the problem in the federal system is outlined by Madison in his commentary on Vice 7:

> A sanction is essential to the idea of law, as coercion is to that of Government. The federal system being destitute of both, wants the great vital principles of a Political Constitution. Under the form of such a Constitution, it is in fact nothing more than a treaty of amity of commerce and of alliance, between so many independent and Sovereign States.[41]

And, in conclusion, he states: "It is no longer doubted that a unanimous and punctual obedience of 13 independent bodies to the acts of the federal Government, ought not be calculated on."[42]

In sum, in his discussion of the vices affecting "the Political system of the U. States," Madison highlighted most the inadequacy of the federal system, the absence of power and coercion, "the great vital principles of a Political Constitution." This vice alone was deemed "fatal" to the whole system; the epithet was applied to none of the other enumerated vices. Wood's assertion that Madison devoted, in his memorandum, "little time to the impotence of the federal government" is not reconcilable with Madison's own words.

Madison's letter of October 24, 1787, to Thomas Jefferson

Wood writes:

> The abuses of the state legislatures, said Madison, were "so frequent and so flagrant as to alarm the most stedfast friends of Republicanism," and these abuses, he told Jefferson in the fall of 1787, "contributed more to that uneasiness which produced the Convention, and prepared the public mind for a general reform, than those which accrued to our national character and interest from the inadequacy of the Confederation to its immediate objects."[43]

41 Madison goes on to ask: "From what cause could so fatal an omission have happened in the articles of Confederation? from a mistaken confidence that the justice, the good faith, the honor, the sound policy, of the several legislative assemblies would render superfluous any appeal to the ordinary motives by which the laws secure the obedience of individuals: a confidence which does honor to the enthusiastic virtue of the compilers, as much as the inexperience of the crisis apologizes for their errors." *Ibid.*, p. 351.

42 *Ibid.*

43 "Interests and Disinterestedness," p. 73.

On the surface, this source appears to be Wood's strongest card. Upon closer examination, however, it is seen to undermine his whole thesis about the ideological purpose of the Constitutional Convention. In order to gain perspective on Madison's comment to Jefferson, it is necessary to complete the picture of Madison's preparations for the Convention and to note how his plan fared at Philadelphia.

While the essay on the "Vices of the Political System" indicated the need for a wholesale revision of the constitutional system, Madison had not, as yet, worked out a detailed plan of government. His correspondence over the first few months of 1787 afforded him the opportunity to put his thoughts into more precise form, preparatory to the Constitutional Convention.

In a letter to Thomas Jefferson, dated March 19, 1787, Madison referred to "the mortal diseases of the existing constitution" and suggested several key points for inclusion in the proposed new document, including national supremacy and the separation of powers.[44] At the heart of his proposals was a suggestion for a national legislative veto:

> Over & above the positive power of regulating trade and sundry other matters in which uniformity is proper, to arm the federal head with a negative *in all cases whatsoever* on the local Legislatures. Without this defensive power . . . however ample the federal powers may be made, or however Clearly their boundaries may be delineated, on paper, they will be easily and continually baffled by the Legislative sovereignties of the States. The effects of this provision would be not only to guard the national rights and interests against invasion, but also to restrain the States from thwarting and molesting each other, and even from oppressing the minority within themselves

44 Madison, *Papers*, vol. 9, pp. 317-22. In his first point, Madison argued for ensuring the supremacy of the federal government over the states. To this end, it was necessary that "the new system" receive "ratification by the people . . . as will render it clearly paramount to their Legislative authorities." *Ibid.*, p. 318. A further point related to the need for instituting the separation of powers on the federal level. "The limited powers now vested in Congs. are frequently mismanaged from the want of such a distribution of them." *Ibid.*, p. 319.

> by paper money and other unrighteous measures which favor the interest of the majority.[45]

In letters to Randolph and Washington, Madison elaborated upon his scheme and stressed that no partial revision of the Articles would be sufficient.[46] His "ideas" of "reform," he said, "strike so deeply at the old Confederation" as to lead to "a systematic change."[47]

The early arrival of the members of the Virginia delegation at Philadelphia enabled them to formulate what is known as the

45 *Ibid.*, p. 318 (emphasis in original). Once again the priority that Madison gives to strengthening and securing the federal prerogative is manifest. The national negative is necessary to prevent encroachment by the states on federal authority and also to prevent the states from interfering with one another. A third, and clearly subsidiary consideration, is the prevention of injustices within the states. The same hierarchy of priorities is evident in Madison's letter to George Washington, 16 April 1787: "A negative *in all cases whatsoever* on the legislative acts of the States, as heretofore exercised by the Kingly prerogative, appears to me to be absolutely necessary, and to be the least possible encroachment on the State jurisdictions. Without this defensive power, every positive power that can be given on paper will be evaded & defeated. The States will continue to invade the national jurisdiction, to violate treaties and the law of nations & to harass each other with rival and spiteful measures dictated by mistaken views of interest. Another happy effect of this prerogative would be its controul on the internal vicissitudes of State policy; and the aggressions of interested majorities on the rights of minorities and of individuals." Ibid, pp. 383-84 (emphasis in original).

46 Madison to Randolph, 8 April 1787, *ibid.*, pp. 368-71; Madison to Washington, 16 April 1787, *ibid.*, pp. 382-87.

47 *Ibid.*, p. 369. On the matter of national supremacy Madison was quite categorical: "I hold it for a fundamental point that an individual independence of the States, is utterly irreconcileable with the idea of an aggregate sovereignty. I think at the same time that a consolidation of the States into one simple republic is not less unattainable than it would be inexpedient. Let it be tried then whether any middle ground can be taken which will at once support a due supremacy of the national authority, and leave in force the local authorities so far as they can be subordinately useful." *Ibid.*; repeated nearly verbatim, *ibid.*, p. 383.
Additionally, Madison now advocated confirming national supremacy over the state judiciaries as well, lest state judges nullify the attempts of the national legislature to control state legislation. Madison to Washington, 16 April 1787, *ibid.*, p. 384.

Virginia Plan.[48] Randolph, as governor of Virginia, was given the honor of presenting the plan to the Convention, but Madison's stamp is clearly visible on all four corners of the document. While the voice was the voice of Randolph, the handiwork was the handiwork of Madison.

In presenting the plan, Randolph "pointed out the various defects of the federal system, [and] the necessity of transforming it into a national efficient Government."[49] The confederation, he declared, was "incompetent to any *one* object for which it was instituted."[50] The full scope of federal power was spelled out in Article 6.

> Resolved . . . that the National Legislature ought to be impowered to enjoy the Legislative Rights vested in Congress by the Confederation & moreover to legislate in all cases to which the separate States are incompetent, or in which the harmony of the United States may be interrupted by the exercise of individual Legislation; to negative all laws passed by the several States, contravening in the opinion of the National Legislature the articles of Union; and to call forth the force of the Union agst. any member of the Union failing to fulfill its duty under the articles thereof.[51]

The penultimate clause spells out the national veto that was so close to Madison's heart and upon which he had expounded in the pre-Convention correspondence. However, the clause incorporated a subtle, but important, change that drastically moderated the scope of the proposed national veto. Madison called for "a negative *in all cases whatsoever* on the legislative acts of the States, as heretofore exercised by the Kingly prerogative." The words emphasized by Madison and his reference to a "Kingly prerogative" indicate that he conceived of the veto as an absolute instrument in the hands of the national legislature with which to control the state govern-

48 See letter of George Mason to his son, 20 May 1787. Farrand, *Records*, vol. 3, p. 23.

49 *Ibid.*, vol. 1, p. 18, n. 7.

50 Notes of James McHenry of Maryland, *ibid.*, p. 26. [Emphasis in original.]

51 *Ibid.*, p. 21.

ments.[52] But the Virginia delegates were obviously unwilling to acquiesce in such a sweeping national negative. At most, they were prepared to arm the legislature with the power to strike down state laws "contravening in the opinion of the National Legislature the articles of the Union." This was an early sign that the delegates to the Constitutional Convention, with all their resolve to enhance the powers of the national government at the expense of the states and to ensure federal supremacy in matters federal, were not inclined to meddle in the strictly internal affairs of the states. The action of the Virginia delegation had significantly modified Madison's scheme and had set clear limits to the federal constitutional enterprise.

Although the Virginia Plan had scotched the absolute legislative veto proposal, Madison adverted to it several times during the Convention debates.[53] The formula espoused by the Virginia Plan was accepted by the Committee of the Whole without "debate or dissent."[54] On June 8, Charles Pinckney of South Carolina moved that the legislative veto extend to "all Laws which they [members of the national legislature] shd. judge to be improper."[55] "A universality of the power was indispensably necessary to render it effectual," he said. "The States must be kept in due subordination to the nation." Madison seconded Pinckney's motion:

> [A]n indefinite power to negative legislative acts of the States . . . [was] absolutely necessary to a perfect system. Experience had evinced a constant tendency in the States to encroach on the federal

52 In the Convention debates Madison described the operation of the veto in the following terms: "The negative (on the State laws) proposed, will make it [the national legislature] an essential branch of the State Legislatures." *Ibid.*, p. 447. One writer has aptly said: "Madison proposed nothing less than an organic union of the general and state governments." Charles F. Hobson, "The Negative on State Laws: James Madison, the Constitution, and the Crisis of Republican Government," *WMQ*, 3d ser., vol. 36 (1979), p. 219.

53 See Farrand, *Records*, vol. 1, pp. 318, 447; vol. 2, pp. 440, 589.

54 The only change introduced was to make the veto also apply to any state act "contravening . . . any treaties subsisting under the authority of the Union." *Ibid.*, vol. 1, pp. 47, 54. This clause, added to the Constitution at the suggestion of Benjamin Franklin, was one of the few emendations that he initiated.

55 *Ibid.*, p. 164.

> authority; to violate national Treaties, to infringe the rights & interests of each other; to oppress the weaker party within their respective jurisdictions. . . . Should no such precaution be engrafted, the only remedy wd. lie in an appeal to coercion. . . . The negative wd. render the use of force unnecessary. The States cd. of themselves then pass no operative act, any more than one branch of a Legislature where there are two branches, can proceed without the other.[56]

The Pinckney-Madison proposal was vigorously attacked. "The Natl. Legislature with such a power," declared Elbridge Gerry of Massachusetts, "may enslave the States. Such an idea as this will never be acceded to."[57] Gunning Bedford of Delaware raised practical considerations that he considered insuperable. "Are the laws of the States to be suspended in the most urgent cases until they can be sent seven or eight hundred miles, and undergo the deliberations of a body who may be incapable of Judging them? Is the National Legislature too to sit continually in order to revise the laws of the States?"[58] Madison attempted to resolve the difficulties by suggesting procedures for implementing the comprehensive negative, but his scheme was dismissed "as cutting off all hope of equal justice to the distant States." Pierce Butler of South Carolina said: "The people there would not . . . [even] give it a hearing." The suggestion to broaden the national legislative veto was voted down by a 3:7:1 majority.[59] The Report of the Committee of the Whole adhered basically to the pattern of the Virginia Plan, both in granting the national legislature power to legislate wherever the

56 *Ibid.*, pp. 164-65.
57 *Ibid.*, p. 165.
58 *Ibid.*, pp. 167-68.
59 *Ibid.*, p. 168. Subsequently, on August 23, Pinckney presented a revised version, under which the legislative veto would be exercised by a two-thirds vote of both houses and would apply to such state laws as "interfered . . . with the general interests and harmony of the Union." His proposal to commit to committee failed by a 5:6 vote. *Ibid.*, vol. 2, pp. 390-91. Rutledge, who had served as chairman of the Committee of Detail, was apparently outraged by the proposal. "If nothing else, this alone would damn and ought to damn the Constitution. Will any State ever agree to be bound hand & foot in this manner." *Ibid.*, p. 391.

"harmony" of the United States was affected and in limiting the legislative veto to instances of unconstitutional state action.[60]

The issue of the national legislative veto was taken up again on July 17, immediately after the question of the composition of the second house was settled. The right of the national legislature to nullify state laws that, in its view, violated the constitution, was vigorously criticized.[61] Gouverneur Morris, a foremost nationalist, opposed the power "as likely to be terrible to the States, and not necessary, if sufficient Legislative authority should be given to the Genl. Government." Roger Sherman of Connecticut "thought it unnecessary, as the Courts of the States would not consider as valid any law contravening the Authority of the Union." Luther Martin of Maryland "considered the power as improper & inadmissable." "Shall all the laws of the States be sent up to the Genl. Legislature before they shall be permitted to operate?" he asked. This criticism prompted Madison once again to expound on the essentiality of the veto "to the efficacy & security of the Genl. Govt." He adverted to the British example where "harmony & subordination of the various parts of the empire" were maintained thanks to "the prerogative by which means the Crown, stifles in the birth every Act of every part tending to discord or encroachment."[62] As the debate wore on, Gouverneur Morris indicated that he was "more & more opposed to the negative." It would, he declared, "disgust all the States. A law that ought to be negatived will be set aside in the Judiciary departmt. and if that security should fail; may be repealed by a Nationl. law." The opposition to the legislative veto was sufficiently strong to lead to its complete elimination from the draft constitution by a vote of 7:3.[63]

60 *Ibid.*, vol. 1, pp. 225, 229.

61 See *ibid.*, vol. 2, pp. 27-28, for Madison's notes on the debate.

62 For the purpose of examining state legislation, he suggested the possibility of some local review authority, empowered to give temporary effect to urgent laws. *Ibid.*, p. 28.

63 *Ibid.* Immediately after the vote, Luther Martin moved the adoption of the supremacy clause, derived from the New Jersey Plan, which bound the state judiciaries to award paramountcy to federal law over contrary state law in their decisions. His proposal was unanimously adopted. *Ibid.*, pp. 28-29.

The foregoing review confirms that, while the Convention was determined to establish federal supremacy, it was equally determined that this supremacy be carefully circumscribed to the federal needs of the Union. Interference in the exclusively internal affairs of the states was not to be entertained. The debate had spotlighted the extreme divergence between Madison, who campaigned vigorously for a blanket legislative veto, and the majority, who were opposed to any legislative role in disallowing state laws, even those deemed manifestly unconstitutional.[64]

Furthermore, in addressing itself to the scope of federal power, the Convention was not content to revise merely one clause in Article 6 of the Virginia Plan (that relating to the legislative veto). It decided, in fact, to revamp the entire format of spelling out federal powers.

The Virginia Plan, it will be recalled, had set up broad categories of powers that the national legislature should control. This pattern was retained throughout the deliberations and incorporated in the draft resolutions conveyed to the Committee of Detail on July 23.[65] By empowering the national government to legislate "in all Cases for the general Interests of the Union, and also in those Cases to which the States are separately incompetent, or in which the Harmony of the United States may be interrupted by the Exercise of individual Legislation," the Convention was saying, in effect, that federal power would be practically limitless. What topics could not be embraced under one of these categories? Members of the Committee of Detail were obviously disturbed by this format and replaced it, early on, with a detailed list of powers that the national

64 In lieu of a national veto, the Convention opted for judicial review as a means of umpiring the federal system and of nullifying state legislation inconsistent with the federal constitution. Judicial review of state legislation should be distinguished from judicial review of federal actions. There was widespread acceptance of the former at the Convention; much less of the latter.

65 *Ibid.*, pp. 131-32.

legislature would exercise.[66] The list was reworked in several drafts by the Committee of Detail until it emerged in the final version on August 6, more or less in the form of the enumerated powers in Article 1, Section 8, of the final Constitution.[67]

In sum, while the Constitutional Convention was intent on providing the national government with both energy and supremacy, it was not prepared to buy the extreme Madisonian model in these matters and opted for the Patersonian model. It rejected any notion of a legislative veto, preferring to allow national supremacy to be enforced by the judiciary; and it circumscribed federal powers carefully by enumerating them one by one in the constitutional provision dealing with the subject. In these two key areas the Constitution is genuinely national *and* federal, as Madison described it in *Federalist*, No. 39. For, although the Constitution goes beyond the New Jersey Plan in the number and scope of the powers allotted the federal government, it does not bestow open-ended authority on that government as the Virginia Plan would have done. In the matter of powers — the central plank of the new

66 See Draft IV, *ibid.*, pp. 142-44. For a conspiratorial interpretation of the work of the Committee of Detail in this matter, see the note by John C. Hueston, "Altering the Course of the Constitutional Convention: The Role of the Committee of Detail in Establishing the Balance of State and Federal Powers," *Yale Law Journal*, vol. 100 (1990), pp. 765-83. Rakove maintains that replacement of the original open-ended formula of the Virginia Plan with a finite list of powers was probably intended from the beginning. *Original Meanings*, pp. 84, 178. This conclusion, however, seems not to coincide with Madison's summation on the subject of powers as cited in the following footnote.

67 See Farrand, *Records*, vol. 2, pp. 181-82. The Convention's handling of the subject of national powers is neatly summarized by Madison in his letter to Jefferson, 24 October 1787: "The second object, the due partition of power, between the General & local Governments, was perhaps of all, the most nice and difficult. A few contended for an entire abolition of the States; some for indefinite power of Legislation in the Congress, with a negative on the laws of the States: some for such a power without a negative: some for a limited power of legislation, with such a negative: the majority finally for a limited power without the negative." Madison, *Papers*, vol. 10, p. 209.

constitution — the end result was a genuine synthesis of both plans.[68]

Given Madison's obsession with the national legislative veto, it is little wonder that he was deeply disappointed that it was not incorporated in the Constitution. So distressed was he by the omission that in two letters to Jefferson he described the Constitution as a failure. In his first letter, dated September 6, even before the Convention rose, he wrote: "I hazard an opinion . . . that the plan should it be adopted will neither effectually answer its national object nor prevent the local mischiefs which every where excite disgusts agst. the state governments. The grounds of this opinion will be the subject of a future letter."[69]

On October 24, 1787, Madison duly sent a lengthy essay to Jefferson analyzing the results of the Convention and explaining, in two numbered paragraphs, why a national legislative veto was critically important: 1) to ensure federal supremacy; and 2) to preclude abuses within the states.[70] The second paragraph contains the extract cited by Wood (supplied here in italics) as evidence that the primary purpose of the Constitutional Convention was reform of the states.

> 1. Without such a check in the whole over the parts, our system involves the evil of imperia in imperio [divided government] . . . Encroachments of the States on the general authority, sacrifices of national to local interests, interferences of the measures of different States, form a great part of the history of our political system . . . It may be said that the Judicial authority under our new system will keep the States within their proper limits, and supply the place of a

68 The foregoing discussion affords a fresh perspective on the relative contribution of the Virginia and New Jersey Plans to the final document of the Constitution.

69 Madison, *Papers*, vol. 10, pp. 163-64.

70 *Ibid.*, pp. 209-14. Jefferson had earlier objected to Madison's proposal for a legislative veto as reaching too far. "It fails in an essential character, that the hole & the patch should be commensurate. But this proposes to mend a small hole by covering the whole garment." *Ibid.*, p. 64 (20 June 1787). Thus, Madison's essay was also a reply to Jefferson's argument.

> negative on their laws.[71] The answer is, that it is more convenient to prevent the passage of a law, than to declare it void after it is passed; . . . and that a recurrence to force, which in the event of disobedience would be necessary, is an evil which the new Constitution meant to exclude as far as possible.
>
> 2. A constitutional negative on the laws of the States seems equally necessary to secure individuals agst. encroachments on their rights. The mutability of the laws of the States is found to be a serious evil. *The injustice of them has been so frequent and so flagrant as to alarm the most stedfast friends of Republicanism. I am persuaded I do not err in saying that the evils issuing from these sources contributed more to that uneasiness which produced the Convention, and prepared the public mind for a general reform, than those which accrued to our national character and interest from the inadequacy of the Confederation to its immediate objects.* A reform therefore which does not make provision for private rights, must be materially defective. The restraints agst. paper emissions, and violations of contracts are not sufficient. Supposing them to be effectual as far as they go, they are short of the mark. Injustice may be effected by such an infinitude of legislative expedients, that where the disposition exists it can only be controuled by some provision which reaches all cases whatsoever.

Before examining the quotation from Madison, it is essential to query Wood's claim that "many delegates" were ready to accept "Madison's radical Virginia Plan and its proposed national authority to veto all state laws." To which veto is Wood referring? As noted, Madison's veto and that of the Virginia Plan were quite dissimilar, with the latter confined to unconstitutional state laws. Madison had little support for his comprehensive legislative veto even within the Virginia delegation, much less in the Convention generally. When Pinckney, seconded by Madison, raised the idea of

71 In his criticism of the proposed legislative veto, Jefferson had suggested that a federal judicial veto would be much better suited to control unconstitutional state legislation. "Would not an appeal from the state judicatures to a federal court, in all cases where the act of Confederation controuled the question, be as effectual a remedy, & exactly commensurate to the defect." *Ibid*. Thus, Madison's reply is directed also to showing why a national legislative veto is more effective than federal judicial review of state legislation. See also Hobson, "The Negative on State Laws," pp. 229-30.

an absolute veto in the plenum, it was roundly rejected.[72] But the plenum went further: it spurned even the Virginia Plan's mild legislative veto. In fact, all of Article 6 of the Virginia Plan was radically revised so as to strictly limit and define federal powers. Consequently, to the extent that Wood's thesis rests on the assumption that the Constitution incorporated intact elements of the Virginia Plan relating to federal powers, it is unsupportable. Even if correcting the abuses of the state legislatures was, for Madison, the principal function of the Convention — a debatable proposition, as will be seen — this was manifestly not the aim of the Federalists, or even of a majority of them. Even a nationalist like Gouverneur Morris refused to entertain a limited legislative veto, much less Madison's absolute variety. Rather than expressing "disgust with the localist and interest-ridden politics of the state legislatures," as Wood would have it, Gouverneur Morris, for one, insisted that any kind of federal veto "would disgust all the States." The Convention did not plan, nor was the Constitution designed, to meddle in the strictly domestic affairs of the states. If the situation within the states was deplorable, that was deemed to be their affair, so long as state action did not encroach on the sphere of federal authority. As summed up by Gouverneur Morris: "Within the State itself a majority must rule, whatever may be the mischief done among themselves."[73] Where the delegates wished to inhibit state conduct, such as in matters of paper money or the validity of contracts, they did not hesitate to impose express prohibitions. But there was no desire to arm the national legislature with a broom with which to cleanse the states of "pollution."[74] Only a few delegates, such as Charles Pinckney, James Wilson, and John Mercer, supported Madison's absolute veto, and they were consistently outvoted.

To establish that for Madison (and his fellow delegates) reform of the states was the primary purpose of the Convention, Wood

72 See above, at n. 59.

73 Farrand, *Records*, vol. 2, p. 439.

74 The expression of Henry Knox, cited by Wood, "Interests and Disinterestedness," p. 76.

cites Madison's letter to Jefferson in which he wrote that the abuses in the states contributed more than the inadequacy of the Confederation "to that uneasiness which produced the Convention, and prepared the public mind for a general reform." More closely scrutinized, however, the cited passage clearly refers not to the aims of the Constitutional Convention but to the atmosphere that prepared public opinion for wholesale reform of the Articles. That atmosphere, Madison maintained, was fed more by the chaotic state of affairs in the states than by the impotent condition of the federal government, which rarely affected the average citizen. Madison, as one writer has said, was talking about "the climate of reform that produced the Federal Convention."[75] He was not talking about the Convention's principal purpose, which, even for him, was to remedy the institutional defects of the national government. In all his correspondence on the national legislative veto Madison gives priority to the need to prevent state encroachment on the sphere of federal powers and mentions only secondarily the benefit of such a veto for remedying the internal vicissitudes in the states. Never does Madison place the reform of the states first.

Wood and Farrand's Records

Wood's thesis, it would seem, progresses through the following steps: 1) Madison's national legislative veto is erroneously equated with the version in the Virginia Plan; 2) that plan, in turn, is said to have been incorporated in the Constitution. In fact, however, not only was the veto idea entirely scrapped; the Virginia Plan's scheme for open-ended federal powers was also abandoned in favor of the New Jersey Plan's format for enumerated and defined legislative powers.[76] The final constitutional document was a far cry from Madison's original conception.

75 Hobson, "The Negative on State Laws," p. 223.

76 Clinton Rossiter writes: "The most important contribution of the committee of detail was to convert the general resolution on the law-making authority of the proposed government to a list of eighteen specific powers of Congress." *1787: The Grand Convention* (N.Y.: Macmillan, 1966), p. 208.

Beyond that, Madison, too, is apparently misconstrued. As noted, his primary focus was and remained the reform of the federal system and the augmentation of national power. Intrastate defects required remedying in a supplementary and subsidiary way, to complete the cycle of reform. As Madison said, "a reform . . . which does not make provision for private rights, must be materially defective."[77]

Even if it could be established that Madison himself accorded intrastate reform priority over federal reform — a questionable assumption — his bitter complaint to Jefferson that the Convention had failed in its task by spurning his veto proposal demonstrates better than anything else that the majority opposed federal interference in state affairs. A program for reforming the states would have to come from within the states themselves, not from the Convention, whose purpose and agenda included no such task.

As noted, the Founding Fathers announced before the Convention that their purpose was to find a means of strengthening the national government. During the Convention they deliberated on how best to achieve that goal. In the subsequent ratification struggle, they debated with their opponents the wisdom and suitability of the institutional arrangements devised to invigorate the federal government. Why should we attribute other motives to them when the records of their private correspondence and the deliberations at Philadelphia are open for all to inspect? The ready availability of this source highlights a crucial deficiency in the evidentiary underpinning of Wood's argument. For if the Convention was actually engaged in a giant conspiracy to reform the social condition of the states, and this, rather than strengthening the federal government, was their real aim, why does Wood not prove his case by quoting chapter and verse from Farrand's minutes of the Convention?[78] The proceedings at Philadelphia were secret, and the

77 Madison, *Papers*, vol. 10, p. 212.

78 For a similar complaint against Beard's *Economic Interpretation*, see above, chap. 2, "Beard's Historiography," at pp. 73-81. Beard "omitted to utilize the one unimpeachable source that could establish the clear motives of the Framers: the records of the Constitutional Convention." *Ibid.*, p. 88.

delegates were at liberty to be absolutely candid. Had their goal been to remedy the social condition in the states, surely this theme would have appeared, and perhaps dominated, the Convention debates. Remarkably, Wood's argument regarding the social motives of the Founders fails to cite this valuable source. Undoubtedly, many delegates were seriously concerned with the spirit of democracy that had gripped parts of the country, as the Records indicate,[79] and Wood correctly draws attention to this fact.[80] But it is one thing to acknowledge such concern as a factor in the search for stability in government,[81] and it is another to allege that the Framers were so alarmed by this development that they organized a whole convention principally to quash, or contain, the democratic spirit in the states.

The Convention records provide ample evidence that property occupied a central place in the political and constitutional thought of the Founding Fathers. Anxiety about the fate of property then

79 See, e.g., the following statements: Edmund Randolph: "Our chief danger arises from the democratic parts of our constitutions . . . None of the constitutions have provided sufficient checks against the democracy." Farrand, *Records*, vol. 1, pp. 26-27. Elbridge Gerry: "The evils we experience flow from the excess of democracy. The people do not want [lack] virtue; but are the dupes of pretended patriots." *Ibid.*, p. 48. On the other hand, George Mason warned against denying the democratic voice its place in the institutions of government. "He admitted that we had been too democratic but was afraid we sd. incautiously run into the opposite extreme. We ought to attend to the rights of every class of the people." *Ibid.*, pp. 48-49. See also Mason's remarks, *ibid.*, pp. 133-34, 359, 364.

80 Reference to the Convention records, it may be noted, would also have confirmed that at least on two occasions in the debate, Madison argued that the turbulent situation in the states led, or at least contributed significantly, to the holding of the Convention. *Ibid.*, pp. 134, 318. Therefore, Wood need not have relied exclusively on the letter to Jefferson to establish that Madison deemed the situation in the states perilous to the future of republicanism in the United States. But, of course, this tells us nothing about Madison's relative rating of the two purposes — revitalizing the federal government, on the one hand, and reforming matters within the states, on the other.

81 See the comment of Randolph regarding the need for "a good Senate" to overcome "the turbulence and follies of democracy." *Ibid.*, p. 51. See also the remarks of Madison on the formation of the upper house of the legislature. *Ibid.*, pp. 421-23, 430-31.

and in the years to come surfaced on numerous occasions.[82] Rakove's examination of the documents has led him to conclude that property was Madison's "deepest concern" and that "his analysis of the dangers to property was paradigmatic for the program of reform he carried to Philadelphia in May 1787."[83] The prohibitions on the states enacted in Article 1, Section 10 of the Constitution reflected this anxiety. To what extent other provisions of the Constitution were also informed by this sentiment is a matter of some debate. Various writers, including Jennifer Nedelsky and Christopher Tomlins, have argued that preoccupation with the protection of property seriously compromised the democratic character of the constitutional document produced at Philadelphia. The notion of limited government, they contend, was devised specifically to ensure that the rights of property would be secured, no matter what the vicissitudes of government.[84] Looking beyond Beard, these writers posit that it was not personal or direct economic interest that motivated the Framers but their broader interest in property as a fundamental right that, more than any other natural right, was peculiarly vulnerable to majoritarian invasion.[85] Other writers have presented the counterargument

82 See the listings under the heading "Property" in the index of the Farrand volumes.

83 Rakove, *Original Meanings*, pp. 332, 314.

84 "The urgent sense that property rights had to be protected from democratic legislatures became the focus for formulating the principle that individual rights set limits to the legitimate power of government. That property-centered formulation shaped the Constitution in 1787." Jennifer Nedelsky, *Private Property and the Limits of American Constitutionalism: The Madisonian Framework and its Legacy* (Chicago: Univ. of Chicago Press, 1990), p. 2. "For Madison the utility of the new American state was heavily bound up in the prospect that it could offer a new model of governance to check unrestrained popular majorities." Christopher L. Tomlins, *Law, Labor, and Ideology in the Early American Republic* (New York: Cambridge Univ. Press, 1993), p. 64.

85 See Nedelsky, *Private Property*, pp. 3-9, and Tomlins, *Law, Labor, and Ideology*, pp. 60-66. Joyce Appleby also concludes: "The Constitution closed the door on simple majoritarian government in the United States. Popular majorities animated by what people wanted to do at a particular moment would be forever constrained." "The American Heritage," p. 804. In so far as Madison saw property as a particularly vulnerable right, see also Rakove, *Original Meanings*, pp. 314-16.

that concern over property, while certainly present at Philadelphia, did not dominate the constitutional debate as much as is often supposed.[86] The Wood thesis, of course, differs from all these approaches. It posits the Founding Fathers' preoccupation not with the property factor as such, but rather with intrastate extravagance and the breakdown of social values. It is in this sense that Wood sees the Constitution as "an aristocratic remedy" to "the excesses of American democracy" in the states. However, nothing in the Convention records substantiates the claim that reforming the social condition of the states was the central purpose of the delegates, Madison included, or of the Constitution that they produced.

Conclusions

On the basis of his analysis of the Founders' motives, Wood concludes that "their Constitution failed, and failed miserably, in what they wanted it to do."[87] This conclusion, of course, is premised on the assumption that the principal concern of the delegates was the turbulent scene in the states and that their Constitution was framed mainly to allow the aristocracy to overcome the tumultuous demands of democracy emanating from there. The foregoing examination of Wood's evidence establishes quite clearly that the Founders did not intend to effect a social revolution in the states. They convened for one essential purpose — to furnish the United States with an effective national government.[88] Since they never sought to produce a social revolution in the states, they cannot be charged with having

86 "Upon examination, . . . it becomes clear that every feature of the federal Constitution that Beard lists as an antimajoritarian device already existed in the state constitutions in one form or another . . . It is one thing to recognize the Founders' desire to ensure the rights of property under the Constitution, in common with other rights, and it is another thing to attribute the very structure of government to a desire to serve a particular form of property by hamstringing popular rule." See above, chap. 2, "Beard's Historiography," pp. 87-90.

87 Wood, "Interests and Disinterestedness," p. 70.

88 Onuf also criticizes Wood's discounting "the significance of 'pressure from above' in the reform movement." "Forum," p. 615.

failed to do so. With the removal of the premise, the conclusion regarding the "failure" of the Founders' constitutional enterprise falls to the ground of its own weight and requires no rebuttal.

The Founding Fathers eminently succeeded in the task they had set for themselves — forestalling the dismemberment of the Union and creating a powerful central government that would promote the national welfare of the United States. Therefore, it can hardly be said that the "farsighted Federalists had their eyes not on what was coming, but on what was passing." Wood's suggestion that the Federalists were "really the victims of events" rather than the "masters," and that, in fact, "it was the Antifederalists who really saw best and farthest,"[89] flies in the face of the facts. The United States in 1787 was on the verge of disintegration, and the Federalists boldly set the nation on the road of national cohesion and integration through the medium of a new constitution. This instrument of government reordered the division of powers between the states and the central government, thereby allowing the latter to weld the country into one powerful entity. The fate and destiny of the United States was determined for generations to come. It is to the credit of the Federalist Founders that they had the foresight and the tenacity with which to promote the realization of their vision, so that the United States could emerge from the crisis of the Critical Period capable of assuming its rightful place "among the Powers of the earth."

While the Antifederalists played a prominent role in securing the adoption of the Bill of Rights, they had no part in the vision underlying the drafting of the Constitution and can therefore scarcely be regarded as modernists. Cecelia Kenyon's description of them as "men of little faith" seems apt.[90] They sought to institute a much weaker national government, and it is questionable whether

89 Wood, "Interests and Disinterestedness," pp. 69-70.
90 See n. 4, above, chap. 2, n. 1, for Kenyon citations.

under their type of constitution the United States would have evolved into the powerful industrial giant that it is today.[91]

In all, Wood's attempt to provide an ideological, sociological interpretation for the Constitutional Convention is unsubstantiated. His portrayal of the Federalists as a retrograde, even reactionary, element and the Antifederalists as farsighted modernists is seen to be quite untenable. If, as Wood acknowledges, Beard's thesis, with its narrow economic analysis, is found wanting as an explanation for the adoption of the Constitution, his own thesis, with its rigid social dichotomy between aristocracy and democracy to define the events of the Constitutional Convention, is no less so. The revolution that the Founding Fathers sought to institute was neither economic, as Beard would have it, nor social, as Wood supposes, but political — reordering the division of powers between the central and state governments — so as to "render the federal constitution adequate to the exigencies of Government & the preservation of the Union."[92]

91 For a different, and more positive, assessment of the role of the Antifederalists in the constitutional debate, see Peter S. Onuf, "Reflections on the Founding: Constitutional Historiography in Bicentennial Perspective," *WMQ*, 3d ser., vol. 46 (1989), pp. 368-71. See also Bernard Bailyn, "Postscript: Fulfillment: A Commentary on the Constitution," in *The Ideological Origins of the American Revolution*, enlarged ed. (Cambridge, Mass.: Belknap Press, 1992), pp. 331-51.

92 Resolution adopted by the United States in Congress Assembled, Feb. 21, 1787. Library of Congress, *Journals of the Continental Congress, 1774-1789* (Washington, D.C.: Govt. Printing Office, 1936), p. 74. Compare Bailyn's observation in the preface to the enlarged edition of his *Ideological Origins*, p. viii: "That document [the Constitution] . . . does not mark a Thermidorean reaction to the idealism of the early period engineered by either a capitalist junta or the proponents of rule by a leisured patriciate; . . . The earlier principles remained, though in new, more complicated forms, embodied in new institutions devised to perpetuate the received tradition into the modern world."

"Motives at Philadelphia": A Comment on Slonim, by Gordon Wood[1]

I am grateful to the editor of *Law and History Review* for the opportunity to respond to Professor Shlomo Slonim's article criticizing my interpretation of the formation of the Constitution. I know Professor Slonim personally from a visit I made over a decade ago to Hebrew University where he was a very gracious host. I know too that he is an earnest and meticulous scholar of the United States Constitution who has spent a great deal of energy refuting Charles Beard. So in this brief response I wish to treat his criticism with respect while at the same time I hope to show where I believe he is wrong or has misunderstood and misinterpreted me.

Slonim is an earnest and meticulous scholar, but he is at the same time a very literal-minded one, someone who I believe sometimes has trouble seeing the woods for the trees. He often tends to miss the political context and the larger significance of the texts he has examined. Too often in dealing with my argument he has created straw men in order to more easily blow them away. His conception of what he calls "the Wood thesis" (p. 123) is a figment of an overheated imagination. Throughout his paper he strains to make his case for the "foresight" (p. 124) of the Federalist Founders and he repeatedly evades contradictory evidence. And finally, he has ignored the works of other historians who have refined and reinforced my interpretation made nearly thirty years ago.

1 Gordon S. Wood is the Alva O. Way University Professor and Professor of History at Brown University. Page numbers in parenthesis refer to the pages in the preceding chapter.

Slonim says at the outset that I believe that correcting the deficiencies of the federal government was "quite incidental" to the aim of the Federalists (p. 98) and that I suggested that "a new constitution was unnecessary" (p. 102). And he claims that I think that the "the primary aim of the Federalists was to redress the chaotic social situation in the states and to restore virtuous government there" (p. 98). None of these claims is true.

I have never suggested that the problems of the Confederation government were "incidental" to the movement to reform the Articles. Quite the contrary. The problems of the Confederation were a major force behind the calling of the Philadelphia Convention. In the since-published lectures on the formation of the Constitution that I gave in January 1987 at Hebrew University, where Professor Slonim was my host, I stated that there were "two levels of explanation for the Constitution, two distinct reform movements in the 1780s that eventually came together to form the Convention of 1787."

> One operated at the national level and involved problems of the Articles of Confederation. The other operated at the state level and involved problems in the state legislatures. The national problems account for the ready willingness of people in 1786-87 to accede to the convening of delegates at Philadelphia. But the state problems, problems that went to the heart of America's experiment in republicanism, account for the radical and unprecedented nature of the federal government created in Philadelphia.[2]

The national problems included the obvious weaknesses of the Confederation, especially its inability to tax, regulate commerce, and pay its debts, and its failure to stand up strong in international

2 Gordon S. Wood, *The Making of the Constitution* (Waco, Tex.: Baylor University Press, 1987), pp. 9-10. I take Slonim's questioning of the amount of my "evidentiary material" (69, 77, 94) to be particularly unfair. Most commentators have accused me of having too much material. I tended to cite quotations only and could have easily piled up citations about the Federalists' concerns for the future of republicanism in the states. But such citations would not by themselves prove my point; that point is proven by the overall context of my argument, which includes my earlier discussion of the state constitutions and the importance of the states to Americans in 1776. Slonim ignores this kind of context.

affairs and protect the territorial integrity of the United States. By 1787 nearly every political leader in the country, including those who later would be Anti-Federalists, was willing to grant substantial powers to the Confederation Congress, including the powers to tax and to regulate commerce. Slonim seems to think that he is refuting me by pointing out that efforts to amend the Articles in the prescribed way had been defeated earlier in the 1780s (pp. 101-103). I do not deny those defeats. In fact, that is why almost every political leader in 1787 more or less willingly acceded to the calling of the Convention in 1787 to reform the Articles — in an unprescribed manner that avoided the problems of getting the unanimous consent of the states. Contrary to what Slonim says, I have never suggested "that a new constitution was unnecessary" for these changes (p. 102). In fact, a new constitution was precisely what was needed. By 1787 many people were prepared for radical change in the Articles. Indeed, so acceptable and necessary seemed some sort of change in the Confederation that later Anti-Federalists like William Findley were remarkably casual about the upcoming meeting at Philadelphia. They expected changes in the Confederation, even a new constitution, that would grant the federal government power to tax and regulate commerce, but they never expected the kinds of fundamental changes the Philadelphia Convention proposed. My argument is that to explain these fundamental changes and the strong and unprecedented nature of the proposed national government, the like of which no one a decade earlier even imagined, we have to go to the second level of problems — those of the states.

I have always believed that both sets of problems — national and state — were important to the reform of the national government in 1787. And I have used Madison's working paper, "Vices of the Political System of the U. States," as important evidence for his thinking about these two sets of problems. Slonim knows that this a crucial document and he devotes a considerable amount of time to it. I believe, however, that he has misinterpreted Madison's memorandum. I meant what I said when I wrote that "Madison spent very little time on the impotence of the Confederation. What was really on his mind was the deficiencies of the state governments" (p. 105). Slonim believes that he is refuting me by pointing out that eight of Madison's twelve "Vices" dealt with problems of the Confederation. But by saying that "Madison was concerned chiefly with the impotence of the national government and only secondarily, and somewhat incidentally, with the domestic situation in the states" (p. 106) he has missed the point of the document, a point that has been fully explained by other historians besides me.[3] He pays no attention, for example, to Charles F. Hobson's contention that "the dominant theme of 'Vices of the Political System' was not the weaknesses of the Confederation government, serious as these were, but the 'multiplicity,' the 'mutability,' and above all the 'injustice' of state laws."[4] More important, Slonim ignores the significance of the fact that Madison attributes nearly all of the problems of the Confederation government, not to its weakness, but to the derelictions and encroachments of the states. So, even in the case of the problems at the national level, it is the states, according to Madison, that were really at fault.

Thus I agree with Madison that it was ultimately the abuses of the state legislatures — abuses "so frequent and so flagrant as to alarm the most stedfast friends of Republicanism" — that "contributed more to that uneasiness which produced the Convention, and prepared the public mind for a general reform, than those which accrued to our national character and interest from the inadequacy of the Confederation to its immediate objects" (p. 107). Slonim realizes that this is a potent piece of evidence for my argument — indeed, I believe it is enough to clinch all I ever claimed to say — but he believes that he has refuted me by saying that this passage refers "not to the aims of the Constitutional

3 Jack N. Rakove, *Original Meanings: Politics and Ideas in the Making of the Constitution* (N.Y.: Alfred A. Knopf, 1996), 46-50; Charles F. Hobson, "The Negative on State Laws: James Madison, the Constitution, and the Crisis of Republican Government," *WMQ*, 3d ser., vol. 36 (1979), pp. 220-22.

4 Hobson, "The Negative on State Laws," pp. 221. Slonim seems to be straining when he explains why Madison devoted so much of his memorandum to internal state affairs by saying that "the first eight vices were deemed so patently fatal to the system as not to require much elaboration" (p. 106, n. 40).

Convention but to the atmosphere that prepared public opinion for wholesale reform of the Articles" (p. 119). How Slonim distinguishes between the aims of the Convention and the public opinion that was ready for wholesale reform of the Articles is unclear, but I certainly agree with Madison (and apparently with Slonim) — it was the central point of my argument — that it was the evils coming out of the states that prepared public opinion for the wholesale reform of the federal government. Or at least the Federalist parts of public opinion. There were after all Anti-Federalists who wanted no such wholesale reform but who were willing to accept the idea of a convention to revise the Articles.

Although Slonim seems to concede that Madison's proposal for a federal negative on all state legislation suggests the reality of his fears of democratic excesses within the states, the fact that this negative was revised in the Virginia plan and was abandoned altogether by the Convention has convinced him that the problems of the states ultimately could not have been all that important to the Convention itself. In the end Slonim's entire case against my argument rests on his distinction between "the chaotic state of affairs in the states" (which he seems to concede) and what he calls "the Convention's principal purpose, which, even for [Madison], was to remedy the institutional defects of the national government" (p. 119).[5]

Slonim points out that the Virginia plan changed the scope of Madison's initial idea of a national veto over all state laws. Instead of granting to the national government "a negative *in all cases whatsoever* on the legislative acts of the States," the Virginia plan's negative could only be exercised over those state laws "contravening in the opinion of the National Legislature the articles of Union" (p. 110-11). Slonim sees this change in the Virginia plan as a real retreat — that the Virginia delegates "were not inclined to meddle in the strictly internal affairs of the states" (p. 111) — but

5 According to the most astute student of Madison's thinking, Jack N. Rakove, Madison's "agenda for the Federal Convention was not addressed to the woes of the Union alone, but to the underlying vices of the Republic." Rakove, *Original Meanings*, pp. 55-56.

his notion that the Virginia plan had turned Madison's negative into simply a "mild legislative veto" (p. 118) seems grossly exaggerated. No doubt Madison's original phrase of *"all cases whatsoever,"* with its echo of Parliament's Declaratory Act, would have been politically suicidal, and some change in wording was necessary. But the change was not as great as Slonim makes it out to be. Not only does the Virginia plan retain the essence of Madison's negative — he, after all, in his "Vices" essay thought that most of the state laws in the 1780s had contravened the articles of Union — but, more important, the Virginia plan left it to the national legislature to decide what state laws could be vetoed or not.

Much of Slonim's case against my interpretation rests on what happened to Madison's veto and other parts of the Virginia plan in the Convention. Since the delegates ultimately modified the Virginia plan in substantial ways, then, according to Slonim, they could not really have shared Madison's fears of democracy in the states. But other historians besides me think differently. "Though not persuaded of the merits of the negative, the framers of the Constitution," writes Hobson, "nevertheless shared Madison's concern to bring about a due subordination of the states and to establish some measure of control over their internal affairs."[6] By concentrating on the changes in the Virginia plan, Slonim misses the significance of what the Convention in the end actually did. It is true that the delegates finally substituted a list of specified powers in place of the Virginia plan's sweeping grant of national authority and eliminated the national negative. But to assume, as Slonim does, that the delegates had "opted for the Patersonian model" (p. 115) and were uninterested in meddling "in the strictly domestic affairs of the states" (p. 118) is mistaken. On June 19 Madison argued that the New Jersey plan would not "provide a Governmt. that will remedy the evils felt by the States both in their united and individual capacities," and the Convention agreed with him, rejecting Paterson's plan seven states to three with one divided.[7]

6 Hobson, "Negative on State Laws," p. 228.
7 Farrand, *Records*, vol. 1, pp. 315-16.

For better or worse the Convention had chosen the Virginia plan for its model. It went on to make all of its subsequent modifications without doing substantial violence to the national character of that plan. Despite its concession to equal state sovereignty in the Senate, the Convention in the end decisively substituted for a confederation of equal separate states a regular tripartite republican government operating directly on the people. To be sure, the Congress was not given a blanket grant of powers, as the Virginia plan proposed, but it was given a substantial list of powers. None has been added since 1787 and the federal government today does all right for itself. Moreover, Slonim passes right over the significance of Article I, Section 10 of the Constitution, which prohibited the states from exercising an extraordinary number of powers, including the powers to levy customs duties, to print paper money, and to pass ex post facto laws and laws impairing contracts. If these prohibitions were not a design "to meddle in the strictly domestic affairs of the states," I do not know what would be. Since customs duties and emitting bills of credit were the principal means by which premodern governments raised money, these prohibitions tended to render the states economically weak. Article I, Section 10 was the Convention's practical substitute for Madison's unwieldy and unworkable proposal for a national veto. In addition, it indicates that, despite many of the delegates' fears of the consolidating and nationalizing implications of the Virginia plan, most were still as worried as Madison about the abuses of democracy in the states. Historian Jack N. Rakove perhaps puts it best: "In the end, the delegates' rejection of Madison's pet scheme of a federal veto matters less than their agreement that what was at stake was the relationship between the institutions of government and the nature of American society, broadly conceived."[8]

Slonim does not seem to appreciate fully the radical nature of the Virginia plan, which dealt with problems that went well beyond the imbecility of the Confederation. "What enabled the Convention to transcend the old boundaries of debate," writes Rakove, "was the

8 Jack N. Rakove, *The Beginnings of National Politics: An Interpretative History of the Continental Congress* (Baltimore: Johns Hopkins Univ. Press, 1979), p. 394.

realization that it had to analyze not merely the specific problems of Congress but, in effect, the whole history of the American republican experiment, thereby subsuming the debility of Congress and the political troubles of the states under one common rubric."[9] That such an outrageous scheme as the Virginia plan could become the Convention's working model and remain virtually intact for half the Convention's life says something about the fears and hopes of the delegates. That it was eventually changed and made less outrageous, of course, says something too about their political realism and the need for compromise. The Constitution as it finally emerged from the Convention was radical enough; it certainly aroused bitter and widespread opposition. The Virginia plan unchanged would never have been ratified, and most of the delegates knew that. Hence the changes. But it does not follow that most of the Federalists therefore were not concerned about constraining or mitigating the democratic excesses of the states.

The real source of the problem is Slonim's basic misreading of my argument. He accuses me of interpretations that I have never made — that the Federalists were "engaged in a giant conspiracy to reform the social condition of the states" (p. 120) and "sought to produce a social revolution in the states" (p. 123). These are outlandish notions, and I have no idea where he got them. All I ever said was that the Federalists through the formation of the new federal government sought to create institutional mechanisms that might evade or mitigate the effects of localist democracy in the states. And they would do this, first, by having the federal government control lawmaking in the states either through a version of a national veto power, which failed of acceptance, or through an out-and-out prohibition of the most parochial and unjust state legislation, which succeeded and became Article I, Section 10 of the Constitution; and secondly, by elevating and expanding the arena of politics and reducing the number of elected officials.

9 Ibid., 390.

This second scheme, resting on a particular insight into the sociology of American politics, was as important to Madison and many other Federalists as the national negative in dealing with the problems of the states, but Slonim pays no attention whatsoever to it. The Federalists hoped that the elevated national government and its expanded electorate would act as a kind of filter, refining the sorts of men who would become national leaders. In a larger arena with a smaller number of representatives, only the most notable, most cosmopolitan, and most well educated were likely to gain political office. If the people of North Carolina, for example, could elect only five men to the federal Congress, in contrast to the 232 they elected to their state assembly, they were more apt to ignore the kinds of obscure, narrow-minded, and parochial politicians who were responsible for the factious, vicious, and unjust state legislation of the 1780s and elect only those "who," as Madison put it in *Federalist*, No. 10, "possess the most attractive merit, and the most diffusive and established characters."

We have only to compare the small number of sixty-five representatives who were designated for the first national Congress with the thousand or more representatives in the state legislatures in order to understand what this narrowing and refining process of the Federalists might mean socially and politically. As one Georgia Federalist put it, in the new national government "none will be distinguished with places of trust but those who possess superior talents and accomplishments."[10]

But there was more to the Federalists' scheme of an extensive and elevated republic than extracting for leadership those "who possess most wisdom to discern, and most virtue to pursue, the common good of the society." Madison and other Federalists likewise believed that in an enlarged national arena "the society itself will be broken into so many parts, interests and classes of citizens, that the rights of individuals, or of the minority, will be in little danger from interested combinations of the majority." In other words, in the extended republic the people's interests would be so

10 Herbert J. Storing, ed., *The Complete Anti-Federalist* (Chicago: Univ. of Chicago Press, 1981), vol. 1, p. 51.

diverse and clashing that they would rarely be able to combine to create tyrannical majorities in the new national government as they had in the state legislatures. Madison understood that this process had worked in American religion: the multiplicity of religious sects in America prevented any one of them from dominating the state and permitted the enlightened reason of liberal gentlemen like Jefferson and himself to shape public policy and church-state relations and to protect the rights of minorities. "In a free government," wrote Madison in *Federalist*, No. 51, "the security for civil rights must be the same as that for religious rights. It consists in the one case in the multiplicity of interests, and in the other in the multiplicity of sects."[11]

None of this has anything to do with "a social revolution in the states," but all of it has social as well as political implications, implications that Slonim disregards completely. Slonim has his nose so close to the ground that he misses entirely the social significance of the new Constitution and its elevated government except to admit that concern for property was central to the Federalist scheme. But what does a concern for property mean? Does it not have social implications? Slonim seems to think that he can finesse the Convention's concern for property simply by denying its social significance and its relation to what was going on in the states. But a struggle over two different kinds of property lay at the heart of the politics in the states during the 1780s.

Madison and many of the other Federalists still conceived of property in premodern, almost classical terms — as rentier property, proprietary property, property as a source of authority and independence, not as a source of productivity and capitalistic investment. The most traditional kind of rentier property was of course land, but it could take other forms as well, such as government bonds and money out on loan. These kinds of fixed property were very vulnerable to inflation, which is why Madison and other Federalists were so frightened by the state assemblies' issuing of so much paper money in the 1780s. Inflation threatened

11 *The Federalist*, Nos. 57, 51.

not simply their livelihood but their authority and independence as citizens. Many of the Federalist gentry could at times regard the factional state majorities that promoted the paper money and debtor relief legislation of the 1780s as little better than levelers. Those majorities, however, were neither the propertyless masses nor radicals opposed to the private ownership of property. Such debtors believed in the sacredness of property as much as Madison and the other Federalists. But it was a different kind of property they were promoting — modern, risk-taking property; not static proprietary wealth, but dynamic venture capital; not money out on loan, but money borrowed; in fact, all the paper money that enterprising farmers and proto-businessmen clamored for in these years. Representatives of these debtor and paper money interests in the states, such as the ex-weaver William Findley of Pennsylvania and the part-time lawyer and shoemaker Abraham Yates of New York, realized only too well that the new Constitution, with its prohibition on the states' issuing bills of credit and passing debtor relief legislation and with its enlarged national arena, was designed to keep them and the interests they represented out of the decision-making processes of government.

Hence they opposed the new Constitution and called it an "aristocratic" scheme designed to constrain much of the democratic majoritarianism of the states. Slonim does not seem to appreciate that this charge was not my invention but was the accusation made by the Anti-Federalists at the time. He may not agree with that charge, but he at least has to confront it and explain what they meant. What Slonim calls my "rigid social dichotomy between aristocracy and democracy" (p. 125) was precisely how many of the contemporaries described the debate over the Constitution. Most of the Anti-Federalists may have been narrow-minded localists, poorly educated, never having attended Harvard or Princeton, but they were not fools; they knew very well what the Constitution intended, and they fought it mainly on the grounds that it was an aristocratic attempt to evade the problems of democracy. In their calls for the most explicit representation of interests, occupations, and ethnicities and in their celebration of localism and equality, the Anti-

Federalists stood for the future of America in a way that the Federalists could not match.

In his literal-minded way Slonim makes much of my whimsical suggestion, made as a hook for my "Interests and Disinterestedness" essay, that the Anti-Federalists ought to replace the Federalists as the bold and far-sighted prophets of the democratic future. Of course, to the extent that former Speaker of the House Tip O'Neill is correct in saying that in America "all politics is local," the Anti-Federalists did foresee the future. But no historical participants ever really foresee the future, and it is no doubt foolish to judge them in these terms. We know that the Federalists furnished the United States with an effective national government, but, contrary to what Slonim says, they by themselves did not and could not determine its fate and destiny for generations to come. That took the turbulent history of several generations and a civil war, and the story is not over yet. Moreover, the Federalists had other aims than creating a national government, and with these they were not very successful. Their prohibition on the states' issuing of bills of credit, for example, was evaded by the states' chartering of banks, hundreds of them, that in turn issued the paper money that the Anti-Federalists and their entrepreneurial supporters wanted. None of the Federalists anticipated the kind of bumptious, liberal, moneymaking, democratic world that emerged in the decades following the creation of the Constitution.

Although he quotes Joyce Appleby's statement that "[t]he Constitution closed the door on simple majoritarian government in the United States," he does not make anything of it (p. 122, n. 85). Perhaps because he is an Israeli and not an American, Slonim may not fully appreciate the extent to which Americans over the past two centuries have sought to constrain and mitigate the effects of localist democratic majorities. We Americans have used a variety of devices to limit the force of what people want to do at any particular moment: we often elevate decision making beyond the reach of popular majorities, we give appointed judges power that no other judges in the world exercise, we insulate important issues like banking and currency control from elected officials, we protect minority and individual rights from popular majorities, and we do all this in the name of democracy. The Federalists were not trying "to effect a social revolution in the states," as Slonim accuses me of saying (p. 123). They could never have done that in any case. All they were trying to do was to find some institutional ways of lessening the turbulent effects of too much localist democracy. They began something that has been used over and over in American history ever since.

Rejoinder to Gordon Wood

Gordon Wood mentions that in 1987, as part of the Hebrew University's program of events marking the bicentennial of the U.S. Constitution, he delivered the annual Samuel Paley Lectures in American Civilization at the University in Jerusalem. If I, as chairman of the Department of American Studies was, as he says, a gracious host, he was no less a gracious guest and, moreover, a fascinating lecturer.[1] A synopsis of his remarks is included in the volume that I edited, *The Constitutional Bases of Political and Social Change in the United States*,[2] comprising lectures delivered at a bicentennial conference later that year and attended by prominent American and Israeli constitutional scholars, including Ruth Bader Ginsburg, now Justice of the U.S. Supreme Court, and Aharon Barak, now President of the Israeli Supreme Court.

It is important to delineate what is at issue. My article contends that the neo-Beardian thesis developed by Wood in the final third of *The Creation of the American Republic* and in "Interests and Disinterestedness," an article published in honor of the bicentennial — that the Constitutional Convention was summoned essentially to arrest the turbulent spirit of democracy allegedly spawned by the Revolution and plaguing the states in the 1780s — does not conform with the historical record. The Federalists, I maintain, convened in order to endow the United States with an effective

1 Wood notes that I reside and teach in Israel. I feel obliged to point out, however, that I was born and educated in Australia (LL.B., Melb.), and received my graduate education in the United States (M.A. and Ph.D., Columbia).

2 N.Y.: Praeger, 1990.

national government, something totally lacking under the Articles of Confederation. Concern over the social condition of the states was subordinate, even in Madison's thought, and never served as the leitmotif of the Framers in the drafting of the Constitution.

To refute my critique of his thesis, Wood cites an expanded version of his above-mentioned lectures published subsequently as an occasional paper, *The Making of the Constitution*, directed to a popular audience. But I never referred to this work; I referred, by chapter and verse, to the central thesis developed in the last third of *Creation* and the "Interests" article, both significant scholarly works. In responding to an argument challenging his thesis, an author could be expected to respond with evidence from the work/s challenged to substantiate the charge that his views have been "misunderstood," "misinterpreted," and "misread," rather than to cite a third, far less prominent, work of his. It is, therefore, quite puzzling that Wood refers to *The Making of the Constitution* to establish the thrust of his thesis, unless, of course, he is suggesting that his current thinking is more accurately reflected in this essay than in his earlier works.

At the risk of repetition, I shall quote some key passages from those two major works to demonstrate the gravamen of my article — that according to Wood, the Constitutional Convention was summoned *primarily* to overcome the democratic turbulence in the states — and that I did not in any way misrepresent his views:

> It was not pressure from above, from the manifest debility of the Confederation, that provided the main impulse for the Federalist movement of 1787; it was rather pressure from below, from the problems of politics within the separate states themselves. (*Creation*, p. 465)

> Their [the Federalists'] focus was not so much on the politics of the Congress as it was on the politics of the states. (*Ibid.*, p. 475)

> More than anything else the Federalists' obsession with disorder in American society and politics accounts for the revolutionary nature of the nationalist proposals offered by men like Madison in 1787 and for the resultant Federalist Constitution. (*Ibid.*, p. 476)

> They conceived of the Constitution as a political device designed to control the social forces the Revolution had released. (*Ibid.*)

> The weaknesses of the Articles of Confederation were not the most important reasons for the making of the Constitution. ("Interests," pp. 72-73)
>
> Not the defects of the Articles of Confederation but . . . promotion of entrepreneurial interests by ordinary people — their endless buying and selling, their bottomless passion for luxurious consumption — was what really frightened the Federalists. (*Ibid.*, pp. 80-81)
>
> They designed the Constitution in order to save American republicanism from the deadly effects of these private pursuits of happiness. (*Ibid.*, p. 81)
>
> [The Framers] failed, and failed miserably in what they wanted it [the Constitution] to do. (*Ibid.*, p. 70)

I also find it strange that, in discussing Madison's listing of "Vices of the Political System of the U. States," Wood states: "Madison attributes nearly all of the problems of the Confederation government, not to its weakness, but to the derelictions and encroachments of the states. So, even in the case of the problems at the national level, it is the states, according to Madison, that were really at fault."[3] But state encroachments on federal powers simply reflect those very weaknesses of the Confederation government that Madison is deploring so strongly. It is not the condition of the states internally that engages his prime attention, as Wood's thesis would have it, but state invasion of national authority. Federal weaknesses and state encroachments were simply two sides of the same coin, and the only way for this fundamental flaw in the Articles to be remedied was to establish a new division of powers between the national and state governments, in a new constitution. Only thus could the federal government defend itself from state infringement of national authority.

I do not see anything new in the discussion of Nos. 10 and 51 of the *Federalist Papers*, nor is there any debate over the Convention's choice of the Virginia Plan over the New Jersey Plan as its working document. My point with regard to the enumeration of specific powers is that, in this matter, the Convention opted for the Paterson

3 See above, p. 129.

format rather than the Virginia model of broad heads of power that would have allowed for greater involvement of the central government in the affairs of the states. On this basis, Madison could subsequently claim (in *Federalist*, No. 39), with justice, that the Constitution was genuinely both national and federal.

I am not alone in taking issue with a genre of writing that seeks to "divine" the motives of historical actors, when the motives of these actors are clearly indicated in their private and public communications. And in the case of the Founders, nothing can match the authenticity of their unguarded comments at the Convention, as revealed in Farrand's *Records*, a source so rarely resorted to by Wood in support of his thesis. Thus, it must be recognized that examining trees can be important, especially when confronting theories based on imagined woods.

I admit that I am a textualist, and for very good reason. Historical analysis, I believe, must be grounded in the documentary record. Any imaginative thesis, as attractive as it may be, that does not coincide with that record remains, in the final analysis, mere speculation. In this regard, I must say that although Wood seeks to enlist noted historians Hobson and Rakove in his support, I find nothing upon which to take issue with them, since I do not read either of them to support the claim that the Constitution was "a political device designed to control the social forces the Revolution had released."[4] And finally, I draw attention to what Bernard Bailyn, doyen of the present generation of historians on the Founding, has written: "That document [the Constitution] . . . does not mark a Thermidorean reaction to the idealism of the early period engineered by either a capitalist junta or the proponents of rule by a leisured patriciate."[5] I believe this comment succinctly sums up my argument regarding the untenability of both the Beardian and neo-Beardian interpretations of the adoption of the U.S. Constitution.

4 Wood, *Creation of American Republic*, p. 476.

5 Bailyn, *The Ideological Origins of the American Revolution*, enlarged ed. (Cambridge, Mass.: Belknap Press, 1992), p. vii.

PART TWO

Constitutional Themes

4

Extrajudicial Activities and the Principle of the Separation of Powers

The constitutional doctrine of the separation of powers[1] has been, throughout the course of American history, a source of keen controversy between the executive and legislative branches of government. Rarely, however, has the doctrine provoked difficulties in relation to the judiciary or any of its members. Indeed, it is a curious fact that judges, since the earliest days of the republic, have assumed non-judicial functions in the service of the executive branch of government.[2] To cite a few examples: John Jay was simultaneously Ambassador to England and Chief Justice of the

1 This doctrine is, of course, nowhere mentioned in the federal Constitution; it is, nevertheless, firmly enshrined as one of the "great structural principles of American Constitutional Law." Edward S. Corwin, "Introductory Essay," *Constitution of the United States of America: Analysis and Interpretation* (Washington, D.C.: Govt. Printing Office, 1953), p. 9.

2 For a careful examination of the manifold activities of the members of the pre-Marshall Court, see Russel Wheeler, "Extrajudicial Activities of the Early Supreme Court," *Supreme Court Review* (1973), pp. 123-58. See also Wheeler, "Extrajudicial Behavior and the Role of the Supreme Court Justice," *University Programs Modular Studies* (1975).
For a rather comprehensive list of judges who have served the executive while still on the bench, see *Report of Senate Judiciary Committee on Abe Fortas*, 90th Congress, 2nd Session (Sept. 20, 1968) pp. 6-8 (Hereinafter cited as *Senate Report on Nomination of Abe Fortas*). See also the list of more recent judges noted in Henry Hart and Herbert Wechsler, *The Federal Courts and the Federal System* (Brooklyn: Foundation Press,1953), pp. 75-77. For extensive discussion of this subject, see *Nonjudicial Activities of Supreme Court Justices and other Federal Judges, Hearing before the Subcommittee on Separation of Powers of the Committee on the Judiciary,*" 91st Congress, 1st Session (July 14, 15, and 16, and Sept. 30, 1969) (Hereinafter cited as *Separation of Powers Hearings).*

Supreme Court. Oliver Ellsworth in 1799 held the posts of Chief Justice and Minister to France. John Marshall served, for a period in 1801, both as Secretary of State and Chief Justice of the Supreme Court.[3] (Marshall's role as Secretary of State, in fact, involved him directly in the events surrounding the appointment of the "midnight" Justices of the Peace which led to the celebrated case of *Marbury v. Madison*).[4] In more recent times, Justice Owen J. Roberts, in 1942, served as chairman of a committee to investigate the Pearl Harbor disaster; Justice Robert H. Jackson was chief counsel for the United States in the prosecution of Nazi war criminals at Nuremberg in 1945-46;[5] and, of course, Chief Justice Earl Warren in 1964 served as head of the Commission appointed by President Johnson to investigate the assassination of President Kennedy. Moreover, on occasions too frequent to enumerate, judges have advised presidents privately on matters of national and of international importance. Chief Justice Taft was particularly active on this score. Indeed, he not only counselled presidents, he actively engaged in promoting their election. It has been said of Taft that he "was the most extrajudicially active Justice of this century"[6] and "exerted enormous influence on legislators, Presidents, Cabinet

3 See Warren, *Supreme Court,* vol. 1, pp. 178, 184-85, 200-1. Marshall's appointment as Chief Justice was confirmed by the Senate on January 27, 1801. The new Administration entered into office on March 4. See also Albert Beveridge, *The Life of John Marshall* (Boston: Houghton Mifflin, 1929), pp. 558-59. Beveridge notes that this was the second time in the history of the United States that the two offices were held simultaneously by the same person. Jay had held the two offices for some six months in 1789-1790 until Jefferson returned from France to assume his post as Secretary of State. Technically, however, Jay's role as Secretary of State was a mere carry-over of his role as Secretary for Foreign Affairs under the Confederation. See F. Monaghan, *John Jay, Defender of Liberty* (N.Y.: Bobbs-Merrill, 1935), p. 300.

4 Warren notes that Marshall had continued to act as Secretary of State at the request of Jefferson. Warren, *Supreme Court,* p 201, n. 1.

5 For the position of Chief Justice Stone on this matter, see Alpheus Mason, "Extra Judicial Work for Judges," *Harvard Law Review,* vol. 67 (1953) pp. 193-216, and Mason, *Harlan Fiske Stone: Pillar of the Law* (N.Y.: Viking Press, 1956), Chap. 42.

6 Peter A. Bell, "Extrajudicial Activity of Supreme Court Justices," *Stanford Law Review,* vol. 22 (1969-70), p. 604.

member, editors, lawyers and friends"[7] while serving as Chief Justice. The close relationship which Justice Felix Frankfurter maintained with President Franklin D. Roosevelt after the latter appointed him to the Court is also a matter of renown.[8] Justice Frankfurter's messages influenced many presidential decisions, one of the more famous of which was the appointment of Henry L. Stimson as Secretary of War in 1940.[9]

On occasion, the extrajudicial executive role of individual judges has given rise to rumblings in Congress. Thus, in 1800 the anti-Federalist Senator Charles Pinckney, angered by the fact that two Federalist judges (Chief Justices Jay and Ellsworth) had successively served as ambassadors, proposed a constitutional amendment to prohibit judges from holding any outside office or appointment. Subsequently he introduced legislation to the same effect. (Nothing came of either of these efforts.)[10]

In 1968, during Senate consideration of the nomination of Associate Justice Fortas to the position of Chief Justice, the issue reached new heights when it was revealed in the course of committee hearings that the Justice had helped draft the 1966 State of the Union message as well as various items of legislation and had also participated in White House discussions on matters relating to the Vietnam war and to the riots in Detroit.[11] Those opposing the

7 Alpheus Mason, *William Howard Taft; Chief Justice* (N.Y.: Simon & Schuster, 1965), p. 287.

8 See in this regard Max Freedman (ed.), *Roosevelt and Frankfurter; Their Correspondence 1928-1945* (Boston: Little, Brown, 1967) pp. 485-744.

9 *Ibid.* pp. 524-25, 529. See also the testimony of Dean Adrian S. Fisher, *Separation of Powers Hearings*, p. 87. Former Secretary of State Dean Acheson, one of Frankfurter's closest friends, vigorously condemned in Senate testimony the Justices's "intimate and notorious friendship with President Roosevelt." His letters to the President, Acheson declared, "should never have been written, preserved or published." *Ibid.* p. 87.

10 *See* Warren, *The Supreme Court* vol. 1, pp. 167-68. In 1804, an attempt to provide for similar legislation was made in the House. *Ibid.* p. 168, n. 1.

11 This episode should be distinguished from the subsequent events and revelations of May 1969 which led to the resignation of Justice Fortas from the bench. The Fortas nomination to the position of Chief Justice was never acted upon by the Senate due to a filibuster from opposing Senators. On October 2, 1968, Mr. Fortas requested President Johnson to withdraw the nomination, which he reluctantly did.

nomination charged, inter alia, that Justice Fortas had violated the principle of the separation of powers, and cited in this context a letter sent by Chief Justice Jay to President Washington on the matter of advisory opinions.[12] (Secretary of State Thomas Jefferson had written the Justices in the name of President Washington requesting their advice on a series of international law questions which the conflict then raging between the British and French had given rise to. Jay and the Associate Justices indicated that the rendering of advisory opinions would be inconsistent "with the lines of separation drawn by the Constitution between the three departments of government.")[13] Other Senators, however, maintained that Justice Fortas had committed no wrong in counselling the President and cited the long list of Justices, including Chief Justice Jay himself, who had served the Executive in one capacity or another.[14]

12 See "Individual Views of Senator McClellan", *Senate Report on Abe Fortas*, pp. 29-30; "Individual Views of Senator Ervin," p. 34; and "Individual Views of Senator Thurmond," p.43.

13 Hart and Wechsler, *Federal Courts* pp. 75-77. For detailed consideration of this episode see Wheeler, *Extrajudicial Activities of United States Supreme Court*, pp. 148-54.

14 See *Senate Report on Nomination of Abe Fortas*, pp 6-8. Senator Ervin subsequently argued that Jay's letter on advisory opinions was not consistent with "the Chief Justice's proclivity on other occasions to engage in extrajudicial public service." *Separation of Powers Hearings*, p. 85. See also in this regard Wheeler, "Extrajudicial Activities of United States Supreme Court Justices; The Constitutional Period, 1790-1809," cited in *ibid.*, p. 783, who considers it "puzzling" that Jay, despite his stand on advisory opinions, was prepared to fulfull the nonjudicial duties of Commissioner of the Sinking Fund and inspector of the United States Mint. See also Wheeler, "Extrajudicial Activities of the Early Supreme Court," pp. 140-44. As a result of these inconsistencies in the conduct of the early Justices in regard to extrajudicial activities, Wheeler is led to the conclusion that it was "at bottom [considered] a question of discretion". Wheeler, p. 131. Fundamentally, it depended on the determination "whether the judge can maintain judicial independence while serving the nation off the bench," *Ibid.* It is submitted that a careful analysis of the rule in Hayburn's Case (see below) removes any basis for a charge of inconsistency in Jay's conduct. Moreover, as will be seen below, the extrajudicial activity of judges was not a matter of simple discretion or whimsy, but derived from sound and consistent constitutional principles.

With regard to the Fortas episode itself, it is arguable that the invocation of the separation of powers doctrine — whether by detractors or defenders of the Justice — was quite misplaced. For clearly, the separation of powers principle relates to the exercise of *powers*, to the performance of *official* acts appertaining to a department other than the one to which the individual concerned belongs; it does not relate to informal, private and unofficial contacts on a personal level. Such informal contacts, however, can in particular instances, raise acutely the issues of judicial ethics, propriety, and conflict-of-interest. And, in fact, in the Fortas case it was this aspect which was central — though it was unjustifiably confused by the Senators with the "separation of powers" doctrine.

Nevertheless, the debates in the Senate on that occasion and the subsequent general Senate deliberations on the separation of powers principle[15] served to highlight a wider question regarding the scope of the separation of powers principle as instituted by the Founding Fathers; was the principle intended to embrace not only the "separation of institutions" — with each branch of government limited to its own proper sphere of operation[16] — but also, as is commonly assumed, the "separation of personnel" so as to bar an individual from belonging to, and exercising the powers of, more

15 Beginning in 1969 the Senate Judiciary Subcommittee on the Separation of Powers, under the chairmanship of Senator Sam Ervin Jr., conducted extensive hearings on the subject of non-judicial activities of judges. See *Separation of Powers Hearings*. Senator Ervin introduced a bill (S. 1097) into the Senate "to enforce the principle of separation of powers . . . to prohibit the exercise or discharge by justices and judges of the United States of nonjudicial governmental powers and duties." *Ibid.*, pp. 7-8. This bill was never reported out of the Senate Committee on the Judiciary. See also in this regard the symposium entitled "Judicial Ethics," in *Law and Contemporary Problems*, Vol. 35 (1970) and, in particular, the article by Senator Ervin, "Separation of Powers: Judicial Independence," pp. 108-27.

16 The classical expression of the "institutional" separation of powers is that found in Part 1, Article 30, of the 1780 Constitution of Massachusetts, which reads as follows: "The legislative department shall never exercise the executive and judicial powers, or either of them; the executive shall never exercise the legislative and judicial powers, or either of them; the judicial shall never exercise the legislative and executive powers, or either of them." Reproduced in Poore, *State Constitutions*, vol. 1, p. 1960. Also cited in *Federalist No. 47* (James Madison).

than one branch of government?[17] Are, then, judges indeed constitutionally barred from serving, even in an official capacity, in another branch of government? Considerable historical and legal evidence, it is submitted, points decisively to negative answers to these questions. This evidence is provided by the discussions at the Constitutional Convention and the state ratifying conventions; Senate confirmation of the nominations of Jay, Ellsworth and Marshall; Pinckney's proposed amendment; and Hayburn's case and subsequent Supreme Court jurisprudence.

The Constitutional Convention

At first glance the "separation of personnel" idea would appear to be embodied in Article 1, Section 6, Clause 2, of the Constitution, which states:

> No Senator or Representative shall, during the Time for which he was elected, be appointed to any civil office under the Authority of the United States, which shall have been created, or the Emoluments whereof shall have been increased during such time; and no person holding any office under the United States, shall be a Member of either House during his continuance in office.

But upon closer scrutiny it becomes evident that this clause is not at all related to the separation of powers doctrine. For if, indeed, the purpose of the provision was the "separation of personnel," then why was it limited by its terms to the legislative and executive departments and not extended to the judiciary? The answer to this lies in the distinction which must be made between the motivation behind the provision and the ultimate consequences of the provision. Admittedly the result of the Constitutional prohibition was effectively to bar the development of any system of cabinet

17 This aspect is best reflected in the Virginia Constitution of 1776, in the following terms: "The legislative, executive and judiciary departments shall be separate and distinct; so that neither exercise the powers properly belonging to the other; *Nor shall any person exercise the powers of more than one of them at the same time.*" (Emphasis supplied.) For text, see Poore, *ibid.*, vol. 2, p. 1910. Also cited in *Federalist No. 47.*

responsibility. Therein, as Clinton Rossiter has noted,[18] lay "its real significance" for the American system of government. But, as Rossiter also observed, the true implication of the clause" naturally escaped their [the Constitutional delegates'] notice." For their concern was *not* with the separation of powers principle but with "'corruption and the low arts of intrigue.'"

There were, in fact, two kinds of corruption which the two parts of Article 1, Section 6, Clause 2, were intended to counteract. On the one hand there was the danger that the members of Congress might create new offices or increase the salaries of old ones and fill these positions themselves. This possibility was precluded by the first half of the provision. The second danger was that the members of Congress could fall prey to the allurements of a patronage-wielding Executive, free to bestow offices upon them. This avenue of Congressional corruption was excluded by the second half of the provision.[19]

The historical roots of Article 1, Section 6, Clause 2, can be traced back to the moves in the British parliament at the beginning of the 18th century to reduce the corrupt influence of the Crown in the lower house.[20] Under the Act of Settlement adopted in 1701, it was provided that "placemen," *i.e.*, persons holding offices of profit under the Crown, should be ineligible for membership in the House of Commons.[21] This provision which, by barring ministers from

18 Clinton Rossiter, *The American Presidency*, 2nd ed. rev., (N.Y.: Harcourt Brace, 1964), p. 75.

19 There can, of course, be more than a little affinity present between the separation of powers and the prevention of undue executive influence on the legislature. They are, however, quite distinct, at least in their purposes. The former aims to ensure that each of the three branches of government is separately administered so as to prevent, as Madison explained, the tyranny which otherwise must arise from the accumulation of all governmental powers in the same hands; the latter is concerned with the probity of the legislator and insuring that he is not given to temptation by office-seeking. Whatever affinity exists, in relation to the independence of the legislature, is thus once again more a matter of result than design.

20 See Edward S. Corwin, *The Constitution and What It Means Today* (Princeton: Princeton Univ. Press, 1965), pp. 21-22.

21 See David Keir, *The Constitutional History of Modern Britain 1485-1937* ,3rd ed. (London: Black, 1947), pp. 268-69; and Wade, *E.C. Constitutional Law* , 5th ed. (London: Longmans, 1955).

Parliament, would have prevented the development of the British cabinet system, was repealed before it took effect. However, the spirit of reform which inspired its adoption in England struck deep roots in the American colonies,[22] and when, subsequently, the Articles of Confederation were drafted, an express provision was included to the following effect: Article V . . . "nor shall any person, being a delegate, be capable of holding any office under the United States, from which he, or another for his benefit receives any salary, fees or emolument of any kind." The inclusion of such a provision in the Articles of Confederation confirms that its purpose was the prevention of legislative corruption and not enforcement of the doctrine of the separation of powers, since the latter doctrine was, of course, never instituted under the Articles at all.[23]

The Virginia Plan strengthened the barrier against venality by proposing that members of Congress be ineligible to hold office under the United States, not only during their term of office, but for a space of time after the expiration thereof.

The debates in the Federal Convention on what ultimately became Article 1, Section 6, Clause 2, fully establish that the overriding concern was with the dangers of bribery and corruption. On a motion to eliminate the foregoing provision of the Virginia plan, Mr. Butler declared:[24]

> This precaution agst. intrigue was necessary . . . . We have no way of judging mankind but by experience. Look at the history of the government of Great Britain, where there is a very flimsy exclusion — Does it not ruin their government? A man takes a seat in parliament to get an office for himself or friends, or both; and this is the great source from which flows its great venality and corruption . . . .[25]
>
> Mr. Mason. It seems as if it was taken for granted, that all offices will be filled by the executive, while I think many will remain in the gift of

22 See discussion in Bernard Bailyn, *The Ideological Origins of the American Revolution* (Boston: Harvard Univ. Press, 1967), pp. 86-92, 102-104.

23 See, on this point, the discussion in Carl Friedrich and Robert McCloskey, *From the Declaration of Independence to the Constitution; The Roots of American Constitutionalism* (N.Y.: Bobbs-Merrill, 1954), pp. 11-13.

24 Farrand, *Records*, vol. 1, p. 376.

25 *Ibid.*, p. 379.

> the legislature. In either case, it is necessary to shut the door against corruption. If otherwise, they may make or multiply offices, in order to fill them . . . . If not checked we shall have ambassadors to every petty state in Europe — the little republic of *St. Marino* not excepted. We must . . . remove the temptation. I consider this clause as the corner-stone on which our liberties depend.[26]

When Charles Pinckney argued that denying members of Congress the right to accept office was "degrading", "inconvenient", and "impolitic",[27] Colonel Mason "ironically proposed to strike out the whole section, as a more effectual expedient for encouraging that exotic corruption which might not otherwise thrive so well in the American Soil . . . for inviting into the Legislative service, those generous & benevolent characters who will do justice to each other's merit, by carving out offices & rewards for it."[28]

Madison himself fought strongly to allow members of Congress to hold office under the United States and wished to limit the scope of the exclusion to newly created positions or those whose salaries had been increased. "He supposed that the unnecessary creation of offices, and increase of salaries, were the evils most experienced, & that if the door was shut agst. them, it might properly be left open for the appointt. of members to other offices as an encouragmt. to the Legislative service."[29] Madison's proposal evoked the only reference to the doctrine of the separation of powers heard in the entire debate, and even then, it was only as a secondary consideration. Mr. Gerry responded as follows to Madison's suggestion:

> This amendment is of great weight, and its consequences ought to be well considered. At the beginning of the war we possessed more than Roman virtue. It appears to me it is now the reverse. We have more land and stock-jobbers than any place on earth. It appears to me, that

26 *Ibid.*, pp. 380-81.
27 *Ibid.*, vol. 2, pp. 283-84. But, cf. below, Pinckney's views on judges holding outside offices.
28 *Ibid.*, p. 284.
29 *Ibid.*, vol. 1, p. 386.

> we have constantly endeavored to keep distinct the three great branches of government; but if we agree to this motion, it must be destroyed by admitting the legislators to share in the executive, or to be too much influenced by the executive, in looking up to him for offices.[30]

This reference to the doctrine of the separation of powers made no impression upon Madison, who continued to fight for his amendment; nor was the argument adverted to by any of the other delegates. Those opposing Madison's motion concentrated on the central issue which had been the mainspring of the provision in the first place — namely, the fear of legislative corruption.[31]

In the respective State Conventions the discussions on Article 1, Section 6, Clause 2, likewise revolved around the question of corruption and bribery. Patrick Henry, in the Virginia Convention, complained that the provision was inadequate — "there is no restraint on corruption." After quoting the provision, he went on to say: "This is an idea strangely expressed . . . If we wish to preclude the inticement to getting offices, there is a clear way of expressing it."[32] It fell to Madison to prove that "the chance of getting an office is . . . so remote, and so very distant, that it cannot be considered as a sufficient reason to operate on their minds to deviate from their duty."[33]

Consequently, since the purpose of the provision was to scotch office-hunting by avaricious Congressmen and not to bolster the doctrine of the separation of powers, it can be readily understood why the provision was limited in its terms to the legislative branch of government. By the same token this explains why the provision

30 *Ibid.*, p. 393.

31 See, for instance, the remarks of Governor Rutledge, *ibid.*, pp. 386, 392; Mr. Mason, *ibid.*, pp. 387, 392, and Mr. Sherman, *ibid.*, pp. 387-88, 393.

32 *Ibid.*, vol. 3, p. 313.

33 *Ibid.*, pp. 315-16.

was inserted in Article 1, dealing with the legislature, and no other.[34]

But perhaps the most significant evidence emerging from the Constitutional Convention is the fact that a specific proposal barring judges from holding outside offices was submitted to the convention, but was never acted upon. On August 20, Charles Pinckney, delegate from South Carolina, presented a motion to the following effect;[35]

> No person holding the office of President of the U.S., a Judge of their Supreme Court, Secretary for the department of Foreign Affairs, of Finance, of Marine, of War, ...shall be capable of holding at the same time any other office of Trust or Emolument under the U.S. or an individual State.

This proposal, together with various other matters, was referred to the Committee of Detail. Nothing more was heard of the suggestion, nor, of course, was anything resembling it ever introduced in the Constitution.[36]

Ambassadorial Nominations and the Pinckney Amendment

The nominations of Chief Justices Jay and Ellsworth as ambassadors to England and France, respectively, received, of course, the "advice

34 In the light of the material and analysis presented in the text, it is respectfully submitted that the suggestion by Corwin, *The Constitution and What It Means Today*, p. 22, to the effect that Article 1, Section 6, Clause 2, was introduced into the Constitution "in conformity with the doctrine of the Separation of Powers" does not fully accord with the documentary record. The earlier cited comment by Clinton Rossiter, it is submitted, more accurately describes the pattern of events surrounding the introduction of this provision into the Constitution.

35 Farrand, *Records* vol. 2, pp. 341-42.

36 Earlier, as noted above, Charles Pinckney had fought for the right of members of the Legislature to hold office under the United States. Obviously, he does not appear to have been overly concerned with strict enforcement of the doctrine of the separation of powers. The proposal cited in the text, upon closer examination, seems directed at preventing double office-holding by members of the Executive or Judiciary and not really related to the separation of powers at all.

and consent" of the Senate. Quite obviously neither President Washington, nor President Adams, nor the nominees, nor the Senate itself, regarded the appointment of an active Justice to an office under the United States as a violation of the Constitution. Neither nominee found it necessary to resign his position on the bench before assuming his ambassadorial post. Each expected to return to the Court upon completion of his tour of duty abroad. (By coincidence, neither subsequently participated in Court proceedings. Jay, after concluding the negotiations for the treaty, was, in 1795, elected Governor of New York, and then resigned from the Court.[37] Ellsworth, in late 1800, after becoming ill in France, informed President Adams that he would no longer be able to serve as Chief Justice.)[38] Similarly, the confirmation of Chief Justice Marshall was not barred because he was Secretary of State. Nor would it be correct to assume that the Senate was unmindful of the constitutional issue involved. The Records of Congress contain no reference to the Senate's discussion on these nominations, but Charles Warren's history of the Supreme Court offers the following information regarding the Jay appointment:[39]

> The choice of a member of the Court for such a mission was not received favorably by the Senate; but after three days' debate, in the course of which a resolution was offered that 'to permit Judges of the Supreme Court to hold at the same time any other office of employment emanating from and holden at the pleasure of the Executive is contrary to the spirit of the Constitution, and as tending to expose them to the influence of the Executive, is mischievous and impolitic,' the nomination was finally confirmed by a vote of 18 to 8, on April 19, 1794.

37 Warren, *The Supreme Court*, vol. 1, p. 124. Thus, Jay not only served as Ambassador, but even ran for the office of Governor, without retiring from the Court. In 1792 he had also run for Governor without resigning, but lost to Clinton. Monaghan, *John Jay*, chap. 16. It is to be noted, however, that Jay did not actively campaign in either contest. *Ibid.*, pp. 326-27, 405.

38 Warren, *The Supreme Court*, vol. 1, pp. 171-72. and see Kathryn Turner, "The Appointment of Chief Justice Marshall," *Wm. & Mary Quarterly*, 3rd series, vol. 17 (1960), p. 143-63.

39 Warren, *The Supreme Court*, vol. 1. p. 119. Also see Monaghan, *John Jay*, p. 367.

Senator Pinckney's efforts to promote a constitutional amendment or Act of Congress to prohibit office-holding by judges while serving on the bench only serve to confirm that the Constitution, as such, was not seen as an effective barrier against such office-holding on the basis of the separation of powers. As Pinckney concedes: "The not preventing, by the Constitution, the Judges from holding other offices may possibly be considered as an omission: it is true, it might as well have been there."[40]

Hayburn's Case and its Subsequent Application

Hayburn's Case, decided in 1792, is early authority for the application of the separation of powers to the judiciary.[41] In that case the Justices of the Supreme Court, sitting in Circuit, held that they would be unable to fulfill a 1792 Act of Congress directing them to rule upon the pension claims of disabled veterans, since the Court's determination would not be final; it would, in fact, be subject to the review of the Secretary of War. The function thus assigned the Court under the Act was deemed to be "not judicial" but administrative, and hence in conflict with the principle of the separation of powers. "That by the Constitution of the United

40 *Annals of the Congress of the United States*, 6th Congress, March 5, 1800, p. 100. For the text of his proposed amendment to the Constitution, see *ibid.*, February 3, 1800, pp. 41-42. Adoption of Pinckney's motion at the Constitutional Convention would, of course, have rendered an amendment unnecessary. In discussing the dangers inherent in members of the Judiciary holding office under the Executive, Pinckney alluded to the possibility of judges declaring laws unconstitutional so as to curry favor with the President. His comments on the power of judicial review, made as they were *before Marbury v. Madison*, are quite illuminating: "It is our duty to guard against . . . this bias, which a Judge, from the nature of his appointment, must inevitably feel in favor of the President. It is more particularly incumbent on us when we recollect that our Judges claim the dangerous right to question the constitutionality of the laws; and either to execute them or not, as they think proper; a right in my judgement as unfounded and as dangerous as any that was ever attempted in a free government; they however do exercise it, and while they are suffered to do so, it is impossible to say to what extent it might be carried." *Ibid.* March 5, 1800, p. 101.

41 2 Dall. 409, 1 L. Ed. 436 (U.S. 1792).

States," declared the Court, "the government thereof is divided into three distinct and independent branches, and that it is the duty of each to abstain from, and to oppose, encroachments on either. Neither the Legislative nor the Executive branches, can constitutionally assign to the judicial any duties, but such as are properly judicial, and to be performed in a judicial manner."[42] Upon a careful reading of the case, however, it becomes clear that that decision does not bar an *individual* judge from undertaking nonjudicial functions. To the contrary, the case appears to establish a distinction between the exercise of nonjudicial powers by the court, as a *body*, or as an *institution*, which is proscribed, and the exercise of such powers by an *individual* judge, in his personal capacity, which is permitted.

The facts in *Hayburn's Case* were as follows: The circuit court for the district of Pennsylvania (together with other circuit courts) had refused to execute the 1792 Pensions Act. Attorney-General Randolph presented a motion for mandamus to the Supreme Court, on behalf of Wm. Hayburn, commanding the Pennsylvania court to examine his petition for his name to be placed on the pension list. The motion was held under advisement by the Supreme Court until the next term, but in the meantime Congress provided in a different manner for the relief of the invalid pensioners. Thus, the Supreme Court never ruled on the motion for mandamus. But in a footnote to the case the reporter indicated that each of three circuit courts which had considered the 1792 Act had concluded that it violated the doctrine of the separation of powers by assigning a nonjudicial function to the court. Two of the circuit courts, however — those for the districts of New York and North Carolina — raise the question whether the statute might not yet be saved, by interpreting it as a directive to the judges personally to act as commissioners in reviewing the pensioners' claims. The members of the Court for the district of New York (Chief Justice Jay, Associate Justice Cushing, and District Judge Duane) were of the opinion that the Act could indeed be interpreted

42 *Ibid.*, n. 2.

"as appointing commissioners for the purposes mentioned in it, by official, instead of personal, descriptions." These judges were prepared to "regard themselves as being the commissioners designated by the act."[43] In contrast, the members of the circuit court for the district of North Carolina (Justice Iredell and District Judge Sitgreaves) concluded that the Act could not bear such an interpretation. "The power appears to be given to the court only, and not to the judges of it."[44]

For more than half a century there was no evidence that the difference of opinion between the circuit courts over the interpretation to be accorded the statute had ever been finally resolved. But in 1852, Chief Justice Taney, in the course of deciding the case of *U.S. v. Ferreira*[45] (to be discussed presently) came upon the unreported Supreme Court decision of *U. S. v. Yale Todd* decided in 1794, and, recognizing its importance for "the nature and extent of judicial power " ordered it to be inserted in the reports immediately after the *Ferreira* decision.[46] The facts of the *Yale Todd* decision were as follows: In 1793, Congress, as noted above, had repealed the 1792 veterans pensions law and had provided for a different method, without recourse to the courts, for determining the strength of veterans' claims. One section, however, of the new act "saved all rights to pensions which might be founded 'upon any legal adjudication,' under the Act of 1792," and defined procedures for obtaining a Supreme Court ruling "on the validity of such rights . . . by the determination of certain persons styling themselves commissioners." Obviously, Chief Justice Jay and Justice Cushing, in accordance with their interpretation of the statute, had proceeded to act as commissioners and in this capacity had awarded pensions, including one to Yale Todd. Hence the law of 1793 provided for the legal testing of the validity of these awards. The United States now brought an action against Yale Todd for the sum of one hundred and seventy-two dollars and ninety-one cents, this being the

43 *Ibid.*, p. 411.
44 *Ibid.*, p. 415.
45 13 How. 40 (U.S. 1852).
46 *Ibid.*, p. 51.

amount he had received since being placed on the pension list. The sole question at issue was whether the judges had been entitled to interpret the 1792 act as a personal designation to them to act as commissioners. In a unanimous decision the Supreme Court ruled for the United States. "It would seem, therefore, . . . that Chief Justice Jay and Justice Cushing became satisfied, on further reflection, that the power given in the Act of 1792 to the Circuit Court, as a court, could not be construed to give it to the judges out of court as commissioners."[47]

What emerges from these decisions is that a statute which assigns, in unambiguous terms, a nonjudicial task to individual judges, in their personal capacity, would not be held to violate the principle of the separation of powers, although the assignment of such a task to a court, in its institutional capacity, would be struck down. This conclusion is confirmed by the Supreme Court decision of *U.S. v. Ferreira,* delivered by Chief Justice Taney in 1852 on behalf of a unanimous court. This case related to the following events:

In 1849, Congress, in accordance with the 1819 peace treaty between the United States and Spain, provided for the settlement of certain outstanding claims by Spanish citizens arising out of the conflict over Florida. Under the terms of the statute, the claims were first to be examined by the Federal Judge for the Northern District of Florida and then reviewed by the Secretary of the Treasury. On being satisfied that the same were "just and equitable" he was to pay out the amount due. The question posed before the Supreme Court was whether an appeal lay from the decision of the District Judge to the Supreme Court. The Court ruled that it did not, since "the decision is not the judgment of a court of justice. It is the award

47 *Ibid*. From the record of the case it would appear that the Court declared categorically that the 1792 Act had been unconstitutional. This case would thus represent a very early instance of judicial review. Warren, however, notes that legal writers, including James B. Thayer and Max Farrand, do not interpret the Court opinion as having declared the Act unconstitutional. *The Supreme Court*, vol. 1, p. 81 n. 2. The statute, of course, had been repealed in the meantime, in any case.

of a commissioner."[48] Naturally enough, in reaching this conclusion, C. J. Taney had occasion to refer to *Hayburn's Case*. He went on to say:

> Every judge [in Hayburn's Case] . . . formally expressed his opinion in writing, that the duty imposed, when the decision was subject to the revision of a secretary and of Congress, could not be executed by the court as a judicial power; and the only question upon which there appears to have been any difference of opinion, was whether it might not be construed as conferring the power on the judges personally as commissioners. And if it would bear that construction, there seems to have been no doubt, at that time, but that they might constitutionally exercise it . . . This law [of 1792] is the same in principle with the one we are now considering, with this difference only, that the Act of 1792 imposed the duty on the court eo nomine, and not personally on the judges. In the case before us it is imposed upon the judge and it appears from the note to the case of Hayburn that a majority of the judges of the Supreme Court were of opinion that if the law of 1792 had conferred the power on the judges, they would have held that it was given to them personally . . . and would have performed the duty as commissioners.[49]

Interestingly enough, Taney, in the course of his opinion, adverted to only one constitutional difficulty which might be raised in regard to a judge performing an extrajudicial function such as that of commissioner — namely, whether the role of commissioner did not constitute the judge "an officer of the United States" warranting appointment by the President, by and with the advice and consent of the Senate, and not by Act of Congress. Taney did not attempt to answer this question since it was not at issue in the case. But what is relevant to the present discussion is that he found no difficulty, on the grounds of the separation of powers, in the judge personally assuming a nonjudicial task. Thus, Taney made explicit the distinction implicit in Hayburn's Case between the actions of the court, qua court, and the actions of individual members of the Judiciary.

48 13 How. 47 (U. S. 1851).
49 *Ibid.*, pp. 49-50.

Conclusions

The principle of the separation of powers as it was established under the Constitution embraces all three branches of the federal government — but solely in relation to institutions, as such. The following description of the separation of powers doctrine given by Madison in his famous *Federalist No. 47*, aptly sums up the restricted nature of the doctrine:

> [Montesquieu's] meaning, as his own words import, and still more conclusively as illustrated by the example in his eye, can amount to no more than this, that where the *whole* power of one department is exercised by the same hands which possess the *whole* power of another department, the fundamental principles of a free constitution are subverted. This would have been the case in the constitution examined by him if the king, who is the sole executive magistrate, had possessed also the complete legislative power, or the supreme administration of justice; or if the entire legislative body had possessed the supreme judiciary, or the supreme executive authority.[50]

It follows from this that an individual in one department of government who belongs to, or exercises the powers of a different department, does not thereby violate the principle of the separation of powers. Only the members of the legislature are bound in this manner, and this, not out of consideration for the doctrine of the separation of powers, but in order to ensure the probity of the legislative body.

In light of the foregoing, the apparent inconsistency in Jay's approach to extrajudicial activities can be satisfactorily explained. Jay and his associate justices regarded the request for an advisory opinion as a matter addressed to the judiciary, as an institution, and therefore precluded by the principle of the separation of powers. Clearly enough, Washington and Jefferson were not content to

50 Emphasis in original. Joseph Story, in his *Commentaries on the Constitution of the United States*, Book 3 (1833), p. 197, defines the doctrine in these terms: "The true meaning is that the whole power of one of these departments should not be exercised by the same hands which possess the whole power of either of the other departments; and that such exercise of the whole would subvert the principle of a free constitution."

receive the advice or counsel of a single judge, be he even the Chief Justice. They sought an institutional answer and it is for this reason that they addressed the questions to the members of the Court. Quite simply, the Cabinet wanted a formal authoritative pronouncement from the judicial branch of the government to guide the actions of the executive.[51] And it was to this "institutional" role which Jay and his brethren took exception. Furnishing advisory opinions, they decided, would not be consistent with the constitutional arrangement of three separate departments of government, "these being in certain respects checks upon each other, and our being judges of a court in the last resort."[52] The rendering of legal advice, as requested, was not meet for the judiciary, "especially as the power given by the Constitution to the President, of calling on the heads of departments for opinions, seems to have been *purposely* as well as expressly united with the *executive* departments."[53] On the other hand, nothing in the Constitution barred the Chief Justice, or any of the individual justices for that matter, from assuming such extrajudicial tasks as Commissioner of the Sinking Fund, inspector of the United States Mint, or ambassador extraordinary to Great Britain. The Court, as such, was not engaged in such enterprises. The same consideration underlay the willingness of certain members of the Court to regard themselves as commissioners in reviewing war pensions.

It is noteworthy that the foregoing distinction was explicitly drawn by Jay in a letter he drafted (and possibly sent)[54] to President Washington. The matter related to the circuit duties of Supreme Court justices, and in his letter Jay wrote: "We are aware of the distinction between a Court and its Judges, and are far from thinking it illegal or unconstitutional, however it may be inexpedient, to employ them for other purposes, provided the latter

51 Thus Jefferson in his requesting letter emphasized that the "authority" "of the opinions of the judges of the Supreme Court" would "insure the respect of all parties." Hart and Wechsler, *Federal Courts*, p. 75.

52 *Ibid.*, p. 76.

53 *Ibid.*, pp. 76-77. Emphasis in original.

54 Cf. Hart and Wechsler, *Federal Courts*, p. 79, with the comment of Wheeler, *Extrajudicial Activities of the Early Supreme Court*, p. 148, n. 117.

purposes be consistent and compatible with the former."[55] Thus, in Jay's eyes, it was clear that individual judges might be able to engage in certain extrajudicial activities even though the Court, as an institution, would be barred from doing so.

Having said all this, it could hardly be maintained that it is a salutary practice for judges to be engaged in extrajudicial activities. Serious questions of propriety, or even conflict of interest, are too often present. These, however, are matters for the statutory or ethical codes; they do not impinge on the constitutional principle which seeks to ensure the separation of the three functions of government, as this principle was instituted in the federal Constitution, interpreted by the courts, and applied in practice.[56]

55 Griffith J. McRee, *Life and Correspondence of James Iredell,* (N.Y.: Appleton, 1878), vol. 2, p. 294 (reprinted 1949, N.Y.: P. Smith).

56 This conclusion raises the question whether the Ervin bill (see footnote 15 above), since it seeks to prohibit nonjudicial activities by individual judges, might not have been better based on something other than "the principle of separation of powers".

5

The U.S. Constitution and Anticipatory Self-Defense under Article 51 of the U.N. Charter

Ever since the U.N. Charter entered into force in 1945 a debate has ensued about the meaning and scope of the right of self-defense under article 51 of the Charter.[1] Two schools of thought have arisen.[2] One school claims that the term "armed attack" must be taken literally and that members of the U.N. have foresworn acts of self-defense even in the face of dire danger or severe provocation. Only when the other side has actually engaged in hostilities by initiating an "armed attack" can the first side resort to the use of force in self-defense.[3] The second school maintains that the provision was not meant to establish new limitations on the

1 Article 51 reads: "Nothing in the present Charter shall impair the right of individual or collective self-defense if an armed attack occurs against a Member of the United Nations, until the Security Council has taken measures necessary to maintain international peace and security."

2 For succinct summaries of these two schools, see J. L. Brierly, *The Law of Nations* (ed. Humphrey Waldock) (6th ed.; Oxford: Oxford Univ. Press, 1963), pp. 413-32; and K. Skubiszewski, "Use of Force by States, Collective Security, Law of War and Neutrality," in Max Sorenson (ed.), *Manual of Public International Law* (London: Macmillan, 1968), pp. 765-68. See also Leland M. Goodrich, Edvard Hambro, and Anne P. Simons, *Charter of the United Nations: Commentary and Documents* (N.Y.: Columbia Univ. Press, 1969), pp. 344-48; and Marjorie M. Whiteman, *Digest of International Law* (Washington, D.C.: Govt. Printing Office, 1965), vol. 5, pp. 971-91.

3 This interpretation is endorsed by such writers as Skubiszewski, "Use of Force by States," pp. 765-68; Hans Kelsen, *Law of the United Nations* (London: Stevens, 1950), pp. 269, 791; Quincy Wright, "The Cuban Quarantine," *AJIL*, vol. 57 (1963), pp. 546-63; and Ian Brownlie, *International Law and the Use of Force by States* (Oxford: Clarendon Press, 1963), pp. 264-80.

traditional right of self-defense, even in the absence of an armed attack. It is noted that the term "self-defense" in article 51 is qualified by the word "inherent," meaning that the natural right of a state to protect itself against threats to its security was left unimpaired. The term "when an armed attack occurs" is held to be merely illustrative.[4] An anticipatory strike against an enemy massing troops or making other signs of preparation for imminent war would be barred by the first interpretation but permitted by the second.

A little-noticed provision of the U.S. Constitution would seem to have a direct bearing on this debate, at least in so far as the United States is concerned. Article 1, section 10, clause 3 of the U.S. Constitution provides: "No State shall, without the Consent of Congress . . . engage in War, unless actually invaded, or in such imminent Danger as will not admit delay." Irrespective of whether the constitutional phrase "unless actually invaded" is equivalent to the Charter condition "if an armed attack occurs," clearly the right of a state to engage in war when it is "in such imminent danger as will not admit of delay" goes beyond the Charter condition; it implies action which is pre-emptive. A state, according to this provision, is given the right to initiate war *in advance of* actual hostilities and is not compelled to wait until after it has been attacked.

The question may be asked: does the word "danger" refer back to the term "invaded" found earlier in the sentence, or does it stand alone — *i.e.*, is a state's right to engage in war limited to danger of actual invasion or does it cover any danger of whatever sort? The Records of the Constitutional Convention offer no guidance. The source for this constitutional clause is to be found in article VI of the Articles of Confederation, which provided: "No State shall engage in any war without the consent of the United States in Congress assembled, unless such State be actually invaded by enemies, or

4 Supporters of this interpretation include Waldock and Brierly *Law of Nations*, pp. 413-32; Julius Stone, *Aggression and World Order* (London: Stevens,1958), pp. 44, 92-104; and Derek Bowett, *Self Defence in International Law* (Manchester: Manchester Univ. Press, 1958), pp. 24, 188-89.

shall have received certain advice of a resolution being formed by some nations of Indians to invade such States, and the danger is so imminent as not to admit a delay till the United States in Congress assembled can be consulted." In the Constitutional Convention, the report of the Committee of Detail closely followed this terminology (except for the reference to the Indians) and prohibited a State to engage in war "unless it shall be actually invaded by enemies, or the danger of invasion be so imminent as not to admit of delay until the Legislature of the United States can be consulted."[5] This formula was retained throughout, even through the report of the Committee of Style on September 12.[6] However, in the final discussions, two days before the Convention adjourned, the provision was refashioned: the word "invasion" in the latter part of the sentence was omitted as was the reference to the legislature, and the provision now read: "or in such imminent danger as will not admit of delay."[7] Since there was no debate on the subject, it is not clear whether the intention was merely to improve the style or actually to broaden the freedom of action with reference to *any* danger — of invasions or otherwise. But in either case, the provision clearly authorizes a state to take action while the danger remains imminent.

The existence of the foregoing constitutional provision would seem to confirm that for the United States, at least, the broader interpretation of article 51 of the Charter, which leaves unimpaired the traditional right of recourse to force in the face of imminent danger, is to be preferred. It might be argued, however, that the federal government of the United States is bound by the Charter, including article 51 in its narrow interpretation, regardless of any rights, including that of self-defense, which the Constitution reserves for the individual states composing the United States. This, however, would produce the rather anomalous state of affairs, whereby the United States would not be permitted to launch anticipatory strikes to ward off a threat of imminent danger, while

5 Farrand, *Records*, vol. 2, pp. 187, 442 n. 26.
6 *Ibid.*, p. 597.
7 *Ibid.*, p. 626.

one of the state governments would be allowed to do so because such a right is preserved for it in the Constitution. Thus, if Florida, for instance, was threatened by action from Cuba, the United States Air-Force could not move, but the Florida Coast-Guard or Air-Patrol would be free to act.

Against this it might be argued that the international commitment of the United States should be equally binding on each of the state governments by virtue of Article VI of the Constitution, the Supremacy clause, which provides that " . . . all treaties made . . . under the Authority of the United States, shall be the supreme Law of the Land. . . . " This argument, however, raises the very interesting question whether the federal government is indeed empowered, by means of a treaty, to affect any of the rights reserved by the Constitution to the individual states. Justice Holmes, in his famous comment on the treaty power of the United States, stated: "Acts of Congress are the supreme law of the land when made in pursuance of the Constitution, while treaties are declared to be so when made under the authority of the United States. It is open to question whether the authority of the United States means more than the formal acts prescribed to make the convention."[8] If this sweeping interpretation of the federal treaty power is law, then the federal government's authority to bind the states would be unaffected by any right which might be reserved to them by virtue of the Constitution. But, as Professor Henkin has written: "Arguments, based on the language of the Supremacy Clause, that treaties are not subject to constitutional prohibitions are now well at rest."[9] The matter was settled by the 1957 Supreme Court decision of *Reid v. Covert* in which Justice Black declared:[10]

> It would be manifestly contrary to the objectives of those who created the Constitution, as well as those who were responsible for the Bill of Rights — let alone alien to our entire constitutional history and tradition — to construe Article VI as permitting the United States to

8 Missouri v. Holland, 252 U.S. 416, 433 (1920).

9 Louis Henkin, *Foreign Affairs and the Constitution* (Mineola, N.Y.: Foundation Press, 1972), p. 137-40.

10 354 U.S. 1 at 17.

> exercise power under an international agreement without observing constitutional prohibitions. In effect, such construction would permit amendment of that document in a manner not sanctioned by Article V.

The right of self-defense inhering in a state, is , of course, not a civil liberty such as those guaranteed individual citizens under the Bill of Rights or the Fourteenth Amendment. Nonetheless, it is an essential assurance regarding the state's very existence, and it is not to be presumed that, if such a right is preserved under the Constitution, the federal government is empowered to nullify it by treaty or otherwise. In the case of *Geofrey v. Riggs*, Justice Field stated (albeit as dictum):[11] "It would not be contended that it [the treaty power] extends so far as to authorize what the Constitution forbids, or a change in the character of the government or in that of one of the States, or cession of any portion of the territory of the latter, without its consent." In accordance with this pronouncement it is generally assumed that the treaty-makers could not modify the republican form of government of the states, or even completely abolish all state militia in the event, for instance, of a treaty prescribing general and complete disarmament.[12]

By the same token, if the terminology of article 1, section 10, clause 3, assures every state in the union a right to engage in war in the face of "such imminent danger as will not admit of delay," it is difficult to see how this right could be abrogated by treaty. Consequently, if such a right inheres in each of the state governments, it must be presumed to inhere no less in the federal government. This is particularly so since, according to article 4, section 4 of the Constitution, the United States is committed to "protect each of them [the States] against Invasion." Thus, the right of self-defense reserved to a state under article 1, section 10, clause 3 must be covered by, and is indeed assumed under, the general protection to which the United States, by virtue of article 4, section 4, is committed.

11 133 U.S. 258 at 267 (1890).

12 See the discussion in Henkin, *Foreign Affairs and the Constitution*, pp. 147-48. See also Louis Henkin, *Arms Control and Inspection in American Law* (N.Y.: Columbia Univ. Press, 1958), pp. 33-36.

If this is the case, then of necessity it must be assumed that for the United States, the broader interpretation of article 51 of the Charter is the correct one, and the traditional concept of self-defense as it existed prior to the Charter, including the right to exercise anticipatory force in certain circumstances, continues to apply.[13]

13 It might be noted, in passing, that if Article 1, section 10, clause 3 of the Constitution sums up the nature of self-defense for the United States, then the definition enunciated by Secretary of State Webster in the case of the *Caroline* would seem to be too narrow. In his correspondence with British Foreign Minister Ashburton in this case, Webster maintained that the right to exercise self-defense by one state against the territory of another was limited to cases in which the "necessity of that self-defense is instant, overwhelming, and leaving no choice of means, and no moment for deliberation." Cited in John Bassett Moore, *A Digest of International Law* (Washington, D.C.: Govt. Printing Office, 1906), vol. 2, p. 412; see also discussion in William W. Bishop Jr., *International Law: Cases and Materials* (2nd ed.; Boston: Little Brown, 1962), p. 777. It does not appear that Webster took note of the foregoing constitutional provision under whose terms it would be sufficient for a state to be confronted by "imminent danger as will not admit of delay" alone, without anything more, for it to be free to exercise the right of self-defense.

6

Congressional-Executive Agreements

The recent demand for a return to the constitutional balance in the realm of foreign affairs has manifested itself in a sharp attack on the use of the executive agreement. In 1972, in an attempt to exercise greater control in this area, Congress passed the Case Act, which requires the Secretary of State to transmit to Congress within sixty days "the text of any international agreement, other than a treaty, to which the United States is a party."[1] In November 1974, the Senate went a step further and passed the Ervin bill, according to which an executive agreement would enter into force only after it had been tabled in Congress for sixty days and only if Congress had not disapproved of the agreement by means of a simple concurrent resolution.[2] The House failed to act on this bill before the Ninety-third Congress adjourned. It is assumed that the measure will be reintroduced.

The underlying assumption in all this legislative activity is that congressional assent to an executive agreement will cure the agreement of any constitutional disability. Similarly, the National Commitments Resolution, adopted by the Senate in 1969, equates congressional-executive agreements with formal treaties as a means of accepting national commitments. Yet in constitutional terms, the authority of Congress to join with the President by majority vote in giving force to an executive agreement is as novel as the "pure"

1 1 U.S.C § 112 (b) (Supp. II 1972). For general background, see J. Wm. Fulbright, *The Crippled Giant: American Foreign Policy and its Domestic Consequences* (N.Y.: Random, 1972), pp. 216-27.

2 S. 3830, 93d Cong., 2d Sess. (1974). For hearings on this bill, see *Hearings on S. 3475 Before the Subcomm. On the Separation of Powers of the Senate Comm. On the Judiciary*, 92d Cong., 2d Sess. (1972).

executive agreement. Neither procedure is mentioned in the Constitution and neither, of course, fulfills the constitutional requirement that the treaty-making power of the President be dependent on the advice and consent of two-thirds of the Senate. In the case of an agreement on a particular subject falling within the scope of one or more of the enumerated legislative powers, such as international trade or postal matters, it might be suggested that Congress is qualified to cure such executive agreements of any possible constitutional defect. It is assumed by the authors of the aforementioned bills, however, that joint congressional-executive action would impart the full force of a treaty even to agreements not falling within this category.

In his definitive study, *Foreign Affairs and the Constitution,*[3] Professor Louis Henkin notes various arguments which have been invoked for validating congressional-executive agreements. One of these runs as follows:

> Before the Constitution all international agreements were made by Congress. The Constitutional Convention considered proposals to require the advice and consent of both houses to the making of treaties, and rejected them largely because they would have made the process too difficult and cumbersome. The requirement of consent of the Senate only can be seen, then, as "settling for less," and the two-thirds requirement in the Senate as a lesser substitute for the consent of the House of Representatives also. If so, the consent of both houses (even if only by simple majority) is an even greater safeguard and should surely be no less effective that the consent of the Senate alone (even by two thirds).[4]

3 Louis Henkin, *Foreign Affairs and the Constitution* (Mineola, N.Y.: Foundation Press, 1972).

4 *Ibid.*, p. 422. Other arguments appear in *ibid.*, pp. 173-76, 85 n. 9. Support for this thesis would appear, at first glance, to arise from the remarks of Convention delegate George Mason, who criticized the final Constitution in these terms:

> By declaring all treaties supreme laws of the land, the executive and the Senate have, in many cases, an exclusive power of legislation which might have been avoided by proper distinctions with respect to treaties and requiring the assent of the House of Representatives, where it could be done with safety.

In general, the possible arguments suggested by Henkin are premised on the assumption that the legislative history of the treaty-making clause is not clear, or at least that it lodges the treaty-making power in the Senate on the basis of technical considerations such as the need for secrecy and dispatch, the greater size of the House, and the frequent changes in House membership.[5] According to these arguments, however, the Founding Fathers would have preferred to vest the power in both Houses of Congress if that had been feasible. Various other authorities, including Quincy Wright, [6] and Myres McDougal and Asher Lans,[7] have likewise maintained that no clear picture emerges from the Constitutional Convention

---

Paul Leicester Ford, *Pamphlets on the Constitution of the United States* (Brooklyn: [s.l.] 1888), p. 331; Farrand, *Records*, vol. 2, p. 639. However, as will be seen below, both the context of Mason's remarks and his subsequent remarks in the Virginia Ratifying Convention, make it clear that he was arguing for a two-thirds, rather than majority, vote in *both* houses of congress. see note 43 *infra*.

5 Certain delegates, both during and after the Convention mentioned these considerations. See *ibid.*, p. 538 (remarks of James Wilson and Roger Sherman); *ibid.*, vol. 3, pp. 251-52 (remarks of Charles Cotesworth Pinckney); *The Federalist No. 75* (Alexander Hamilton). It might also be noted that Mason, in advocating inclusion of the House in the treaty-making process, made such inclusion conditional on the "safety" factor. None of this, however, detracts from the clear-cut evidence of fundamental policy considerations in the formulation of the provision.

6 Wright, "The United States and International Agreements," *AJIL.*, vol. 38 (1944), pp. 341-55.

7 McDougal and Lans, "Treaties and Congressional-Executive or Presidential Agreements: Interchangeable Instruments of National Policy, Parts 1 and 2," *Yale L.J.* vol. 54 (1945), pp. 181-351, 534-615. This two-part article was written toward the end of World War II, on the eve of the drafting of the United Nations Charter. The views of the authors reflected the widespread fear that a small number of Senators might block United States membership in a world organization as had occurred previously in the case of the League of Nations. This article was designed to establish the validity of an alternative form of ratification by means of a congressional-executive agreement or an executive agreement alone.
For a contrary view, see Edwin Borchard, "Shall the Executive Agreements Replace the Treaty?" *Yale L.J.*, vol. 53 (1944), pp. 664-83; "Treaties and Executive Agreements — A Reply, *Yale L.J.*, vol. 54 (1945) pp. 616-64. On the topic generally, see Wallace M. McClure, *International Executive Agreements: Democratic Proceedure Under the Constitution of the United States* (N.Y.: Columbia Univ. Press, 1941).

concerning the motives behind the formulation of the treaty-making clause, and that policy considerations were not determinative. They conclude, therefore, that "an executive agreement ratified by joint resolution differs from a treaty largely in name only."[8]

It is respectfully submitted that when taken together with evidence supplementary to the debates, the full record of the Constitutional Convention (the " Convention") demonstrates quite convincingly that the underlying consideration prompting the delegates to vest the treaty-making power in the Senate was the desire of the States to retain maximal control over foreign affairs. The final clause on the treaty-making power emerged as the product of several basic conflicts which had beset the Constitutional Convention: clashes between "nationalists" and "federalists," between large and small States, and between North and South. By means of a compromise, the President was given a role in the treaty-making process, while the vote required in the Senate was raised from a simple majority to two-thirds. Against this background, it becomes evident that the latter requirement was a deliberate policy decision designed to ensure protection of factional interests, rather than merely a less stringent alternative to a majority vote in both Houses.

Neither the Virginia Plan[9] nor the New Jersey Plan[10] proposed any change in the treaty-making arrangements made operative under the Articles of Confederation. Each would have continued to assign the power to Congress.[11] Even when the Committee of the Whole accepted the revised Virginia Plan, which provided for a select upper chamber, no change was proposed regarding the status of the treaty-making power.[12] The foreign affairs power, *i.e.*, the competence to make treaties and to appoint ambassadors, became lodged exclusively in the Senate only upon adoption of the

8 Statement of Representative J. William Fulbright in October 1945, cited by Wright, "The United States and International Agreements", p. 341.

9 Farrand, *Records*, vol. 1, pp. 20-22

10 *Ibid.*, pp. 242-45.

11 Under the Articles of Confederation, nine votes out of a possible thirteen votes were required for treaty ratification. *Articles of Confederation*, art. IX.

12 Farrand, *Records*, vol. 1, pp. 228-32.

Connecticut Compromise, which introduced the principle of equal state representation in the upper House.[13] This circumstance permits the inference that the states, and perhaps the smaller states in particular, were jealous of the authority accorded the national government over foreign affairs and therefore sought to retain control over foreign relations through the Senate. The remarks of William Davie, delegate to the North Carolina Ratifying Convention, lends weight to this inference:

> The extreme jealousy of the little states, and between the commercial and non-importing states, produced the necessity of giving an equality of suffrage to the Senate. The same causes made it indispensable to give to the senators, as representatives of states, the power of making, or rather ratifying, treaties. . . . The small states would not consent to confederate without an equal voice in the formation of treaties. Without the equality, they apprehended that their interest would be neglected or sacrificed in negotiations. This difficulty could not be got over. . . . [Because] of the inflexibility of the little states in this point it . . . became necessary to give them an absolute equality in making treaties.[14]

As Farrand concludes:

> In place of allowing congress to appoint ambassadors [and] to make treaties . . . as had been the case under the confederation, those functions were now transferred to the senate, the body which most nearly corresponded to the old congress as the representative of the states.[15]

At this point, the President had not been accorded any role in the making of treaties. It apparently was assumed that the Senate itself, in collective form, would both negotiate and ratify treaties. The relevant provision, as reported by the Committee of Detail, read as follows: "The Senate of the U.S. shall have power to make treaties, and to appoint Ambassadors . . . "[16]

13 See the various drafts of the Committee of Detail, vol. 2, *ibid.*, pp. 143, 155, 169.

14 *Ibid.*, vol. 3, p. 348. See also *ibid.*, p. 342 (remarks of Richard Spaight). But see Ford, *Pamphlets*, p. 356 (remarks of Iredell) for an answer to Mason's objections.

15 Farrand, *Framing of Constitution*, p. 131.

16 Farrand, *Records*, vol. 2, p. 392

When the Convention commenced consideration of the provision on August 23, Madison criticized the exclusive Senate control over treaty-making, "observ(ing) that the Senate represented the States alone, and that for this as well as other obvious reasons it was proper that the President should be an agent in Treaties."[17] The complaint reflected not only a more "national" perspective on the foreign affairs power, but also the dissatisfaction of the larger States over the disproportionate authority in national management which had been made available to the smaller states by means of the Senate. Madison therefore suggested that the President, the only truly national figure in the framework of government, be included in the treaty-making process. Gouverneur Morris went a step further, proposing that under certain circumstances the lower House be brought into the picture. On the same day, the convention had adopted the Supremacy Clause, which made treaties the supreme law of the land.[18] Apparently with that clause in mind, Gouverneur Morris proposed an amendment of the treaty-making provision to avoid binding the United States by any treaty "not ratified by a law."[19] Wilson and other nationalists supported the motion. The significance of the amendment was revealed by Mr. Dickinson of Delaware, who "concurred in the amendment, as most safe and proper, tho' he was sensible it was unfavorable to the little States; which would otherwise have an *equal* share in making Treaties."[20] Gouverneur Morris's motion, however, was defeated by a wide margin, being supported only by the delegation from his home state, Pennsylvania (the most "national" of the delegations).[21] The states, and particularly the smaller states, obviously were not

17 *Ibid.* Nevertheless, Madison refrained from submitting a formal proposal.
18 *Ibid.*, p. 389.
19 *Ibid.*, p. 320.
20 *Ibid.*, p. 393.
21 *Ibid.*, p. 394

anxious to share the foreign affairs power with the popularly-elected branch of the legislature.[22]

The ultimate form of the treaty-making provision was a product of the last stages of the Convention. Madison's earlier suggestion for Presidential participation in the treaty-making process was revived by the Committee of Postponed Parts, which also instituted the two-thirds voting requirement in the Senate.[23] With these two major revisions, the final product was presented to the plenum and approved. The considerations which had prompted these changes are not readily apparent, since that committee's deliberations were not preserved, and the Convention itself approved the changes "with surprising unanimity and surprisingly little debate."[24] Comments made by George Mason, however, both at the Convention and immediately thereafter shed light on the motives behind the formulation of the final provision.

In the first place, a written note entered by Mason at the Convention reveals a link between the treaty clause and the Convention debate on navigation laws. This comment, uncovered by Farrand in his 1937 supplement to the *Records of the Federal Convention of 1787,* was written by Mason in the margin of a printed copy of the *Report of the Committee of Detail,* which had vested the treaty-making power in the Senate.[25] Mason noted:

22 In theory, once the Senate was granted a veto in the treaty-making process, the inclusion of the House in the implementation of treaties should have been unobjectional to those concerned with ensuring the equality of States. Similarly, it might have been assumed that the nationalists, anxious to make treaties automatically binding upon the states, would oppose burdening the treaty-making process with an additional requirement of legislative implementation. Yet, strangely enough, the positions in this debate were reversed: only the nationalists favored such a step. The opposing delegates obviously felt that the conferral upon the House of any role in relation to treaties, even a legislative role, represented a corresponding diminution of Senate (*i.e.,* state) control. (Additionally, some delegates undoubtedly hesitated to encumber the treaty-making process with a legislative requirement.)

23 Farrand, *Records,* vol. 2, pp. 498-99. The appointment of ambassadors was likewise transferred to the President, subject to the advice and consent of the Senate, but in this case, the simple majority requirement was not changed.

24 Farrand, *Framing of Constitution,* p. 171.

25 Cited in text at n. 16 above.

> As treaties are to be the Laws of the Land & commercial Treaties may be so framed as to be partially injurious, there seems to be some necessity for the same Security upon this Subject as in the 6th Section of the 6th Article.[26]

The latter provision, relating to navigation laws, required a two-thirds majority for adoption.[27] Ever since the United States had declared independence, the Southern States had been concerned that the North, like pre-revolutionary Great Britain, might adopt legislation restricting the shipment of export or import goods to American ships,[28] thus benefitting the commercial and ship-building states of the North, but adversely affecting the South by raising the price of finished goods imported from abroad and by restricting the free dispatch of produce in any ship available. Throughout the convention, the Southern states successfully retained a clause in the draft constitution which required a two-thirds majority in both Houses of Congress for the adoption of any navigation law. Since the Northern states alone could not command such a majority, the interests of the South were made secure. It was in this context that Mason had entered the comment on the treaty-making provision. The conclusion of commercial treaties clearly could disadvantage the South no less injuriously than the adoption of navigation laws; hence it was necessary to extend the two-thirds requirement to treaty-making as well. Indeed, if, as Mason suggested, the safeguards applicable to treaties were to be equalized with those adopted for navigation laws, then Mason would seem implicitly to have advocated a two-thirds requirement for treaties in

26 Farrand, *Records*, vol. 4, pp. 52-53. Since this material first came to light in 1937, it was not noted in earlier works on the treaty power. For examples of such works see Charles H. Butler, *The Treaty Making Power of the United States* (N.Y.: Banks Law Publishing, 1902); Samuel B. Crandall, *Treaties – Their Making and Enforcement* (N.Y.: Columbia Univ. Press, 1904). However, it is surprising that later writers also have failed to note the significance of Mason's marginal comment and the other documents uncovered by Farrand in his 1937 revision.

27 Farrand, *Records*, vol. 2, p. 183.

28 See Andrew C. McLaughlin, *The Confederation and the Constitution; 1783-1789* (N.Y.: Macmillan, 1905) pp. 84-86, 260-62; Farrand, *Framing of Constitution*, pp. 147-52; Warren, *Making of Constitution*, pp. 579-86.

both Houses of Congress. Yet despite his comment in the margin, there is no indication that Mason raised the issue in the debates. Nonetheless, there are signs that Mason was not alone in thinking that special interests needed as much protection against adverse treaties as against adverse laws. In one of the earlier drafts of the *Report of the Committee of Detail*, the provisions on navigation laws and treaties were juxtaposed as follows:

> Restrictions
> I. A navigation act shall not be passed, but with the consent of (eleven states in) <2/3d. of the Members present of> the senate and (10 in) <the like No. of> the house of representatives.
>
> . . .
>
> (3. the lawful territory To make treaties of commerce
> (qu: as to senate) Under the foregoing restrictions)
> 4. (To make treaties of peace or alliance
> (qu: as to senate) under the foregoing restrictions, and without the surrender of territory for an equivalent, and in no case, unless a superior title.)[29]

The link between the treaty clause and navigation law questions appears in fact to have been caught up in a broader debate involving North-South differences at the Convention. On August 23, at the same time that the Convention was considering the treaty-making clause,[30] it was also grappling with three other difficult items: importation of slaves, taxes on exports, and the vote required for the adoption of navigation laws. These latter questions were moved to a special committee of eleven.[31] The hope expressed by Gouverneur Morris that the three items might "form a bargain among the Northern and Southern States" was realized by means of one of the well-known compromises of the Convention: the two-thirds requirement for navigation laws was dropped in return for the right to continue the importation of slaves for a further twelve years (which ultimately became twenty years) and a prohibition on

29 Farrand, *Records*, vol. 2, p. 143. Farrand indicates that this document is in the handwriting of Edmund Randolph of Virginia, with corrections by John Rutledge of South Carolina. Those portions in parentheses were crossed out in the original, while those in brackets represent Rutledge's emendations.

30 *Ibid.*, pp. 392-94

31 *Ibid.*, pp. 359-75.

the imposition of export taxes.[32] It is less well-known, however, that the treaty clause was affected directly by this overall compromise, and may well have been one of the elements of it. The testimony of George Mason during the course of the debates at the Virginia Ratifying Convention is illuminating in this regard:

> Mr. Chairman — With respect to commerce and navigation . . . I will give you, to the best of my recollection, the history of that affair. This business was discussed at Philadelphia for four months . . . and I assert, that eight states out of twelve, for more than three months, voted for requiring two-thirds of the members present in each house to pass commercial and navigation laws. True it is, that afterwards it was carried by a majority, as it stands. If I am right, there was a great majority for requiring two-thirds of the states in this business, till a compromise took place between the northern and southern states; the northern states agreeing to the temporary importation of slaves, and the southern states conceding, in return, that navigation and commercial laws should be on the footing on which they now stand . . . The Newfoundland fisheries will require the consent of two-thirds of the members present in the senate.[33]

It is not clear whether Mason was suggesting that the two-thirds requirement for treaties actually had been part of the *quid pro quo* in the compromise, or whether in the case of treaties, in contrast to the situation regarding navigation acts, the South had won on a qualified majority, since the fisheries interest of the East had coincided with the South's interest in staples. Yet it is clear that the fear of adverse effects of commercial treaties on sectional interests had prompted the raising of the majority vote to two-thirds. When the treaty-making clause came up for discussion on September 7, the delegates overwhelmingly rejected proposals made by Wilson, the Pennsylvania nationalist, to include the House in the treaty-making process[34] and to eliminate the two-thirds voting requirement.[35] An understanding between South and East had been

32 *Ibid.* pp. 400 *ff.*

33 *Ibid., vol. 3,* pp. 334-35.

34 *Ibid.*, vol. 2, p. 538. Wilson contended: "As treaties . . . are to have the operation of laws, they ought to have the sanction of laws also." The vote was one to ten against the inclusion of Wilson's proposals. *Ibid.*

35 *Ibid.*, pp. 540, 549. Wilson argued: "To require the concurrence of 2/3 . . . puts it in the power of the minority to controul the will of a majority." *Ibid.*, p. 540. The vote was one to nine with one vote divided. *Ibid.*, p. 549.

reached, and the delegates, not prepared to forego any of the safeguards incorporated into the provision, were committed to the preservation of the treaty power in the Senate and to guaranteeing that no treaty injurious to sectional interests be adopted.

At the same time, however, the delegates were not averse to modification of the two-thirds requirement where vital interests were not affected. Thus Madison's proposal to exclude peace treaties, "allowing these to be made with less difficulty than other treaties," was accepted unanimously.[36] Immediately upon adoption, however, certain delegates began to entertain second thoughts. Mr. Gerry of Massachusetts argued that:

> [I]n treaties of peace a greater rather than less proportion of votes [is] necessary, than in other treaties. In Treaties of peace the dearest interests will be at stake, as the fisheries, territory & c. In treaties of peace also there is more danger to the extremities of the Continent, of being sacrificed, than on any other occasions.[37]

Gerry's remarks undoubtedly served to remind the delegates, and particularly the Southern delegates, if a reminder were in fact necessary, of the rather sharp controversy which had racked the Confederacy only a year earlier. In 1786, Secretary of Foreign Affairs John Jay had proposed the conclusion of a treaty with Spain according to which the United States would relinquish the right to sail the Mississippi to its outlet for some 25 to 30 years, in return for certain diplomatic and economic benefits. The suggestion had aroused a storm of protest from the South which charged that the North and the East were intent on gaining commercial advantages at its expense.[38] Initially, it would seem, the delegates had not

36 *Ibid.* p. 540. Madison also moved to empower two-thirds of the Senate "to make treaties of peace without the concurrence of the President." The President, Madison argued, "would necessarily derive so much power and importance from a state of war that he might be tempted, if authorized, to impede a treaty of peace." *Ibid.* The motion was rejected by a vote of three to eight. *Ibid.*, p. 541.

37 *Ibid.*, p. 540.

38 For further discussion of this episode, known as the Jay-Gardoqui negotiations, see Samuel F. Bemis, *A Diplomatic History of the United States* (4th ed., Holt, Rinehart and Winston, 1955), pp. 78-80; McLaughlin, *Confedaration and Constitution*, pp. 94-101; Frank Monaghan, *John Jay: Defender of Liberty* (N.Y.: Bobbs-Merrill, 1935), pp. 255-61; Julius Pratt, *A History of United States Foreign*

perceived that the terms of a peace treaty could be as harmful to their interests as commercial treaties, if not more so. But Gerry's remarks alerted them to the dangers, and they now moved to ensure that the exception from the two-thirds rule, applicable to peace treaties, would not serve as an avenue for the conclusion of agreements affecting essential states' rights. Before the end of the day's session, Mr. Williamson and Mr. Spaight moved the following amendment: "But no treaty of peace shall be entered into, whereby the United States shall be deprived of any of their present Territory or rights without the concurrence of two-thirds of the Members of the Senate present."[39] In his 1937 supplement, Farrand presented a different version of this proposal which specifically links the two interests — navigation (of the Mississippi, presumably) and fishery — which had so engaged the delegates:

> But no treaty (of peace) shall be made without the concurrence of the House of Representatives, by which the territorial boundaries of the U.S. may be contracted, or by which the common rights of *navigation* or *fishery* recognized to the U. States by the late treaty of peace, or accruing to them by virtue of the laws of nations may be abridged.[40]

The motion was not voted upon in either form and Mr. King moved the next morning "to strike out the 'exception of Treaties of peace' completely from the general clause requiring two-thirds of the Senate for making Treaties."[41] After short deliberation, the Convention readily agreed, and all treaties without exception were made subject to the advice and consent of two-thirds of the Senate.[42]

Policy (Englewood Cliffs, N.J.: Prentice-Hall, 1963), pp. 62-65; Warren, *Making of Constitution*, pp. 24-30.

39 Farrand, *Records*, vol. 2, pp. 534, 543.

40 *Ibid.*, vol. 4, p. 58. Emphasis in original. McDougal and Lans do not mention this document in their historical analysis. The proposal to include the House represented an attempt to institute a minimal additional safeguard in lieu of the two-thirds rule, which had been lifted from provisions relating to peace treaties. The modified form of protection for sectional interests, however, apparently was not regarded as adequate. Thus, as noted in the text, on the following day it was moved to eliminate the peace treaties exception completely by reinstituting the two-thirds requirement for all treaties.

41 *Ibid.*, vol. 2, p. 547.

42 *Ibid.*, p. 549. The vote was eight to three in favor.

The importance of the Mississippi in this episode is highlighted by the following account of the discussions by Hugh Williamson, delegate from North Carolina, in a letter to James Madison:

> It is said that some antifed in Maryland on the last Winter fastened on the Ear of Genl Wilkinson . . . and persuaded him that in case of a new Govt. the Navigation of the Mississippi would infallibly be given up. Your Recollection must certainly enable you to say that there is a proviso in the new Sistem which was inserted for the express purpose of preventing a majority of the Senate or of the States which is considered as the same thing from giving up the Mississippi. It is provided that two-thirds of the Members present in the senate shall be required to concur in making Treaties and if the southern states attend to their Duty, this will imply 2/3. of the States in the Union together with the President, a security rather better than the present 9 States especially as Vermont & the Province of Main may be added to the Eastern Interest and you may recollect that when a Member, Mr. Wilson objected to this Proviso, saying that in all Govts. the Majority should govern it was replyed that the Navigation of the Mississippi after what had already happened in Congress was not to be risqued in the Hands of a meer Majority and the Objection was withdrawn.[43]

When the treaty-making clause was taken up in the state ratifying conventions, criticism was directed mainly at the ease with which treaties could be adopted and at the vulnerability of critical sectional interests. Various amendments were proposed for tightening the treaty-making procedure. The Virginia Convention

43 *Ibid.*, vol. 3, pp. 306-307. The letter was dated June 2, 1788. Warren, *Making of Constitution*, pp. 657-58, cites this letter and concludes that

> the provision for a two-thirds, rather than a majority, vote of the Senate was inserted for the express purpose of calming the fears of Virginia, North Carolina and the West lest the North and East should relinquish the navigation right on the Mississippi.

See generally Bemis, *Diplomatic History*, p. 80; Pratt, *History of U.S. Foreign Policy*, p. 65 n. 7. This conclusion seems to disregard the other factors that were involved. The coincidence of the Eastern interest in fisheries, it would appear, was crucial in gaining adoption of the two-thirds rule. See in this regard McLendon, "Origin of the Two-thirds Rule in Senate Action Upon Treaties," *AHR* vol. 36 (1931), pp. 768-72. Moreover, Warren fails to take account of the straightforward commercial interests of the South — aside from Mississippi — which had moved it to fight for a qualified majority in the making of treaties involving navigation laws.

subsequently voted on the following amendment, which, incidentally, highlights each of the specific interests discussed above — commercial, fishery, and Mississippi navigation — as well as calling, in certain cases, for a qualified majority in *both* Houses.[44]

> That no commercial treaty shall be ratified without the concurrence of two-thirds of the whole number of the members of the Senate; and no treaty, ceding, contracting, restraining or suspending, the territorial rights or claims of the United States, or any of them, or their, or any of their rights or claims to fishing in the American seas, or navigating the American rivers shall be made, but in cases of the most urgent and extreme necessity; nor shall any such treaty be ratified without the concurrence of three fourths of the whole number of the members of both Houses respectively.[45]

In assessing the intentions of the Founding Fathers, it is also relevant to recall President Washington's message to the House of Representatives regarding the Jay Treaty.[46] In refusing to convey the background papers to the House, Washington stressed that the function of advice and consent had been vested exclusively in the Senate, since in this body large and small States had equal representation. "For, on the equal participation of those powers [of the Senate], the sovereignty and political safety of the smaller States were deemed essentially to depend."[47] Washington also

44 Mason's call for inclusion of the House in the treaty-making process (see n. 4 above), also represented a demand for a qualified majority in *both* Houses, as illustrated by the following comment made by him at the Virginia Convention: "The Senate alone ought not to have this power [to dismember the empire]; much less ought a few states to have it. No treaty to dismember the empire ought to be made without the consent of three fourths of the legislature in all its branches." Elliot, *Debates in State Conventions*, vol. 3, p. 509.

45 *Ibid.*, p. 660. It is interesting to observe that Warren, in accordance with his de-emphasis of the commercial factor in the drafting of the treaty-making provision, cites this proposal for an amendment, but omits the first sentence regarding commercial treaties. Warren, *Making of Constitution*, p. 658.

46 *Annals of Cong.*, vol. 5 (1796) [1789-1824], p. 760.

47 *Ibid.*, p. 761.

noted that a proposal to include the House in the treaty-making process was explicitly rejected.[48]

In the light of the foregoing review, and especially the material furnished by Farrand, it is hard to accept the conclusion of McDougal and Lans that it is "difficult to assay the exact extent to which transient sectional considerations may have been persuasive in the framing of the treaty-making clause."[49] It would seem that conferral of the treaty-making power on the Senate exclusively was very much a deliberate policy decision, as was the institution of the two-thirds rule. The denial by McDougal and Lans that sectional interests played any role is premised *inter alia*, on the following evidence. After the two-thirds rule had been extended to embrace all treaties, Mr. Sherman of Connecticut moved that "no Treaty be made without a majority of the whole number [of the Senate]."[50] Mr. Gerry seconded the motion, which was narrowly defeated by a vote of 5 to 6. McDougal and Lans state that the five supporters of the motion were two small States (Connecticut and Delaware), the great fishing State of Massachusetts, and two Southern States (South Carolina and Georgia), which should have been concerned about the Mississippi and the West. On the basis of this evidence, the authors conclude that neither "protection of small states [n]or protection of sectional interests" underlay the two-thirds requirement in the Senate.[51]

Immediately preceding the vote to which they refer, however, the Convention overwhelmingly defeated a motion by Wilson to eliminate the two-thirds requirement.[52] This action might serve as a

48 *Ibid.* McDougal and Lans stress the fact that the Senate, as part of the function of giving "advice," was expected to participate actively with the President "in the detailed negotiation of treaties," thus precluding the participation of the 65-member House in the treaty-making process. McDougal and Lans, "Treaties and Executive Agreements," p. 539. This however, does not explain why the Convention twice rejected the suggestion that the House be accorded the legislative function of ratifying treaties so as to give them the force of law.

49 *Ibid.*, p. 543.

50 Farrand, *Records*, vol. 2, p. 549.

51 McDougal and Lans, "Treaties and Executive Agreements," pp. 542-43. See also *ibid.*, p. 541.

52 Farrand, *Records*, vol. 2, p. 549.

more reliable measure of the sectional interests of such States as Massachusetts, Virginia, the Carolinas, and Georgia, all of which voted against the Wilson proposal. Similarly, all of the above States joined in striking the peace treaty exception form the treaty clause.[53] The 5 to 6 vote can be explained by the fact that according to the treaty clause, no treaty could be made "without the consent of two-thirds of the members present." Since a majority of fourteen constituted a quorum, this meant that ten Senators alone could adopt a treaty. Under a proposal for a majority of the entire Senate, at least fourteen votes would be needed. Furthermore, the requirement based on the entire number would enable members of the Senate to defeat consideration of a treaty simply by absenting themselves from the session. This indeed had happened frequently in the Confederate Congress.[54] Thus the move of Mr. Sherman of Connecticut and Mr. Gerry of Massachusetts to replace "two-thirds of the Senate present" with "a majority of the whole Senate" was simply a better means of safeguarding the interests which they yearned to protect. As to the effectiveness of the means, however, the delegates, despite sectional interests, were quite naturally divided.[55] The following exchange occurring after submission of the Sherman-Gerry proposal, confirms the significance of the issue:

> Mr. Williamson. This will be less security than 2/3 as now required.
> Mr. Sherman — It will be less embarrassing.[56]

53 *Ibid.*, pp. 548-49.

54 See Warren, *Making of Constitution*, p. 655. During the South Carolina Ratifying Convention, General Pinckney stated:

> It was frequently difficult to obtain a representation from nine states; and if only nine states were present, they must all concur in making a treaty. A single member would frequently prevent the business from being concluded. . . . This actually happened when a treaty of importance was about to be concluded with the Indians; and several states, being satisfied, at particular junctures, that the nine states present would not concur . . . were indifferent whether their members attended or not.

Elliot, *Debates in State Conventions*, vol. 4, p. 280.

55 It should be noted that a move made by Madison for a two-thirds Senate quorum to consider treaties was narrowly defeated by a vote of five to six. Farrand, *Records*, vol. 2, p. 549.

56 *Ibid.*

The key word is "security," the gist of the entire battle. The episode, then, far from discrediting a "sectional interests" thesis in the origin of the treaty-making clause, lends further credence to it.[57]

In conclusion, formulation of the treaty-making clause constituted a three-step process at the Constitutional Convention. Once the Senate was established as the repository of state power, the smaller states, intent on ensuring an equal role, shifted the treaty-making power to the Senate. The dissatisfied nationalists, representatives of the large States, succeeded in bringing into the picture the President, the only truly national figure in government. Finally, sectional interests from both the Northeast and the South prevailed upon the Convention to raise the voting requirement from a simple majority to two-thirds. The end result was a composite compromise reflecting the wishes of each of the three groups: small States, nationalists, and sectional interests.

Thus, if indeed the protection of small States and sectional interests was a crucial factor, if not *the* crucial factor, in the formulation of the treaty-making provision, it appears highly unlikely that a majority vote in both houses of Congress would represent a superior title to a two-thirds vote in the Senate alone, for the safeguards originally built into the latter provision would be obliterated. Yet, while the attempt to equate congressional-executive agreements with treaties on the basis of the Framers' *intentions* is shaky at best, the same cannot be said of validation of congressional-executive agreements by reference to subsequent *constitutional practice.* As Henkin notes: "Neither Congress nor Presidents nor courts have been troubled by . . . conceptual difficulties. Whatever their theoretical merits, it is now widely accepted that the congressional-executive agreement is a complete alternative to a treaty."[58]

57 One noted scholar apparently accepts the McDougal and Lans theory. Pratt, *History of U.S. Foreign Policy*, p. 65, n. 7.

58 Henkin, *Foreign Affairs and Constitution*, p. 175.

This development undoubtedly was aided by the Constitution's contemplation of congressional approval of certain categories of international agreements, those concluded between separate states and foreign powers, coupled with the inclusion of the subject matter of certain international agreements in areas such as international postal service, trade, and copyrights, within the purview of the enumerated powers of Congress.[59] With the extension of international trade and communications, more and more items were handled by means of congressional-executive agreements so that the distinction between such agreements and treaties ultimately became quite blurred.[60] Moreover, the enumerated powers of Congress aside, the vast expansion in the implied foreign affairs power which occurred during the twentieth century has further tended to modify the distinction between the legitimate subject matter of congressional-executive agreements and of full-fledged treaties. In other words, if Congress's legislative power over matters bearing on foreign affairs is broad enough today to encompass any area which can be made the subject-matter of a treaty, then it may be argued that by implication, through the interaction of its broadened substantive powers and the necessary and proper clause, Congress can authorize agreements on a host of subjects previously considered outside the scope of congressional authority.[61] Nevertheless, there still remain various categories of international agreements which do not fall within the scope of congressional powers, whether enumerated or implied.[62] If the intentions of the Founding Fathers were adhered to, these matters would require the advice and consent of two-thirds of the Senate. But, as noted, practice, by and large, has modified this assumption of the Founding Fathers.

59 The Supreme Court early held that postal conventions have equal standing with treaties as the law of the land, *Cotzhausen v. Nazro*, 107 U.S. (1882), p. 215.

60 For a discussion of this evolution, see Butler, *Treaty Making Power*, pp. 88-98; Henkin, *Foreign Affairs and Constitution*, pp. 173-76, 420-25.

61 *See* Louis Henkin, "The Treaty Makers and the Law Makers: The Law of the Land and Foreign Relations" *U. Pa. L. Rev.*, vol. 107 (1959), pp. 903-36.

62 See Henkin, *Foreign Affairs and Constitution*, p. 174.

7

The Founders' Fears of Foreign Influence

The possibility that the 1996 elections were marked by foreign influence-peddling and even bribery was widely noted and commented upon in the media;[1] it also became the subject of Congressional investigation.[2] In particular, there was concern that the Chinese government might have contributed heavily to the Democratic National Committee in support of the Clinton-Gore election campaign, and might have received, in return, promises regarding the maintenance and even expansion of U.S. trade with China.[3] Even after the decision of Attorney-General Janet Reno not to request the appointment of an independent counsel to investigate the case against Vice-President Gore, because of insufficient evidence, media and public attention continued to be focused, as never before, on the broader issues of illegal campaign financing and on the attempts by foreign governments to purvey influence in the United States.[4]

Regardless of the truth or falsity of the specific charges which have propelled these broader questions to center stage, it may be

1 See, for example, the news reports in *N.Y. Times* of Feb. 4, 5, 7, 8, 9, 11, 15, 18, 25, 26, 27, Mar. 2 and 4, 1998. See also editorials of Feb. 5, 15 and 25, 1998.

2 Congressional investigations were conducted by the Senate Governmental Affairs Committee under the chairmanship of Senator Fred Thompson of Tennessee.

3 See excerpts from report of the Senate Governmental Affairs Committee, *N.Y. Times*, Feb. 10 and 11, 1998. It should be noted, however, that the Committee acknowledged that it could not establish that the Chinese Government "funded, directed or encouraged the illegal contributions." *Ibid.*, Feb. 10, 1998.

4 For the decision of Attorney-General Reno, see *ibid.*, Nov. 24, 1998. And see the editorial criticism by the *New York Times* of her decision: "The White House was at the center of a pervasively reckless fund-raising operation, and

helpful and of more than passing academic interest to add a historical dimension to the current debate. In particular, it might be useful to explore how, in shaping the U.S. Constitution of 1787 as the basic document of American governance, the Founding Fathers sought to guard against the dangers of foreign influence as perceived at the time, and what the lessons might be for the present, radically changed U.S. position in the world.

A review of the debates at the Constitutional Convention reveals great awareness of the vulnerability of American officials and legislators to financial inducements from foreign agents and of the dangers of foreign influence in the fledgling republic, in general. It also demonstrates the determination of the Framers to anchor in the Constitution provisions which would curtail such undesired influence and effectively minimize the possibility that Americans in positions of power would readily succumb to the temptations of foreign largesse.

The perspective of the Framers can best be culled by reference to the following matters: the Virginia Plan and its legislative veto v. the New Jersey Plan; foreign gifts and honors; naturalization and eligibility for election to office; the method for selecting the executive; the executive veto; and the impeachment of the executive.

The Virginia Plan and its Legislative Veto v. the New Jersey Plan

The central debate at the 1787 Constitutional Convention, between proponents of the Virginia Plan and supporters of the rival New Jersey Plan, occasioned several references to the danger of foreign intrigue. James Madison, "Father" of the Constitution and probable author of the Virginia Plan, contended that the New Jersey Plan left the United States exposed to the threat of corruption from foreign sources. In a lengthy address, Madison presented a veritable battery

---

the Government still does not know the full extent of the shadowy fund-raising from foreign sources, the extent to which favors were traded to China or its business allies, and whether Chinese Government money went into campaign accounts." *Ibid.*, Nov. 29, 1998.

of reasons for rejecting the New Jersey Plan as inadequate. In Point 6, he posed the question: "Will it secure the Union agst. the influence of foreign powers over its members?"[5] The word "members" in this sentence refers to the individual states, and Madison was expressing the fear that under the New Jersey Plan they would be vulnerable to foreign influence. Madison was not purporting to suggest that such influence had already "been tried: but it naturally [was] to be expected that occasions would produce it." He illustrated his argument with various historical references: the record of the Amphictonic Confederation, where intrigue was first practiced by the Kings of Persia and then by Philip of Macedonia; the inroads made among the Acheans by Macedon and Rome; the influence exercised in the Swiss Confederation by Austria, France and others; what occurred in the Germanic (body), and in the Belgic Republic. He concluded his remarks with the following comment: "The plan of Mr. Patterson, not giving to the general Councils [the national government] any negative on the will of the particular States, left the door open for the like pernicious machinations among ourselves."

In order to understand why Madison felt that the states would be susceptible to such foreign influence under the New Jersey Plan but not under the Virginia Plan, it is necessary to appreciate a central plank of the latter which was missing in the former. Among the powers accorded the federal government under Article 6 of the Virginia Plan was the authority "to negative all laws passed by the several States, contravening in the opinion of the National Legislature the articles of Union."[6] The notion of a federal legislative veto over state laws was a crucial feature of Madison's scheme of government.[7] Without it, the states would continue to

5 Farrand, *Records*, vol. 1, p. 319.
6 *Ibid.*, p. 21.
7 On Madison's commitment to the legislative veto, see Charles F. Hobson, "The Negative on State Laws: James Madison, the Constitution, and the Crisis of Republican Government," *WMQ*, 3d. ser., vol. 36 (1979), *passim*. See also Chap. 3 above, pp. 108-113.

invade the federal sphere of authority as they had done with impunity under the Articles of Confederation. In a letter to George Washington in advance of the Constitutional Convention, Madison had called for the adoption of: "A negative *in all cases whatsoever* on the legislative acts of the States, as heretofore exercised by the Kingly prerogative." "Without this defensive power," he declared, "every positive power that can be given on paper will be evaded & defeated."[8] Thus, Madison advocated an absolute negative which would enable the national legislature to disallow any and every state law which it regarded as unwarranted or harmful.[9] The Virginia delegation, meeting in caucus before the opening of the Convention, was not prepared to go so far, and modified Madison's recommendation by proposing that the national legislature only be empowered to veto state laws which it deemed unconstitutional, as noted above. But in either case, this was a vast power and would authorize the federal government to veto any state move to, for instance, provide a foreign government with some special privilege or engage the credit of the state. Special state concessions might be unconstitutional as militating against the national interest and would be struck down. Alternatively, state grants of this nature might be suspected of being the product of undue influence on state legislators and executives alike and lacking validity on that ground. Since under the New Jersey Plan the federal government would lack any such national legislative veto, the states, Madison argued, would be open to foreign influence-peddling, and there would be no way of counteracting, or canceling, the consequences of such influence.[10]

8 16 April 1787. Madison, *Papers*, vol. 9, pp. 383-84 (emphasis in original). Madison made the same point in letters to Thomas Jefferson, March 19, 1787, and to Edmund Randolph, April 8, 1787. *Ibid.*, pp. 317-22 and 368-71.

9 In the Convention debates Madison described the operation of the veto as follows: "The negative (on the State laws) proposed, will make it [the national legislature] an essential branch of the State Legislatures." Farrand, *Records*, vol. 1, p. 447. Hobson has correctly pointed out that under this scheme, "Madison proposed nothing less than an organic union of the general and state governments." "Negative on State Laws," p. 219.

10 Although the Virginia delegation qualified Madison's concept of the legislative veto and limited its application to unconstitutional state measures,

In fact, the debate on the legislative veto itself prompted contrasting arguments, both of which were based on a fear of foreign influence. In support of the legislative veto, James Wilson stated:

> Unless this power is vested in the Genl. Govt. the States will be used by foreign powers as Engines agt the Whole – New States will be soon formed, the Inhabitants may be foreigners and possess foreign affections, unless the Genl. Govt. can check their State laws they may involve the Nation in Tumult and Confusion.[11]

Refuting this line of reasoning, Elbridge Gerry used the fear of foreign influence to dismiss the notion of a legislative veto. Throughout the Convention Gerry warned of the danger that the original Eastern states would be overwhelmed by the new Western states, and he sought to incorporate within the Constitution provisions which would forestall such an eventuality. New states coming into the Union, he cautioned, "may even be under some foreign influence; are they in such case to participate in the negative on the will of the other States?"[12]

Madison won his battle, and the Virginia Plan, rather than the New Jersey Plan, was chosen by the Convention as its working document.[13] The final Constitution, with emendations and substantive changes, evolved from the Virginia Plan.[14] But Madison lost his battle over the legislative veto. To his dire regret, this feature of his plan was eliminated from the Constitution in the course of the

---

Madison never tired, during the course of the Convention, of lobbying for the adoption of an absolute form of legislative veto. The delegates, however, not only failed to endorse the absolute variety, they completely eliminated the legislative veto from the Constitution, as will be seen below. Nonetheless, in Article 1, Section 10 of the Constitution, they instituted prohibitions on the states to enter into an agreement or compact with foreign countries without the authorization of Congress.

11 Farrand, *Records*, vol. 1, p. 172.

12 *Ibid.*, p. 166

13 *Ibid.*, pp. 313, 322.

14 As Catherine Drinker Bowen has written: "The fifteen Resolves [of the Virginia Plan] were . . . the core and foundation of the United States Constitution." *Miracle at Philadelphia: The Story of the Constitutional Convention May to September 1787* (Boston: Little Brown, 1966), p. 14.

Convention debates.[15] It was left to the federal judiciary, under the Constitution's supremacy clause (Article 6), to serve as umpire of the federal system of government and to invalidate state legislation violating the federal Constitution. But concern over the vulnerability of the federal and state governments to foreign influence remained a constant feature of the Convention's deliberations.

Foreign Gifts and Honors

One clause in the Constitution stands out as a clearly designed bar to the possibility of foreign governments attempting to bribe American officials. The clause was introduced by Charles Pinckney late in the Convention's proceedings, on August 23. According to Madison's minutes, "Mr Pinkney urged the necessity of preserving foreign Ministers & other officers of the U.S. independent of external influence."[16] He moved the following provision:

> No person holding any office of profit or trust under the U.S. shall without the consent of the Legislature, accept of any present, emolument, office or title of any kind whatsoever, from any King, Prince or foreign state.

The proposal was adopted unanimously without debate.[17] Only minor stylistic emendations were made in the final version as it appeared in Article 1, section 9 of the Constitution.

15 The grounds for rejecting the legislative veto were both practical and conceptual. For one thing, how would the veto be applied? As Luther Martin asked: "Shall all the laws of the States be sent up to the Genl. Legislature before they shall be permitted to operate? Farrand, *Records*, vol. 2, p. 28. Secondly, many delegates regarded a national legislative veto as an infringement of state sovereignty and violative of the federal principle. In the words of Gouverneur Morris, it would "disgust all the States." *Ibid.*
It might be noted that Madison was so convinced of the essentiality of a national legislative veto that in a letter to Jefferson immediately upon the conclusion of the Convention, he labelled the Constitution a failure. See Hobson, "Negative on State Laws," pp. 228-33; and chap. 3 above, pp. 116-17.

16 Farrand, *Records*, vol. 2, p. 389.

17 *Ibid.*

In the Virginia Ratifying Convention, Edmund Randolph commented on the provision as follows: "This restriction is provided to prevent corruption . . . It was thought proper, in order to exclude corruption and foreign influence, to prohibit any one in office from receiving or holding any emoluments from foreign states." Randolph related that it was as a result of an "accident" that the clause was introduced. During the War of Independence, Benjamin Franklin, U.S. minister to France, had received a snuff-box bearing a "beautiful portrait of Louis XVI." "I believe," said Randolph, "that if at that moment, when we were in harmony with the King of France, we had supposed that he was corrupting our ambassador, it might have disturbed that confidence, and diminished that mutual friendship, which contributed to carry us through the war . . . "[18]

Naturalization and Eligibility for Election to Office

Debate over the period of citizenship required of a naturalized immigrant before he could qualify to stand for elective office also reflected the Founders' fears of scheming foreign states intent on gaining influence in the councils of government.

George Mason of Virginia was the first to call for some citizenship requirement for members of the national legislature.[19] His motion of July 26, that the Committee of Detail introduce a clause to this effect into the draft constitution, was endorsed by a vote of 8:3.[20] The report of the Committee of Detail, issued on August 6, stipulated that every member of the House of Representatives had to be at least twenty-five years old and to have been a citizen of the United States for at least three years prior to election, while a Senator had to be at least thirty years old and a citizen of at least four years' standing.[21] Mason found this inadequate. For one thing, "so short a term" was not enough "for

18 *Ibid.*, vol. 3, p. 327.
19 *Ibid.*, vol. 2, p. 121.
20 *Ibid.*, pp. 116-17, 124-25.
21 Art. IV, sec. 2, and Art. V, sec. 3, *ibid.*, pp. 178-79.

ensuring that local knowledge" which a Representative ought to possess. Secondly, "it might also happen that a rich foreign Nation, for example Great Britain, might send over her tools who might bribe their way into the Legislature for insidious purposes." While he favored "opening a wide door" for immigrants, he "did not chuse to let foreigners and adventurers make laws for us & govern us."[22] He moved that in the lower house, "seven" be substituted for "three," and his motion was carried by all states except Connecticut.[23] Subsequently, on August 13, James Wilson of Pennsylvania, himself an immigrant from Scotland, joined with Edmund Randolph of Virginia to propose substituting four years for the seven-year citizenship requirement for Representatives.[24] Elbridge Gerry of Massachusetts objected. He wished that "in future the eligibility might be confined to Natives." "Foreign powers," he warned, "will intermeddle in our affairs, and spare no expense to influence them"; and "Persons having foreign attachments will be sent among us & insinuated into our councils, in order to be made instruments for their purposes." And he added: "Every one knows the vast sums laid out in Europe for secret services."[25] Hugh Williamson, of North Carolina, recommended requiring nine years of citizenship rather than seven.[26] Dissenting from such restrictive views, Hamilton proposed that citizenship alone be sufficient to run for office, bearing in mind that the legislature would be free to fix the terms of naturalization.[27] His proposal was seconded by Madison who spoke of "maintaining the character of liberality" which had been regularly "professed" in America. "He wished to invite foreigners of merit & republican principles among us. That

22 *Ibid.*, p. 216. At a later point in the debate, Mason said: "If persons among us attached to G-B. should work themselves into our Councils, a turn might be given to our affairs & particularly to our Commercial regulations which might have pernicious consequences. The great Houses of British Merchants would spare no pains to insinuate the instruments of their views {into the Govt –}." *Ibid.*, pp. 271-72

23 *Ibid.*, pp. 213, 216.

24 *Ibid.*, pp. 267-68.

25 *Ibid.*, p. 268.

26 *Ibid.*

27 *Ibid.*

part of America which had encouraged them most had advanced most rapidly in population, agriculture & the arts."[28] The sentiment of the majority, however, was more accurately mirrored in the attitude of Pierce Butler of South Carolina, who "was strenuous agst. admitting foreigners into our public Councils."[29] The motions of both Hamilton and Wilson were rejected, by a vote of 4:7 and 3:8, respectively.[30] The Convention then proceeded to endorse a citizenship requirement of seven years.[31] An attempt, by Gouverneur Morris, to have current citizens exempted from the restriction was also rejected.[32]

The citizenship requirement for Senators occasioned a similar spirited exchange. Stressing the danger "of admitting strangers into our public Councils," Gouverneur Morris moved to substitute fourteen years for the four-year requirement prescribed by the Committee of Detail.[33] He was supported by Charles Pinckney, who noted that the Senate was "to have the power of making treaties & managing our foreign affairs." Consequently, there was "peculiar danger and impropriety in opening its door to those who have foreign attachments." He cited "the jealousy of the Athenians on this subject who made it death for any stranger to intrude his voice into their legislative proceedings."[34] George Mason was vehement in his support of Morris's move,[35] while Madison, once again, argued against any constitutional restriction. Since naturalization was a subject of Congressional regulation, there was no need for the Convention to set fixed terms of citizenship to qualify for elective office, he opined. He could not accept anything like the Morris proposal, as it would give "a tincture of illiberality to the Constitution." On the assumption that "the proposed Constitution" would give "stability and reputation" to the United States, Madison

28 *Ibid.*, pp. 268-69.
29 *Ibid.*, p. 269.
30 *Ibid.*, pp. 265, 269.
31 *Ibid.*, pp. 266, 272.
32 *Ibid.*, pp. 265, 270, 272.
33 *Ibid.*, p. 235.
34 *Ibid.*
35 *Ibid.*

anticipated that "great numbers of respectable Europeans . . . who love liberty" would want to settle in the United States. "All such would feel the mortification of being marked with suspicious incapacitations." Moreover, he did not fear that foreign powers would make use of strangers "as instruments for their purposes." They would be more inclined to direct their bribes to native Americans, who would be less carefully watched than strangers.[36]

Benjamin Franklin likewise deplored the inclusion of "illiberality" in the Constitution,[37] and Edmund Randolph, rejecting the fourteen-year proposal, was prepared, at most, to endorse a seven-year restriction.[38] James Wilson, noting that he was himself an immigrant, also addressed "the illiberal complexion which the motion would give to the System."[39] A good system, he said, would have the effect of "inviting meritorious foreigners among us, but the "degrading discrimination" proposed would make them feel a sense of "discouragement & mortification." "To be appointed to a place may be a matter of indifference. To be incapable of being appointed, is a circumstance grating, and mortifying," Wilson declared.

Gouverneur Morris was unyielding. Reason must prevail over feelings, he insisted, and "we should not be polite at the expense of prudence." He noted that "some tribes of Indians, carried their hospitality so far as to offer to strangers their wives and daughters." "Was this a proper model for us?" he asked. "He would admit them [foreigners] to his house, he would invite them to his table, would provide for them comfortable lodgings; but would not carry the complaisance so far as, to bed them with his wife. He would let them worship at the same altar, but did not choose to make Priests of them." And "as to those philosophical gentlemen, those Citizens of the World, as they called themselves, He owned he did not wish to see any of them in our public Councils." "He would not trust them," Morris stated. "The men who can shake off their attach-

36 *Ibid.*, pp. 235-36.
37 *Ibid.*, pp. 236-37.
38 *Ibid.*, p. 237.
39 *Ibid.* Wilson had arrived in America from Scotland some twenty years earlier.

ments to their own Country can never love any other." "Admit a Frenchman into your Senate, and he will study to increase the commerce of France." The same was true for an Englishman, he asserted.[40]

Notwithstanding Gouverneur Morris's vivid portrayal of alien mores, the majority was not prepared to go as far as he proposed, and his suggestion for a fourteen-year requirement was defeated by a vote of 7:4.[41] At this point, John Rutledge contended that with seven years' citizenship being required for membership in the House, the Senate, "which will have more power," should surely have a longer term.[42] Hugh Williamson, his colleague from North Carolina, reasoned that it was necessary to guard the Senate even more than the House, since "Bribery and Cabal can be more easily practised in the choice of the Senate which is to be made by the [state] Legislatures composed of a few men, than of the House of Represents. who will be chosen by the people."[43] Thereupon, the Convention, by a vote of 6:4, with one divided, settled for a nine-year citizenship requirement for Senators.[44]

Paradoxically, perhaps, the requirement that the President be a native-born American was inserted in the Constitution (Article II, section 1) very late in the Convention, and occasioned no debate or discussion whatsoever. As noted earlier, the Committee of Detail was instructed to prescribe "certain qualifications" of citizenship also for "the Executive, [the Judiciary, and the Members of both branches of the Legislature]."[45] Despite this request, the final plan of the Committee of Detail, submitted to the Convention on August 6, contained no citizenship conditions for the executive. This was in stark contrast to its citizenship requirement for members of both houses of the legislature. On August 20, Elbridge Gerry moved "that the Committee be instructed to report proper qualifications for

40 *Ibid.*, pp. 237-38.
41 *Ibid.*, pp. 228, 238.
42 *Ibid.*, p. 239.
43 *Ibid.*
44 *Ibid.*, pp. 228, 239.
45 *Ibid.*, pp. 116-17.

the President."[46] The Committee, headed by Rutledge duly reported on August 22, and stipulated that the executive be "of the age of thirty five years, and a Citizen of the United States, and shall have been an Inhabitant thereof for Twenty one years."[47] Subsequently, the Brearley Committee on Unfinished Parts revised the provision on the executive and provided for his election by means of an Electoral College. Its report contained, for the first time, the requirement of native birth for serving as President.[48] This draft provision was agreed to unanimously without debate, on September 7, barely ten days before the close of the Convention.[49] The final version provides:

> No Person except a natural born Citizen, or a Citizen of the United States, at the time of the Adoption of this Constitution, shall be eligible to the Office of President; neither shall any Person be eligible to that Office who shall not have attained to the Age of thirty five Years, and been fourteen Years a Resident within the United States.[50]

What is noteworthy, indeed remarkable, about this formulation, is that the Convention was prepared to be more lenient on the qualifications for President than on those required for members of Congress. It will be recalled that Gouverneur Morris had attempted in vain to have the Convention exempt current citizens of the United States from the citizenship requirements stipulated for members of Congress. Why, then, the willingness of the delegates to incorporate the more liberal criterion of current citizenship in the case of the President? Perhaps they believed that no one but a native would in any case be acceptable to the electorate under the Electoral College scheme. Or perhaps they simply did not wish to preclude the possibility of the future election to the highest office of some of the prominent political figures of the time (such as Alexander Hamilton, born in the West Indies, and Scottish-born James Wilson, both delegates at the Convention).

46 *Ibid.*, p. 344.
47 *Ibid.*, p. 367.
48 *Ibid.*, p. 494.
49 *Ibid.*, p. 536.
50 U.S. Constitution, Art. II, sec. 1, para. 5, *ibid.*, p. 659.

Method for Selecting the Executive

In choosing a method for selecting the executive, the Convention was again concerned to ensure that foreign influence not compromise the selection process. On July 24, the Convention reverted to its initial preference and decided that the choice be made by the legislature.[51] Madison criticized this proposal on several grounds, among them the danger of alien interference.[52]

> The Ministers of foreign powers would have and make use of, the opportunity to mix their intrigues & influence with the Election. Limited as the powers of the Executive are, it will be an object of great moment with the great rival powers of Europe who have American possessions, to have at the head of our Governmt. a man attached to their respective politics & interests. No pains, nor perhaps expence, will be spared, to gain from the Legislature an appointmt. favorable to their wishes.

To illustrate his point, Madison cited the cases of Germany and Poland where the election of the head of government was a matter that "interested all Europe, and was much influenced by foreign interference." Indeed, in Poland, according to Madison, the choice of chief executive "has in fact at length slid entirely into foreign hands."

Similar considerations prompted Madison to object to the appointment of the national executive by the state executives. Since these executives were "standing bodies," undoubtedly "they could & would be courted, and intrigued with by the Candidates, by their partizans, and by the Ministers of foreign powers."

Other delegates echoed Madison's concern. Thus, Pierce Butler of South Carolina felt that "the two great evils to be avoided are cabal at home, & influence from abroad";[53] and both of these would be difficult to avoid, were the choice of an executive to be made by the legislature. He was supported by Hugh Williamson, who

51 *Ibid.*, pp. 97, 101. For discussion of the Convention's deliberations on procedures for selection of an executive, see chap. 1, above.

52 Farrand, *Records*, vol. 2, pp. 109-111.

53 *Ibid.*, p. 112.

declared that election by the legislature "opened a door for foreign influence."[54] "Candor obliged" George Mason "to admit, that there was great danger of foreign influence, as had been suggested." Indeed, he acknowledged that "this was the most serious objection with him that had been urged."[55] Nonetheless, he adhered to his previous preference for selection by the legislature as the least objectionable method proposed. Only when the Brearley Committee came up with the scheme for an electoral college were the fears of foreign intervention mitigated. Gouverneur Morris indicated that "the principal advantage aimed at" in choosing this method "was that of taking away the opportunity of cabal."[56] "As the Electors would vote at the same time throughout the U.S. and at so great a distance from each other, the great evil of cabal was avoided," he explained.[57] James Wilson concurred. "It gets rid of one great evil, that of cabal & corruption."[58]

However, granting the Senate a contingency choice in the event that no candidate gained a majority in the Electoral College, proved disturbing to many delegates. Opposition to vesting this power in the Senate was based primarily on the fear that the Senate was accumulating too much power and becoming a center of aristocracy.[59] Others voiced the fear that the Senate was composed of too

54 *Ibid.*, p. 113.
55 *Ibid.*, p. 112.
56 *Ibid.*, p. 501
57 *Ibid.*, p. 500.
58 *Ibid*. p. 501. In *Federalist No. 68*, Hamilton highlighted the fact that the electoral college arrangement was designed to preclude "cabal, intrigue and corruption" in the choice of a chief executive. "Chiefly," he said, it would frustrate "the desire in foreign powers to gain an improper ascendant in our councils . . . by raising a creature of their own to the chief magistracy of the union." The Convention, Hamilton contended, had guarded against "all danger of this sort with the most provident and judicious attention."

> They have not made the appointment of the president to depend on any pre-existing bodies of men who might be tampered with before hand to prostitute their votes; but they have referred it in the first instance to an immediate act of the people of America, to be exerted in the choice of persons for the temporary and sole purpose of making the appointment.

59 See discussion, Farrand, *Records*, vol. 2, p. 522.

small a number and therefore more readily exposed to corruption from abroad. Thus, James Wilson, in opposing Senatorial choice of a President even on a contingency basis, alluded to the fact that "the power of making Treaties involves the case of subsidies, and here as an additional evil, foreign influence is to be dreaded."[60] Elbridge Gerry repeatedly "enlarged on the danger of putting the essential rights of the Union in the hands of so small a number as a majority of the Senate, representing perhaps, not one fifth of the people." "The Senate," he feared, "will be corrupted by foreign influence."[61]

Only when it was decided that the contingency choice be moved from the Senate to the House of Representatives voting by states, were the delegates prepared to endorse the Electoral College system for selecting a President. Unlike the sparsely populated Senate, the House was deemed to be less prone to foreign interference and also less characterized by aristocratic tendencies.

Executive Veto

Under Resolution 8 of the Virginia Plan, the Executive, together with a convenient number of the judiciary, would act as a council of revision to veto any law of the national legislature.[62] Subsequently, on separation-of-powers grounds, the judiciary was excluded from any share in the veto.[63] But on June 6, James Wilson moved that the judiciary be restored to its position in the council of revision.[64] In seconding the motion, Madison contended that the executive in a republic needed strengthening since he lacked that "settled pre-eminence in the eyes of the rest, that weight of property, that

60 *Ibid.*, p. 523. For Wilson's misgivings regarding the concentration of power in the Senate, see *ibid.*, vol. 3, p. 162.

61 *Ibid.*, vol. 2, p. 548. It is noteworthy that in the debate on the treaty power, Gerry favored vesting the power to make treaties of peace in the legislature rather than the Senate alone, since "The Senate are more liable to be corrupted by an Enemy than the whole Legislature." *Ibid.*, p. 319.

62 *Ibid.*, vol. 1, p. 21.

63 *Ibid.*, p. 104.

64 *Ibid.*, p. 138.

personal interest agst. betraying the National interest, which appertain to an hereditary magistrate."

> The Executive Magistrate would be envied & assailed by disappointed competitors: His firmness therefore wd. need support. He would not possess those great emoluments from his station, nor that permanent stake in the public interest which wd. place him out of the reach of foreign corruption: He would stand in need therefore of being controuled as well as supported. An association of the Judges in his revisionary function wd both double the advantage and diminish the danger.[65]

Despite Madison's powerful plea, the Convention decided by a vote of 3:8 to exclude the judiciary from any role in the reversionary council.[66] The executive would exercise the veto unilaterally.

The size of the Congressional majority required in order to override a Presidential veto was also a subject which occasioned expressions of anxiety regarding possible corruption. If the majority required was made too high, e.g. three-fourths, it would enable the President to spurn threats of an override. Thus, Randolph acknowledged: "Foreign influence would also be more likely to be exerted on the President who could require three fourths by his negative."[67] This consideration contributed to the ultimate decision of the Convention to institute a two-thirds vote to override a Presidential veto.

65 *Ibid.*, pp. 138-39.

66 *Ibid.*, pp. 131, 140.

67 *Ibid.*, vol. 2, p. 453. In *Federalist No. 22*, Hamilton writes that giving "a minority a negative upon the majority (which is always the case where more than a majority is requisite to a decision) . . . gives greater scope to foreign corruption as well as to domestic faction." He illustrates this argument by instancing a case where the U.S. government, contrary to the preferences of an ally, might be intent on concluding a peace treaty with an erstwhile enemy. "This ally . . . would evidently find it much easier by his bribes and intrigues to tie up the hands of government from making peace, where two-thirds of all the votes were requisite to that object, than where a simple majority would suffice." Likewise, said Hamilton, "it would be much easier for a foreign power with which we were at war, to perplex our councils and embarrass our exertions." Commercial arrangements might "be subjected to similar inconveniences."

Impeachment of the Executive

The Report of the Committee of the Whole, presented to the plenum on June 13, had provided that the National Executive would "be removeable on impeachment and conviction of malpractices or neglect of duty."[68] When the Convention took up this provision for debate on July 20, Charles Pinckney and Gouverneur Morris moved that the clause be struck out since, as Pinckney put it, "he {ought not to} be impeachable whilst in office."[69] Impeachments, he insisted, "ought not issue from the Legislature who would in that case hold them as a rod over the Executive and by that means effectually destroy his independence."[70] In the course of the debate, Pinckney stated that he "apprehended that some gentlemen reasoned on a supposition that the Executive was to have powers which would not be committed to him." To the contrary, "{He presumed} that his powers would be so circumscribed as to render impeachment unnecessary."[71] Morris maintained that since the test for any executive would lie in his re-election bid, an overarching threat of impeachment was not required. "Besides," he asked, "who is to impeach?" "The impeachment will be nearly equivalent to a displacement, and will render the Executive dependent on those who are to impeach."[72] In response, George Mason stated that "no point is of more importance than that . . . of impeachment." "Shall any man be

68 Farrand, *Records*, vol. 1, p. 236.
69 *Ibid.*, vol. 2, p. 64.
70 *Ibid.*, p. 66.
71 *Ibid.*, p. 68. This remark would appear highly pertinent to the subsequent debate between Hamilton and Madison as to whether the opening words of Article 2 of the Constitution, "The executive power shall be vested in a President," constitute an independent grant of power. On this topic generally, see Edward S. Corwin, *The President: Office and Powers*, 4th rev. ed., (N.Y.: New York Univ. Press, 1957), pp.178-80; and Louis Henkin, *Foreign Affairs and the Constitution* (N.Y.: Norton, 1975), pp. 42-44. To the best of my knowledge, the significance of Pinckney's remark has never previously been noted in the literature.
72 Farrand, *Records*, vol. 2, pp. 64-65.

above Justice?" he asked. "Above all shall that man be above it, who can commit the most extensive injustice?"[73]

Madison "thought it indispensable that some provision should be made for defending the Community agst the incapacity, negligence or perfidy of the chief Magistrate . . . . He might pervert his administration into a scheme of peculation or oppression. He might betray his trust to foreign powers."[74] Madison proceeded to elaborate on the factors which, though they would not disqualify any other part of the government, would disqualify the executive, making the possibility of his impeachment imperative:

> The case of the Executive Magistracy was very distinguishable from that of the Legislative or of any other public body, holding offices of limited duration. It could not be presumed that all or even a majority of the members of an Assembly would either lose their capacity for discharging, or be bribed to betray, their trust. Besides the restraints of their personal integrity & honor, the difficulty of acting in concert for purposes of corruption was a security to the public. And if one or a few members only should be seduced, the soundness of the remaining members, would maintain the integrity and fidelity of the body. In the case of the Executive Magistracy which was to be administered by a single man, loss of capacity or corruption was more within the compass of probable events, and either of them might be fatal to the Republic.

Benjamin Franklin supported Madison's argument with an illustration from the Dutch Prince of Orange who was suspected of having come under foreign influence, as a result of which the Dutch fleet had failed to act in "the late war."[75]

Apparently, the remarks of Madison and Franklin on the dangers of corruption led Gouverneur Morris to announce that his "opinion had been changed by the arguments used in the discussion."

> Our Executive was not like a Magistrate having a life interest [term], much less like one having an hereditary interest in his office. He may be bribed by a greater interest to betray his trust; and no one would

73 *Ibid.*, p. 65.
74 *Ibid.*, pp. 65-66.
75 *Ibid.*, pp. 67-68.

> say that we ought to expose ourselves to the danger of seeing the first Magistrate in foreign pay without being able to guard agst it by displacing him . . . . Corrupting his electors, and incapacity were other causes of impeachment.[76] . . . No man wd. say, that an Executive known to be in the pay of an Enemy, should not be removeable in some way or other.[77]

By a vote of 8:2, the Convention voted to make the executive removeable by the process of impeachment.[78]

"Foreign Influence" Anxiety: Then and Now

That the Founding Fathers were acutely conscious of the dangers of foreign inroads on the operation of the governmental system that they were establishing is well reflected in the debates at Philadelphia in 1787. So pervasive was the fear of foreign influence that its specter was repeatedly reverted to, often to bolster opposite stands on the same issue. More significantly, various key Constitutional provisions were explicitly formulated with the aim of averting (or, at least, minimizing) the dreaded alien intrusions. The President, most prominently, was to be shielded from foreign taint and corruption by a variety of devices: restriction of the office to native born Americans; the complex Electoral-College mode of selection; the overriding of a presidential veto by no less, but also no more, than a two-thirds majority; and the impeachment procedure for removal from office. Likewise, the citizenship requirements for other candidates for elective office were linked to the Founders' felt need to guard against foreign intrigue.

The fact that the Framers were committed to establishing a republican government heightened their concern. In contrast to a monarchy, a republic was assumed to be particularly susceptible to

76 *Ibid.*, pp. 68-69.

77 *Ibid.*, pp. 103-4. While conceding that a power of impeachment was essential, Morris stressed his earlier fear about compromising the executive's independence. "When we make him amenable to Justice however we should take care to provide some mode that will not make him dependent on the Legislature." *Ibid.*, p. 69.

78 *Ibid.*

corruption from foreign sources. This belief was echoed by various delegates at the Convention,[79] and is illustrated in the following remark by Hamilton:

> The Hereditary interest of the King was so interwoven with that of the Nation, and his personal emoluments so great, that he was placed above the danger of being corrupted from abroad . . . . [O]ne of the weak sides of Republics was their being liable to foreign influence & corruption. Men of little character, acquiring great power became easily the tools of intermedling neighbours."[80]

Of course, disquiet over the perils of foreign influence did not end with the Constitutional Convention and the entry into force of the Constitution; it has been echoed and re-echoed throughout the history of the republic. Among the first and strongest cautionary voices was that of George Washington, in his famous Farewell Address to the American people.[81] In ringing passages, oft-cited yet today, he warned that the evil of faction "opens the door to foreign influence and corruption, which find a facilitated access to the government itself through the channels of party passion."[82] He wished to exclude both "permanent, inveterate antipathies against particular nations and passionate attachments for others," believing that such attachments provide "avenues to foreign influence in innumerable ways." "How many opportunities do they afford to tamper with domestic factions, to practice the arts of seduction, to mislead public opinion, to influence or awe the public councils!" he declared.[83] And he entered a strong plea: "Against the insidious wiles of foreign influence (I conjure you to believe me, fellow-citizens) the jealousy of a free people ought to be *constantly* awake, since history and experience prove that foreign influence is one of the most baneful foes of republican government."[84]

79 See remarks of Gouverneur Morris, cited above in text at n. 73.

80 Farrand, *Records*, vol. 1, p. 289. This same line of argument is also repeated by Hamilton in *Federalist*, Nos. 22 and 75.

81 James D. Richardson, *A Compilation of the Messages and Papers of the Presidents* (1902), vol. 1, pp. 213-224.

82 *Ibid.*, p. 219.

83 *Ibid.*, pp. 221-22.

84 *Ibid.*, p. 222. [Emphasis in original.]

The concerns of today with respect to foreign influence surely cannot be equated with those of the Framers and of George Washington at the end of the eighteenth century. Then it was felt necessary to protect the independence of a vulnerable, isolated, United States from the "intrigues" and bribes of powerful trans-Atlantic imperialist powers whose yokes the fledgling republic had so recently shed.[85] In the metamorphosed world of the present *fin de siecle,* the United States finds itself in the position of sole global superpower, a natural target of attempts by trans-Pacific and other aspiring powers to influence American policies, contracts and largesse. The products of those early anxieties — including the constitutional provisions informed so largely by fears of foreign intrigue — remain, of course, relevant even today. But present

85 The early years of the Republic provided several instances in which the British, French, or Spaniards sought to take advantage of American susceptibility with the aim of influencing policy. Two episodes, in particular, illustrate America's exposure to pressures and possible bribe taking.
The first is that of Edmund Randolph in 1795, then serving as Secretary of State in Washington's second administration, and who was suspected by the President of soliciting a bribe from the French minister, Joseph Fauchet. The charge has never been determined with finality, but from all indications, Randolph was guilty of imparting information to Fauchet which the latter could exploit to disrupt the domestic harmony of the United States, and thus affect its international relations, as well. While Randolph was busy advising President Washington to delay his approval of the Jay treaty with Great Britain, he was fomenting trouble for the President by suggesting to Fauchet that money for state officials would encourage them in their defiance of the federal government, then engaged in subduing the Whiskey Rebellion. Fauchet's despatch to Paris summed it up as follows: "Thus with some thousands of dollars the [French] Republic would have decided on civil war [in the United States] or in favor of peace." For a full discussion of the Randolph episode see, Stanley Elkins and Eric McKitrick, *The Age of Federalism; The Early American Republic, 1788-1800* (N.Y.: Oxford, 1993), pp. 393-431.
The second episode, also not free of controversy, is the Burr conspiracy of 1805-6. Aaron Burr, former Vice-President of the United States, in conjunction with General James Wilkinson of the U.S. army and several state officials, is alleged to have conspired with Spanish authorities to detach the western states from the United States. Some thousands of dollars changed hands, but the plot failed miserably. For a short review of this episode see, Marshall Smelser, *The Democratic Republic, 1801-1815* (N.Y.: Harper, 1968), pp. 111-24.

anxieties must be examined and addressed in a manner adapted to the changed circumstances in which the United States now operates, so as to secure the system of government which the Framers established and shield it from disruptive and destructive influences.

PART THREE

The Federal Impulse at Philadelphia

8

The Philosophy of a Dissenting Father: George Mason at the Constitutional Convention of 1787

Three of the delegates present at the close of the Constitutional Convention on 17 September 1787 declined to sign the completed document.[1] One of the three was George Mason, delegate from Virginia. (The other two were fellow Virginian, Governor Edmund Randolph, and Elbridge Gerry from Massachusetts.) Mason, of course, is renowned as the author of the 1776 Virginia Declaration of Rights, the forerunner of the bills of rights in the other state constitutions. But Mason's refusal to sign, coupled with certain remarks he made in the course of the Convention discussions, might be taken as evidence that Mason was opposed to popular government. His remarks were delivered during the Convention debate on devising procedures for electing an executive. The Convention had initially decided to provide for selection by the "National Legislature."[2] Subsequently, Gouverneur Morris of Pennsylvania had moved that the executive be chosen, instead, by "citizens of U.S.,"[3] i.e. by popular election. In support of his proposal Morris had argued that:

> He ought to be elected by the people at large, by the freeholders of the Country . . . If the people should elect they will never fail to prefer

1 See Farrand, *Records*, vol. 2, pp. 631-33.
2 *Ibid*. vol. 1, p. 230; vol. 2, p. 29.
3 *Ibid* vol. 2, pp. 22, 29.

> some man of distinguished character or services; some man . . . of continental reputation.[4]

To this, Mason retorted as follows:

> A Government which is to last ought at least to be practicable. Would this be the case if the proposed election should be left to the people at large . . . it would be as unnatural to refer the choice of a proper character for a Chief Magistrate to the people, as it would, to refer a trial of colours to a blind man. The extent of the Country renders it impossible the people can have the requisite capacity to judge of the respective pretensions of the Candidates.[5]

At a later stage of the debate Mason said:

> It has been proposed that the election [of the executive] should be made by the people at large: that is that an act which ought to be performed by those who know most of Eminent characters & qualifications, should be performed by those who know least.[6]

These remarks would seem to reflect a decidedly elitist, even aristocratic, philosophy of government. They would appear to be quite averse to democratic notions.

Remarkably enough, not one of the three biographers of Mason[7] draws attention to his severely critical comments on the popular election of an executive, nor do any of them attempt to reconcile Mason's remarks with his general liberal philosophy. One of his biographers, Robert Rutland, even goes so far as to assert:

> That "all power is vested in, and consequently derived from the people" moved him [Mason] even to consider supporting popular elections for president, an advanced suggestion that he made no further show of favoring when it grew obvious that most of the convention was appalled by it.[8]

4 *Ibid* p. 29

5 *Ibid.*, p. 31

6 *Ibid.*, p. 119

7 Kate Mason Rowland, *The Life of George Mason, 1725-1792* (N.Y.: Putnam, 1892); Helen Hill Miller, *George Mason: Constitutionalist* (Cambridge, Mass.: Harvard Univ. Press, 1938 and 1966); and Robert A. Rutland, *George Mason: Reluctant Statesman* (Charlottesville, Va.: Dominion, 1961).

8 *George Mason: Reluctant Statesman*, p. 84. See also his "George Mason: The Revolutionist as Conservative," in Ralph A. Rossum and Gary L. McDowell, eds. *The American Founding: Politics, Statesmanship and the Constitution* (Port Washington, N.Y.: National Univ. Publishers, 1981), p. 103.

No one was more appalled by it than Mason himself, as the foregoing extracts make clear. It is true that Mason on one occasion states that he "favors the idea [of popular election of the executive] but thinks it impracticable."[9] However, this remark only makes his subsequent comment comparing popular election to a trial of colors by a blind man even more puzzling and demanding of an explanation. Rutland does not address himself to this question at all.

The present paper, in an effort to elucidate Mason's philosophy of government as revealed at the Constitutional Convention, will seek answers to the following three question: 1) To what extent did Mason's known liberal views project themselves into the Convention debates? 2) How can Mason's liberal views be squared with his comments on popular selection of the executive? 3) Does Mason, notwithstanding his refusal to sign the final document, qualify as a Founding Father?

In order to ascertain Mason's real views on the philosophy of government and to assess the measure of his contribution to the drafting of the Constitution, it is proposed to examine his comments on certain key features of the Constitution as these arose for discussion in the course of the Convention.[10]

Mode of Election of the Members of the Lower House of the Legislature

As one of its first acts, the Convention on 31 May took up for consideration the composition of the lower house of the legislature and the mode of election of its members.[11] The Virginia Plan, which Governor Randolph had two days earlier presented to the

9 Farrand, *Records*, vol. 1 p. 69. On the convention's consideration of procedures for electing an executive see chapter 1, above.

10 George Mason was one of the first delegates to arrive at Philadelphia, 17 May (even before there was a quorum), and he remained to the very final day of the Convention, 17 September. See Farrand, *Records*, vol. 3, pp. 22-28 and vol. 2, pp. 632, 648-49.

11 *Ibid.*, vol. 1, pp. 46, 48.

Convention, provided for popular election of the representatives.[12] This proposal was criticized by several delegates who charged that it allowed too much sway to democracy. Thus, Elbridge Gerry of Massachusetts averred: "The evils we experience flow from the excess of democracy. The people do not want [lack] virtue; but are the dupes of pretended patriots."[13] The same thought was echoed in the remarks of Roger Sherman of Connecticut: "The people . . . should have as little to do as may be about the Government. They want [lack] information and are constantly liable to be misled."[14] The minutes record Mason's response as follows:

> Mr. Mason argued strongly for an election of the larger branch by the people. It was to be the grand depository of the democratic principle of the Govt. It was, so to speak, to be our House of Commons — It ought to know & sympathise with every part of the community; and ought therefore to be taken not only from different parts of the whole republic, but also from different districts of the larger members of it, which had in several instances particularly in Virga., different interests and views arising from difference of produce, of habits &c &. He admitted that we had been too democratic but was afraid we sd. incautiously run into the opposite extreme. We ought to attend to the rights of every class of the people. He had often wondered at the indifference of the superior classes of society to this dictate of humanity & policy, considering that however affluent their circumstances, or elevated their situations, might be, the course of a few years, not only might but certainly would, distribute their posterity throughout the lowest classes of Society. Every selfish motive therefore, every family attachment, ought to recommend such a system of policy as would provide no less carefully for the rights — and happiness of the lowest than of the highest orders of Citizens.[15]

These views were warmly endorsed by James Wilson of Pennsylvania and by James Madison of Virginia and,[16] as a result, the Convention, by a decisive margin, (6:2:2), adopted on 31 May a

12 *Ibid.*, p. 20.
13 *Ibid.*, p. 48.
14 *Ibid.*
15 *Ibid.*, pp. 48-49.
16 Thus, according to Yates, "Virginia supported the resolve, alledging that this ought to be the democratic branch of government, and as such, immediately vested in the people." *Ibid.*, p. 55.

resolution providing for "election of the first branch of the national Legislature by the people."[17]

Despite the overwhelming majority which endorsed this decision, supporters of state sovereignty repeatedly endeavoured to have it reversed. On each occasion Mason spoke out firmly on behalf of a popularly elected lower house. On 6 June Mr. Pinckney of South Carolina moved "that the first branch of the national Legislature be elected by the State Legislatures, and not by the people." Mason objected as follows:[18]

> Under the existing Confederacy, Congs. represent the *States* not the *people* of the States: their acts operate on the *States* not on the individuals. The case will be changed in the new plan of Govt. The people will be represented; they ought therefore to choose the Representatives. The requisites in actual representation are that the Reps. should sympathize with their constituents; shd. think as they think, & feel as they feel; and that for these purposes shd. even be residents among them. Much he sd. had been alledged agst. democratic elections. He admitted that much might be said; but it was to be considered that no Govt. was free from imperfections & evils; and that improper elections in many instances, were inseparable from Republican Govts. But compare these with the advantage of this Form in favor of the rights of the people.[19]

Upon this occasion the Convention by an even greater margin than before (8:3), rejected Pinckney's proposal and confirmed popular election of the lower house.[20]

Barely two weeks later, however, two attempts, on 20 and 21 June, were made to revise this decision. On 20 June, Lansing of New York proposed that the Convention abandon the idea of a bicameral legislature altogether and retain the state-appointed one house Congress of the Articles of Confederation.[21] Mason declared he "did not expect this point would have been reagitated."

17 *Ibid.*, pp. 46, 50.
18 *Ibid.*, pp. 130, 132.
19 *Ibid.*, pp. 133-34. [Emphasis in original.]
20 *Ibid.*, pp. 130, 137-38.
21 *Ibid.*, pp. 334, 336.

> Is it to be thought that the people of America, so watchful over their interests; so jealous of their liberties, will give up their all, will surrender both the sword and the purse, to the same body, and that too not chosen immediately by themselves? They never will. They never ought. Will they trust such a body, with the regulation of their trade, with the regulation of their taxes; with all the other great powers, which are in contemplation?[22]

Lansing's proposal was defeated by a vote of 6:4:1.[23]

On the morrow, 21 June, Pinckney once again revived his proposal for having the state legislatures, rather than the people, choose the members of the lower house of the national legislature.[24] Mason once again condemned the proposal.

> Whatever inconveniency may attend the democratic principle, it must actuate one part of the Govt. It is the only security for the rights of the people.[25]

In Yate's version of the debate Mason's remarks are reported as follows:

> I am for preserving inviolably the democratic branch of the government — True, we have found inconveniences from pure democracies; but if we mean to preserve peace, and real freedom, they must necessarily become a component part of a national government.[26]

By a vote of 4:6:1 the Convention rejected Pinckney's proposal and reconfirmed its earlier stand in favor of a democratically elected lower house.[27]

22 *Ibid.*, pp. 338-39
23 *Ibid.*, pp. 334, 344.
24 *Ibid.*, pp. 353, 358.
25 *Ibid.*, p. 359.
26 *Ibid.*, p. 364. In a similar vein, in discussing the nature of the executive branch of government Mason declared: "Notwithstanding the oppressions & injustice experienced among us from democracy; the genius of the people is in favor of it, and the genius of the people must be consulted." *Ibid.*, p. 101.
27 *Ibid.*, pp. 353, 360.

Qualification of Electors to Lower House

Mason had occasion to demonstrate a liberal viewpoint not only in advocating popular election of the lower house but also in rejecting proposals for a property qualification for exercising the right of suffrage to that chamber.

The revised draft of the constitution reported upon by the Committee of Detail on 6 August provided as follows:

> The members of the House of Representatives shall be chosen every second year, by the people of the several States comprehended within this Union. The qualifications of the electors shall be the same from time to time, as those of the electors in the several States, of the most numerous branch of their own legislatures.[28]

In the debate, Gouverneur Morris moved to strike out the last part of the paragraph so as to limit the right of suffrage to freeholders.[29] Once again, Mason, joined forces with Madison and James Wilson in opposing an anti-democratic proposal.

> Eight or nine States have extended the right of suffrage beyond the freeholders. What will the people there say, if they should be disfranchised . . .
> We all feel too strongly the remains of antient prejudices, and view things too much through a British Medium. A Freehold is the qualification in England, & hence it is imagined to be the only proper one. The true idea in his opinion was that every man having evidence of attachment to & permanent common interest with the Society ought to share in all its rights & privileges. Was this qualification restrained to freeholders? Does no other kind of property but land evidence a common interest in the proprietor? does nothing besides property mark a permanent attachment. Ought the merchant, the monied man, the parent of a number of children whose fortunes are to be pursued in their own <Country>, to be viewed as suspicious characters, and unworthy to be trusted with the common rights of their fellow Citizens.[30]

In the minutes recorded by Rufus King, Mason's remarks are reported as follows:

28 *Ibid.*, vol. 2, p. 178.
29 *Ibid.*, pp. 194, 201.
30 *Ibid.*, pp. 201-3.

> I think every person of full age and who can give evidence of a common Interest with the community shd. be an Elector — under this definition has a Freeholder alone ys [this] common Interest? I think the Father of a Family has this interest — his Children will remain — this is a natural Interest — a Farm & other property is an artificial interest — we are governed by our prejudices in favr. of Engd. — there a Twig, a Turf is the Elector — .[31]

The liberal alliance held firm and Gouverneur Morris's attempt to limit the franchise to freeholders was defeated by a vote of 1:7:1.[32]

Although Mason was opposed to the imposition of property qualifications for the right of suffrage to, or membership in, the lower house, he did, however, advocate a property test for membership in the Senate. "One important object in constituting the Senate," he declared "was to secure the rights of property." He therefore favored "the propriety of annexing to the office a qualification of property."[33] This suggestion reveals that Mason, notwithstanding his liberal views, embraced the then popular notion of "mixed or balanced government" i.e. a government composed of three elements — democracy, aristocracy and monarchy. The lower house would represent democracy; the upper house, aristocracy; and the executive, monarchy. The doctrine was particularly popular with the Convention delegates.[34] Thus, in discussion on the Senate, General Charles C. Pinckney of South Carolina, supported by the venerable Benjamin Franklin, recom-

31 *Ibid.*, pp. 207-8.

32 *Ibid.*, pp. 194, 206.

33 *Ibid.*, vol. 1, pp. 428, 433.

34 See discussion on the term of office for Senators, ibid., pp. 421-34. On the subject of mixed government as reflected in the writings of John Adams, and his influence on constitution making at both the state and federal levels from 1776 to 1787, see Bernard Bailyn, *The Ideological Origins of the American Revolution* (Cambridge, Mass.: Harvard, 1967), pp. 272 ff. and Wood, *Creation*, chaps. 6 and 14. See also the letter from Convention delegate Benjamin Rush to Richard Price on 2 June 1787. "Mr. Adam's book has diffused such excellent principles among us, that there is little doubt of our adopting a vigorous and compounded federal legislature. Our illustrious minister in this gift to his country has done us more service than if he had obtained alliances for us with all the nations of Europe." Farrand, *Records*, vol. 3, p. 33.

mended that no salary be paid to members of the upper house. "as this branch was meant to represent the wealth of the country, it ought to be composed of persons of wealth; and if no allowance was to be made the wealthy alone would undertake the service."[35] Likewise, Pierce Butler of South Carolina declared: "This second branch I consider as the aristocratic part of our government,"[36] It was in this vein that Mason recommended a property qualification for membership in the Senate.

Underlying this approach lay the notion that the aristocracy should be isolated in one part of the legislature to ensure that it would not dominate the popularly elected lower house. Gouverneur Morris expressed this sentiment in the strongest terms.

> The Rich will strive to establish their dominion and enslave the rest. They always did. They always will. The proper security agst. them is to form them into a separate interest. The two forces will then controul each other. Let the rich mix with the poor and in a Commercial Country, they will establish an Oligarchy. . . . By thus combining & setting apart, the aristocratic interest, the popular interest will be combined agst. it. There will be a mutual check and mutual security.[37]

But with all his solicitude for the Senate, Mason remained "jealous" of its aggrandizing tendencies. Albeit sound government required a balancing process, this did not mean that the two parts of the legislature should be on an absolute par. As will be seen in the next section, Mason opposed allowing the Senate an equal voice with the House on money bills. Subsequently, he complained bitterly about the range of powers conferred on the Senate. In listing the factors which prompted him to abjure from signing the Constitution, the dominant role of the Senate, operating independently or in conjunction with the President, was a key consideration.[38]

35 Farrand, *Records*, vol. 1, pp. 426-27.

36 *Ibid.*, p. 434.

37 *Ibid.*, pp. 512-13; see also p. 517. Later Morris said: "There never was, nor ever will be a civilized Society without an Aristocracy. His endeavor was to keep it as much as possible from doing mischief." *Ibid.*, p. 545.

38 See text below, at n. 57 ff.

The Initiation of Money Bills

As part of the Connecticut Compromise which accorded each state an equal vote in the Senate, it was also provided that money bills should originate only in the lower house.[39] The debate on this clause presented a further occasion for Mason, who was a member of the committee which hammered out the Connecticut Compromise, to give voice to what could best be labeled populist views.

> The consideration which weighed with the Committee was that the 1st. branch would be the immediate representatives of the people, the 2d. would not. Should the latter have the power of giving away the peoples money, they might soon forget the Source from whence they received it. We might soon have an aristocracy.[40]

Subsequently, on this same issue, he had the following to say on the Senate.

> An aristocratic body, like the screw in mechanics, workig. its way by slow degrees, and holding fast whatever it gains, should ever be suspected of an encroaching tendency — The purse strings should never be put into its hands.[41]

And, at a later point in the debate,

> The Senate did not represent the *people*, but the *States* in their political character. It was improper therefore that it should tax the people . . . the Senate is not like the H. of Reps. chosen frequently and obliged to return frequently among the people . . . The pursestrings should be in the hands of the Representatives of the people.[42]

Admission of New States

Various delegates, and most prominently Gouverneur Morris, expressed fears that, in accordance wit the principle of equality of representation in the Senate, the new states to be formed out of the western territories would gain power in the legislature out of all

39 Farrand, *Records*, vol. 1, pp. 524-26.
40 *Ibid.*, p. 544.
41 *Ibid.*, p. vol. 2, p. 224.
42 *Ibid.*, pp. 273-74. [Emphasis in original.]

proportion to their wealth. Morris, therefore, recommended that the Atlantic States should be accorded a permanent advantage in representation so that the western states should not be able to overwhelm them.[43] As he put it, "The rule of representation ought to be so fixed as to secure to the Atlantic States a prevalence in the National Councils. . . . If the Western people get the power into their hands they will ruin the Atlantic interests. The Back members are always most averse to the best measures."[44] The suggestion outraged Mason's sense of egalitarianism.

> Strong objections had been drawn from the danger to the Atlantic interests from new Western States. Ought we to sacrifice what we know to be right in itself, lest it should prove favorable to States which are not yet in existence. If the Western States are to be admitted into the Union as they arise, they must, he wd. repeat, be treated as equals, and subjected to no degrading discriminations. They will have the same pride & other passions which we have, and will either not unite with or will speedily revolt from the Union, if they are not in all respects placed on an equal footing with their brethren. It has been said they will be poor, and unable to make equal contributions to the general Treasury. He did not know but that in time they would be both more numerous & more wealthy than their Atlantic brethren.[45]

Gouverneur Morris's suggestion (moved by Mr. Rutledge) to discriminate against the west and provide for representation to be proportionate to both population and wealth was roundly defeated.[46]

Ratification of the Constitution by the States

The Committee of the Whole House, in Resolution 19, recommended that the completed constitution be submitted to Assemblies "to be chosen by the people for the express purpose of ratifying it."[47] In discussion it was proposed by Ellsworth of Connecticut that

43 *Ibid.*, vol. 1, pp. 533-34, 583-84.
44 *Ibid.*, pp. 533, 583.
45 *Ibid.*, pp. 578-79. See also p. 534.
46 *Ibid.*, pp. 525, 534; cf. also pp. 575, 586.
47 *Ibid.*, pp. 232, 237.

this decision be revised to provide for ratification by the state legislatures.[48] Mason was the first to react. He objected strongly:

> Mason considered a reference of the plan to the authority of the people as one of the most important and essential of the Resolutions. The Legislatures have no power to ratify it. They are the mere creatures of the State Constitutions, and cannot be greater than their creators. . . . Whither then must we resort? To the people with whom all power remains that has not been given up in the Constitutions derived from them. It was of great moment he observed that this doctrine should be cherished as the basis of free Government. . . . In some of the States the Govts. were <not> derived from the clear & undisputed authority of the people. This was the case in Virginia. Some of the best & wisest citizens considered the Constitution as established by an assumed authority. A National Constitution derived from such a source would be exposed to the severest criticisms.[49]

Mason's colleagues agreed with him and the proposal to exclude the people from any direct role in the ratification of the Constitution was overwhelmingly defeated (3:7).[50]

Subsequently, a different question arose in relation to the ratification procedure. How many state conventions would have to ratify before the Constitution could enter into force?[51] Some delegates maintained that the unanimous consent of the states was necessary. Others suggested approval by a majority of states having a majority of the population. Still others advocated the consent of ten states. Mason intervened to urge preservation of "ideas familiar to the people. Nine States had been required in all great cases under the Confederation and that number was on that account preferable."[52] His recommendation to adhere to "ideas familiar to the people" was overwhelmingly endorsed by the delegates (8:3).[53]

48 *Ibid.*, vol. 2, pp. 84-85, 88.
49 *Ibid.*, pp. 88-89.
50 *Ibid.*, pp. 84-85, 93.
51 See *ibid.*, pp. 471-72, 475-77.
52 *Ibid.*, pp. 472, 477.
53 *Idem.*

Mason's liberal conviction, of course, did not emerge for the first time in 1787 at Philadelphia. As noted earlier, Mason was the author (in 1776) of the Virginia Declaration of Rights which served as the forerunner of the various Bills of Rights which appeared in the state constitutions, and subsequently in the Federal Constitution.[54] He condemned slavery (notwithstanding the fact the fact that he was a Virginia plantation owner himself) and at the Constitutional Convention vigorously opposed the slave trade.[55] His words ring with the moral tone of a preacher:

> Every master of slaves is born a petty tyrant. They bring the judgment of heaven on a Country. As nations can not be rewarded or punished in the next world they must be in this. By an inevitable chain of causes & effects providence punishes national sins, by national calamities. He lamented that some of our Eastern brethren had from a lust of gain embarked in this nefarious traffic. As to the States being in possession of the Right to import, this was the case with many other rights, now to be properly given up. He held it essential in every point of view, that the Genl. Govt. should have power to prevent the increase of slavery.[56]

Given Mason's enlightened views and, in particular, his support for democratic rights, two things remain to be explained. One is his refusal to sign the completed Constitution and the other, his outburst against popular election of the executive. With regard to his refusal to sign, the brief answer is that in his view the final product was insufficiently democratic. At the close of the proceedings Mason penned a series of "Objections to this Constitution of Government."[57] Fully eight of the fifteen objections could be labelled as "populist." For one thing, the Constitution contained no bill of rights; and since the laws of the "general government" are made paramount to the state constitutions "the Declaration of Rights in the

54 See Rutland, *George Mason*, pp. 49-61.

55 "As early as 1765 he had questioned the practice of slavery both for its economic principle and for its effect on the 'morals and manners of our people'." *Ibid.* p. 53.

56 Farrand, *Records*, vol. 2, p. 370.

57 *Ibid.*, pp. 637-40.

separate States are no security,"[58] There was no declaration "for preserving liberty of the press . . . trial by jury in civil causes nor against the danger of standing armies in time of peace." Congress was free to create monopolies, to "constitute new crimes [and] inflict unusual and severe punishments." Representation in the House of Representatives, even with one to thirty thousand population, rather than the forty thousand originally contemplated, offered only the "shadow" not the "substance" of representation. Such a legislature "can never . . . inspire confidence in the people." Also, it was improper to grant the Senate power to amend money (tax) bills and originate appropriations of money since "they are not the representatives of the people or amenable to them." The close links which tie the Senate to the Executive in such matters as treaty making and appointments, coupled with the fact that the Senate will be "a constantly existing body, almost continually sitting . . . will destroy any balance in the government and enable them to accomplish what usurpations they please upon the rights and liberties of the people." The structure of the Federal Judiciary and the scope of its powers to prevail over state judiciaries will render the law "tedious,, intricate and expensive" and enable "the rich to oppress and ruin the poor." In conclusion, declared Mason:

> This government will set out <commence> a moderate aristocracy: it is at present impossible to foresee whether it will, in its operation, produce a monarchy, or a corrupt tyrannical <oppressive> aristocracy; it will most probably vibrate some years between the two, and then terminate in the one or the other.[59]

58 At the last stages of the Convention Mason strove valiantly to have a bill of rights attached to the Constitution. His remarks on 12 September, five days before the signing ceremony, are reported as follows: "He wished the plan had been prefaced with a Bill of Rights, & would second a motion if made for the purpose — It would give great quiet to the people; and with the aid of the State declarations, a bill might be prepared in a few hours." *Ibid.*, pp. 587-88. Gerry of Massachusetts took up Mason's suggestion and presented a formal proposal for a committee to prepare a Bill of Rights. The matter was dismissed out of hand by a vote of 0:10. *Ibid.*, pp. 582, 588. No doubt, "the impatience which prevailed towards the close of business," noted subsequently by Madison, precluded serious consideration of the suggestion. *Ibid.*, vol. 3, p. 136.

59 *Ibid.*, vol. 2, p. 640 and see also *ibid.*, p. 632.

Whatever else his objections reveal, they demonstrate most clearly that Mason was not opposed to the Constitution because it was excessively democratic, but precisely because it was insufficiently responsive to the wishes of the people. Moreover, in his view, it lacked the safeguards which would preserve the liberties of the people. Since it could not protect them from an overbearing aristocracy, ultimately it would end up as a frightful tyranny. Mason's refusal to sign the Constitution reflected his profound commitment to popular government and his belief, fortunately mistaken, that the 1787 Constitution was not the vehicle for providing such a government for the American people.

This stand makes Mason's condemnation of popular elections for choosing the executive even more puzzling. His comment, that such elections would be the equivalent of a trial of colors for a blind man, would seem to suggest an utter lack of faith in democracy. If, however, Mason's remarks are examined in their context, it becomes quite evident that Mason was not challenging the *right* of the people to choose but rather their *ability* to do so given the size of the electoral district within which they would have to exercise that right. The vast expanse of the United States, the difficulty of communication, and the unfamiliarity of the general populace with national personalities, all militated against an informed choice. In fact, as noted above,[60] Mason had earlier in the debate expressed himself in favor of popular election but considered it "impracticable," for the reasons, no doubt, which he subsequently enumerated by reference to "the extent of the Country."[61]

Republican government, or representative democracy, in the eyes of the generation of the Founding Fathers, as is well recognized, meant a system of government in which the people participate directly, or nearly directly, in the operation of the organs of government. Of necessity, therefore, popular participation, or representative democracy, was feasible only over a small area. The wider the expanse of territory the less acquainted the people would be with the merits or demerits of the respective candidates and the

60 See text above at n. 9.
61 See text above at n. 5.

less capable they would be of making meaningful choices. Inevitably they would be prey to manipulators and schemers. It was in this sense that Mason found fault with nationwide elections of the executive. Essentially, his complaint was that under the circumstances, popular election of the executive would have the trappings of representative democracy but not the essence.

As Cecelia Kenyon has written: "The Anti-Federalist theory of representation was closely allied to the belief that republican government could operate only over a small area. . . . One of the basic fears of the Anti-Federalists [was]: loss of personal, direct contact with and knowledge of their representatives."[62] "The fundamental issue over which Federalists and Anti-Federalists split was the question whether republican government could be extended to embrace a nation, or whether it must be limited to the comparatively small political and geographical units which the separate American states then constituted. The Anti-Federalists took the latter view."[63] And on the indirect mode of electing an executive Kenyon writes:

> This belief that larger electoral districts would inevitably be to the advantage of the well-to-do partially explains the almost complete lack of criticism of the indirect election of the Senate and the President. If the "middling" class could not be expected to compete successfully with the upper class in Congressional elections, still less could they do so in state-wide or nation-wide elections. It was a matter where size was of the essence. True representation . . . could be achieved only where electoral districts were small.[64]

James Wilson, in the Pennsylvania Ratifying Convention, stressed this point in explaining why the Constitutional Convention had not

62 Cecelia M. Kenyon, "Men of Little Faith: The Anti-Federalists on the Nature of Representative Government," *WMQ*, 3d ser., vol. 12 (1955), pp. 10-11. Kenyon cites Mason at the Virginia Ratifying Convention to illustrate this concern. "To make representation real and actual, the number of representatives ought to be adequate; they ought to mix with the people, think as they think, feel as they feel, — ought to be perfectly amenable to them, and thoroughly acquainted with their interest and condition," *Ibid.*, p. 10.

63 *Ibid.*, p. 38.

64 *Ibid.*, p. 13.

instituted nationwide elections for the presidency. "If gentlemen object, that an eighth part of our country forms a district too large for election, how much more would they object, if it was extended to the whole Union! On this subject it was the opinion of a great majority in Convention, that the thing was impracticable."[65] No one in the Antifederalist camp disputed Wilson's claim.

The foregoing review allows us to draw several conclusions about George Mason's role at the Constitutional Convention. Clearly, Mason was not a passive bystander at Philadelphia; his role was substantial and influential. He campaigned vigorously on behalf of his concepts of republican representative government. His stand on popular election to the lower house, his objection to any property test for electors to that house, his insistence that only the popularly elected body be permitted to initiate money bills, and his refusal to tolerate discrimination against the nascent western states — all were confirmed by his fellow delegates. In each case Mason articulated the views accepted by a majority of the Convention. Notwithstanding his failure to sign the completed document, Mason's contribution to the Convention clearly stamps him as a Founding Father of the Constitution.

In presenting his viewpoint Mason consistently espoused an enlightened liberal philosophy of government. As he stated, "the basis of free government" is the "doctrine" that "all power" "remains" with "the people" and constitutions can only be "derived from them" His remarks on representation reflected a strong sense of egalitarianism. Equality of representation meant equality regardless of personal wealth and regardless of geographic location, east or west. Mason's refusal to sign the completed constitution was but a reflection (at least in part) of his deeply held democratic convictions. Mason's belief in popular government also informed his concept of balanced government. Even if the doctrine of mixed government, which Mason in common with so many other

65 Elliot, *Debates in the State Conventions*, vol. 2, p. 511; also in Farrand, *Records*, vol. 3, p. 167.

delegates espoused, called for one part of the legislature to be reserved for the propertied minority, it did not mean that this aristocratic part should dominate. To the contrary — all steps were to be taken to restrict the influence of the aristocratic body and to ensure the responsiveness of the legislature to the wishes of the popular electorate, the sole source of ultimate authority. Mason's views have a remarkably modern, and even "populist," ring to them. Thus, it has justifiably been said of Mason: He "was an outstanding liberal of late eighteenth-century America . . . [who] was far ahead of his time in his democratic social philosophy.[66] This same philosophy prompted Mason's criticism of the proposal to institute popular nationwide elections of the executive. Representation in Mason's view entailed intelligent and informed choice. Democracy could only function in a circumscribed area which allowed the populace to be aware of the merits or faults of the respective candidates. Broadening the electorate to a nationwide choice where no one could be expected to be acquainted with the record or stand of the candidates would distort, rather than fulfill, true democracy. In short, in Mason's view, democracy could not exist without information. Perhaps in this regard he was only anticipating the populist views of a later generation of political philosophers.

66 Alfred H. Kelley and Winfred A Harbison, *The American Constitution: Its Origins and Development* (4th ed; New York: Norton, 1979), p. 120. According to Gordon Wood, "Mason throughout the duration of the Philadelphia Convention acted as the conscience of an old republicanism he thought his Virginia colleagues had forgotten and continually reminded them of what the Revolution had been about." Wood, *Creation*, p. 514.

9

Securing States' Interests at the 1787 Constitutional Convention: A Reassessment

Delegates to the Constitutional Convention of 1787 were convinced that their meeting represented the last great chance to save the Union from dismemberment.[1] By the same token, they recognized that the constitution they were to draft would determine the fate of the states composing the Union. In a letter to Edmund Randolph in advance of the Convention, James Madison highlighted the dichotomous nature of the task confronting the delegates intent on strengthening the national government without eliminating the states as political entities.

> [A]n individual independence of the States, is utterly irreconcileable with the idea of an aggregate sovereignty. I think at the same time

1 See, e.g., the following observations by George Washington, Elbridge Gerry, and Edmund Randolph, respectively:
"That something is necessary, none will deny; for the situation of the general government, if it can be called a government, is shaken to its foundation, and liable to be overturned by every blast. In a word, it is at an end; and, unless a remedy is soon applied, anarchy and confusion, will inevitably ensue." Letter of George Washington to Thomas Jefferson, May 30, 1787. Farrand, *Records*, vol. 3, p. 31.
"The object of this Meeting is very important in my Mind–unless a System of Government is adopted by *Compact, Force* I expect will plant the Standard: for such an anarchy as now exists cannot last long." Letter of Elbridge Gerry to James Monroe, June 11, 1787. *Ibid*., p. 45.
"Are we not on the eve of war, which is only prevented by the hopes from this convention." Opening remarks of Edmund Randolph as recorded by James McHenry of Maryland, May 29, 1787. *Ibid*., vol. 1, p. 26.

> that a consolidation of the States into one simple republic is not less unattainable than it would be inexpedient. Let it be tried then whether any middle ground can be taken which will at once support a due supremacy of the national authority, and leave in force the local authorities so far as they can be subordinately useful.[2]

Clearly, Madison envisaged that the states would have no role or, at most, a very restricted role, in the operation of the national government. They would be confined to attending to strictly local matters. If the Virginia Plan captured Madison's vision of a system of national government unfettered by state interference or control, the New Jersey Plan reflected the view of those delegates intent on preserving a goodly measure of state sovereignty, so as to prevent the larger states from "swallow[ing] up the smaller ones by addition, division, or by impoverishment."[3] Once the Convention opted for the Virginia Plan over the New Jersey Plan, it could be assumed that the smaller states, and any other group promoting states' interests, had very little influence on the ultimate shape of the

2 James Madison to Edmund Randolph, April 8, 1787. Madison, *Papers*, vol. 9, p. 368.

3 Letter of Delaware delegate George Read to his colleague John Dickinson, urging him to hasten his attendance at the Convention. May 21, 1787. Farrand, *Records*, vol. 3, p. 26.
The New Jersey Plan, of course, reflected more than just the demand of the smaller states for equality. Were that all that was involved, the Plan might have consisted of one clause spelling out a demand for a one-house national legislature, with each state having an equal vote. But the Plan also represented a demand for the survival of the states as sovereign political entities in a more decentralized federal system than envisaged by the Virginia Plan. In this sense, the New Jersey Plan was statal, and called for a detailed enumeration of federal powers so that the line of demarcation between national and state authority would be clearly delineated. This explains why delegates of some of the larger states also favored the New Jersey Plan's call for an enumeration of national powers while, on the other hand, some of the smaller states were not averse to voting for the broad Virginia formula on powers, since this subject was not exclusively a small state-large state issue. See, on this topic, the discussion in Andrew C. McLaughlin, *A Constitutional History of the United States* (N.Y.: Appleton-Century-Crofts, 1935), pp. 160-61, and esp. n. 18. See also Michael P. Zuckert, "Federalism and the Founding: Toward a Reinterpretation of the Constitutional Convention," *Review of Politics*, vol. 48 (1986), pp. 166-210, and esp. pp. 169-72.

Constitution. This coincides with scholarly assessment of the impact of the Virginia Plan. As Catherine Drinker Bowen has written: "The fifteen Resolves [of the Virginia Plan] were . . . the core and foundation of the United States Constitution."[4] And in the words of Max Farrand: "These [Resolves] are important, because amended and expanded they were developed step by step until they finally became the constitution of the United States."[5] The one major provision in the Constitution said to reflect a concession to state sovereignty is that providing for equal representation for all states in the upper house of the legislature.[6] The belief that the composition of the Senate represents the solitary significant departure from the Virginia Plan appears to be sustained by the oft-quoted statement of Charles Pinckney during the Convention debate: "[T]he whole comes to this . . . Give N. Jersey an equal vote, and she will dismiss her scruples and concur in the Natil. system."[7]

The purpose of the present paper is to question the facile assumption that the Constitution was a product almost exclusively of the Virginia Plan and to demonstrate that those concerned with states' interests inspired, or at least significantly influenced, the formulation of many more Constitutional provisions than the one dealing with the Senate. Close scrutiny of the Convention debates reveals a complex interplay between the contending interests and groups at Philadelphia and a nuanced response to the need to balance the requirements of the emerging national government with

4 Catherine Drinker Bowen, *Miracle at Philadelphia: The Story of the Constitutional Convention May to September 1787* (Boston: Little, Brown, 1966), p. 18.

5 Farrand, *Framing of Constitution*, p. 68. Clinton Rossiter sums it up tersely: "Elaborated, tightened, amended, and refined . . . the Virginia Plan became the Constitution of the United States." *1787: The Grand Convention* (N.Y.: Norton, 1966), p. 161.

6 See, for example, the discussion in Alfred H. Kelly, Winfred A. Harbison, and Herman Belz, *The American Constitution: Its Origins and Development*, 6th ed. (N.Y.: Norton, 1983), pp. 93-97.
The New Jersey Plan, as is well known, also contributed the supremacy clause to the final Constitution, but this hardly represents a concession to states' interests.

7 Farrand, *Records*, vol. 1, p. 255.

the preservation of state influence. As will be seen, in their dissent from the Virginia Plan, the small states received crucial support, at critical junctures, from the slave states and those devoted generally to preserving state sovereignty.[8] Nearly all spheres of discussion at Philadelphia were permeated by large state-small state differences, and the final document reflected a much more ubiquitous compromise between large and small states, as also between

8 However, care should be taken not to confuse the stand of proponents of the New Jersey Plan, such as William Paterson, with the demand of states' righters Yates and Lansing, who were not prepared to see any significant enhancement of national power at the expense of the states. The two latter fought for retention of the basic principle of the Articles of Confederation, whereby the central government would remain the creature of the states. Once the Convention voted to endorse the Virginia Plan as its working document, they left Philadelphia in protest over the process of "consolidation" which they claimed the Convention was instituting. In contrast, Paterson and his colleagues were prepared to embrace national supremacy but sought to accord the states, and more specifically the smaller states, an effective role in the operation of the national government. They refused to allow the larger states exclusive control of the machinery of government. In this regard, as the present article makes clear, their campaign for an effective voice for the smaller states extended throughout the course of the Convention. See Farrand, *Records*, vol. 3, p. 244.

Herman Belz likewise observes that the smaller states "clearly supported a stronger central authority, but they insisted that institutional changes resulting in a stronger Union should rest on an affirmation of states' rights." He goes on to say: "The New Jersey Plan showed that the basic division in the convention was not between centralizers and localists, but between centralizers like Madison, who at best thought the states might be retained merely as subordinate administrative units, and states'-rights men, who supported both state sovereignty and a stronger central government." Kelly, Harbison and Belz, *The American Constitution*, pp. 95, 96. See also Merrill Jensen, *The Making of the Constitution* (N.Y.: Van Nostrand, 1964), pp. 55, 59. But cf. Warren, *Making of Constitution*, pp. 150-51, for a different view of the nationalist attitude towards the states. See also the more recent study: Lance Banning, *The Sacred Fire of Liberty: James Madison and the Founding of the Federal Republic* (Ithaca, N.Y.: Cornell Univ. Press, 1995), *passim*.

On the subject of American sovereignty, see Akhil Reed Amar, "Of Sovereignty and Federalism," *Yale Law Journal*, vol. 96 (1987), pp. 1425-1520. In the matter of nomenclature, in the present article the term "states' righters" is reserved for Yates and Lansing, in order to distinguish them from proponents of the New Jersey Plan and their allies who are here classified as "supporters of states' interests."

nationalists and those intent on preserving states' interests, than is commonly recognized. In place of Madison's vision of a national government freed from any reliance on the states, the final version of the Constitution accorded the states a significant role and essential involvement in the operation of the national government. Madison's later comment, in *Federalist No. 39*, that the Constitution "is, in strictness, neither a national nor a federal Constitution, but a composition of both" is far closer to the mark than is generally supposed.[9]

Recognition of how the proponents of states' interests influenced the drafting of the Constitution is, of course, highly significant for legal as well as historiographic considerations. From the legal perspective, appreciating the factors which, for instance, brought about an enumeration of the powers of Congress in place of wide open-ended heads of power adds an entirely new dimension to the Tenth Amendment. The current forensic debate over state sovereignty and the scope of federal authority can draw fresh insights from an analysis of the drafting history of various provisions of the Constitution.[10]

Historiographically, a reassessment of the contribution of the smaller states is relevant to the controversy which has persisted ever since members of the Progressive school of historical interpretation of the Constitution — most prominently, Charles Beard — presented their version of the 1787 events at Philadelphia. The basic premise of that school was that the Constitutional Convention was devoted essentially to fashioning a document which would serve to protect the economic interests of an elitist class in society. "From this point of view," Beard postulates, "the old conception of the battle at Philadelphia as a contest between small and large

9 Needless to say, Madison is using the term "federal" to mean a system of government that provides for the participation of the states, in contra-distinction to "national."

10 See *National League of Cities v. Usery*, 426 U.S. 833 (1976), *Garcia v. San Antonio Metropolitan Transit Authority*, 469 U.S. 528 (1985), and the literature they have spawned. See also the more recent cases, *U.S. v. Lopez*, 514 U.S. 549, 115 S. Ct. 1624, 131 L. Ed. 2d 626 (1995). *Alden v. Maine*, 119 S. Ct. 224; 144 L. Ed. 2d 636 (1999).

states — as political entities — will have to be severely modified."[11] Establishing the pervasiveness of the "small state"-"large state" dispute throughout the Convention debates constitutes, therefore, a further source of evidence to refute the already severely challenged economic interpretation of the Philadelphia assembly.

The salience of state influence on the final contents and contours of key constitutional provisions may be discerned by focussing on the following four major issues and their denouement at Philadelphia: federal powers; a federal legislative veto; the advice and consent of the Senate; and the Electoral College.

Federal Powers

Article 6 of the Virginia Plan, as presented by Edmund Randolph to the Convention plenum on May 29, 1787, contained the following provision on the subject of federal power:

> Resolved . . . that the National Legislature ought to be impowered to enjoy the Legislative Rights vested in Congress by the Confederation & moreover to legislate in all cases to which the separate States are incompetent, or in which the harmony of the United States may be interrupted by the exercise of individual Legislation.[12]

Even a cursory glance reveals that this formula of the Virginia Plan confers practically unlimited power on the federal government. Unlike the Articles of Confederation, the provision contains heads of power rather than specified, enumerated, powers. Any subject which the legislature would deem national in scope or impact would justly come within the purview of federal legislation; an individual state would automatically be considered "incompetent" to legislate thereon; and attempted state legislation in such spheres would unquestionably be held to "interrupt" the "harmony of the United States." In effect, the provision would emasculate the power of the states, rendering the federal government all-powerful in any

11 Beard, *Economic Interpretation*, p. 153, n. 1.
12 Farrand, *Records*, vol. 1, p. 21.

matter in which it sought to ensure national uniformity. No sphere of operation would be immune from federal authority.[13]

The Virginia formula of according the national legislature heads of power to legislate where the separate states are "incompetent" or where "the harmony of the United States is affected" was discussed by the Convention no less than three times. On each occasion, the extremely broad formulation of national power provoked critical comment, even from some noted nationalists. The first discussion took place on May 31 in the Committee of the Whole, and the following colloquy ensued:

> Mr. Butler [of South Carolina] apprehended that the taking so many powers out of the hands of the States as was proposed, tended to destroy all that balance {and security} of interests among the States which it was necessary to preserve; and called on Mr. Randolph the mover of the propositions, to explain the extent of his ideas . . .
> Mr. Pinkney & Mr. Rutledge [both from South Carolina] objected to the vagueness of the term *incompetent*, and said they could not well decide how to vote until they should see an exact enumeration of the powers comprehended by this definition.[14]
> Mr. Butler repeated his fears that we were running into an extreme in taking away the powers of the States, and called on Mr. Randolp[h] for the extent of his meaning.
> Mr. Randolph [of Virginia] disclaimed any intention to give indefinite powers to the national Legislature, declaring that he was entirely opposed to such an inroad on the State jurisdictions. and that he did not think any considerations whatever could ever change his determination. His opinion was fixed on this point.[15]

13 "This proposal, had it been allowed to stand, would have given Congress vast authority of a vague and undefined character, inconsistent with the very nature of a federal state." Alfred H. Kelly and Winfred A. Harbison, *The American Constitution: Its Origins and Development*, 3rd ed. (N.Y.: Norton, 1955), p. 143.

14 Farrand, *Records*, vol. 1, pp. 51, 53. The queries of the South Carolina delegates regarding the scope of national powers under the Virginia Plan probably reflected concern about the possibility of national interference in the system of slavery.

15 *Ibid.*, p. 53. Randolph's remarks at this point and in the debate on July 16, noted below, seem strangely at variance with the import of the Virginia Plan's provision on powers. Randolph's biographer, John Reardon, describes the episode as follows: "He [Randolph] found it necessary to reassure . . . the

Mr. Madison said that he had brought with him into the Convention a strong bias in favor of an enumeration and definition of the powers necessary to be exercised by the national Legislature; but had also brought doubts concerning the practicability. His wishes remained unaltered; but his doubts had become stronger. What his opinion might ultimately be he could not yet tell. But he should shrink from nothing which should be found essential to such a form of Govt. as

---

delegates that the Virginia Plan did not, in fact, seek to destroy the power of the states . . . At one point he strongly implied that he considered the preservation of the legitimate power of the states more important than the Union itself, an observation that must have sent a shiver down Madison's spine." *Edmund Randolph: A Biography* (N.Y.: Macmillan, 1975), p. 101. It is possible that in presenting the Virginia Plan, Randolph did not fully appreciate all of its implications. This seems to be the conclusion of Clinton Rossiter, who writes that the Virginia Plan "suggested a government so different from the Confederation in form, scope, and basis that no one could have been fooled — except perhaps the unsuspecting Randolph himself." *The Grand Convention*, p. 169. A letter written by Madison close to the end of his days offers perhaps a more credible explanation: "It was perfectly understood that the [Virginia] propositions committed no one to their precise tenor or form; and that the members of the [Virginia] deputation would be as free in discussing and shaping them as the other members of the Convention." Cited by Warren, *Making of Constitution*, p. 141.

Whatever his considerations, Randolph consistently strove to modify the broad grant of powers proposed. On July 16 he (and George Mason) obviously voted in favor of committing the clause for "a specification of the powers comprised in the general terms." This determined that Virginia's vote would be in the aye column. Farrand, *Records*, vol. 2, pp. 15, 17. Likewise, he (and again Mason) must have swung Virginia's vote in favor of eliminating the legislative veto, although it was an essential part of Resolution 6 on powers. *Ibid.*, pp. 24, 29. And, of course, Randolph served on the Committee of Detail which replaced the Virginia formula on powers with a detailed enumeration. *Ibid.*, pp. 97, 106. That Randolph never considered himself tied to the particulars of the Virginia Plan is also evident from the fact that he campaigned for a plural executive, although a single executive was certainly implicit in the Plan. *Ibid.*, vol. 1, pp. 88, 90, 92. Moreover, by the end of the Convention Randolph was deploring the "indefinite and dangerous" nature of national power and pointing to the "necessary and proper" clause as a reason for refusing to sign the Constitution. Obviously, neither his presentation of the Virginia Plan to the Convention nor his membership in the Committee of Detail that produced the provision on powers deterred him from voicing this objection. *Ibid.*, vol. 2, pp. 563, 631. The Constitution, he charged, threatened to undermine state sovereignty. The "definition of the powers of the Government was so loose as to give it opportunities of usurping all the State powers." *Ibid.*, p. 489.

> would provide for the safety, liberty and happiness of the Community. This being the end of all our deliberations, all the necessary means for attaining it must, however reluctantly, be submitted to.[16]

The vote to grant powers in cases "to which the States are incompetent" was 9 in favor, with none opposed and 1 divided; and the other clause, giving powers "necessary to preserve harmony among the States" was agreed to unanimously.[17] The report of the Committee of the Whole, submitted to the Convention on June 13, endorsed the formulation of Article 6 of the Virginia Plan on powers.[18]

On June 15, William Paterson presented the New Jersey Plan to the Convention.[19] In contrast to the Virginia formula, Paterson's proposal would have granted the federal government only specific supplementary powers "in addition to" those already "vested in the U. States in Congress, by the present existing articles of

16 *Ibid.*, vol. 1, p. 53. William Pierce of Georgia records Madison's remarks as follows:

> Mr. Maddison said he had brought with him a strong prepossession for the defining of the limits and powers of the federal Legislature, but he brought with him some doubts about the practicability of doing it: — at present he was convinced it could not be done. *Ibid.*, p. 60.

Many years later, in 1833, Madison sought to convey the impression that the broad formulation of powers in the Virginia Plan was never intended to be adopted as is. He wrote:

> It can not be supposed that these descriptive phrases were to be left in their indefinite extent to Legislative discretion. A selection & definition of the cases embraced by them was to be the task of the Convention. If there could be any doubt that this was intended, & so understood by the Convention, it would be removed by the course of proceeding on them as recorded, in its Journal. many of the propositions made in the Convention, fall within this remark: being, as is not unusual general in their phrase, but if adopted to be reduced to their proper shape & specification.

Ibid., vol. 3, pp. 526-27. This interpretation does not seem to coincide with the views he expressed at the Convention, as indicated in the text and in Pierce's minutes. Nor does it coincide with the description of the debate on powers he subsequently conveyed to Jefferson, as will be seen below. See text at n. 78. See also Warren, *Making of Constitution*, p. 164. See also below n. 44.

17 Farrand, *Records*, vol. 1, pp. 47, 54.

18 *Ibid.*, pp. 229, 236.

19 *Ibid.*, pp. 242-45.

Confederation." The new powers would authorize "the U. States in Congress" to raise revenue by means of duties and stamp charges, to regulate trade and commerce between the states and with foreign nations, and to enforce requisitions. This format of distinct enumerated powers would reflect and reinforce the federal (as against national) character of the union, since the Congress, under the New Jersey Plan, would, of course, remain the representative organ of the states, with each state wielding one vote therein.[20] On June 19, the Convention was called upon to decide whether it wished to continue discussion on the Virginia Plan or switch to the New Jersey Plan. After a major address by Madison highlighting the latter's inadequacy, the Convention voted, 7 to 3 with one abstention, to continue with the Virginia Plan.[21]

Thereby the Convention signalled its determination to promote a national solution to the problems confronting the Confederation. According to Catherine Drinker Bowen, the vote also confirmed that "the New Jersey Plan was dead, finished. Madison had given it the crowning blow."[22] "The vote to bury the New Jersey Plan was cast," Clinton Rossiter wrote, "and the Convention turned dutifully to a clause-by-clause consideration of the resolutions reported by the committee of the whole."[23] In fact, even if this vote signalled the end of the road for the New Jersey Plan as such, it by no means signalled the end of efforts by states-minded delegates, especially those of the smaller states, to ensure that the provisions of the Constitution would be drafted in a way that would accommodate their views as well. These delegates would make their influence felt for the duration of the discussions, indeed up to the very last day of the Convention.

20 Implicitly, the New Jersey Plan would also have retained the same system of representation that operated under the Articles of Confederation, namely, state delegates subject to recall and whose salaries are covered by the state governments. All this was rejected when the Convention voted in favor of the Virginia Plan.

21 *Ibid.*, pp. 313, 322.

22 Bowen, *Miracle at Philadelphia*, p. 117.

23 *The Grand Convention*, p. 179.

When the provision in the Virginia Plan on the powers of the national legislature came up for reconsideration on July 16, Butler once again rose to object to the sweeping nature of the powers granted.[24] He called for "some explanation of the extent of this [legislative] power; particularly of the word *incompetent*." "The vagueness of the terms," he said, "rendered it impossible for any precise judgment to be formed." In response, Mr. Gorham of Massachusetts sought to allay Butler's fears by explaining that "the vagueness of the terms constitutes the propriety of them. We are now establishing general principles, to be extended hereafter into details which will be precise & explicit."[25] This explanation left Rutledge less than satisfied. If details were to be supplied, he wanted them to be supplied here and now. He "moved that the clause should be committed [to committee,] to the end that a specification of the powers comprised in the general terms, might be reported."[26] But the vote on his motion failed, the delegates being equally divided.[27] Apparently, a considerable number of the delegates were quite content to leave the provision on powers in its present pristine form which offered the greatest scope for federal action.

The tie vote, however, did not quell agitation for greater specification of the national legislature's powers. The very next day, July 17, Roger Sherman of Connecticut "observed that it would be difficult to draw the line between the powers of the Genl. Legislatures, and those to be left with the States; that he did not like the definition contained in the Resolution." He therefore proposed that the following clause be inserted in the provision on powers:

> To make laws binding on the people of the United States in all cases which may concern the common interests of the Union; but not to interfere with the government of the individual States in any matters of internal police which respect the government of such States only,

24 Farrand, *Records*, vol. 2, p. 17. (Emphasis in original).
25 *Ibid*.
26 *Ibid*.
27 *Ibid*.

> and wherein the general welfare of the United States is not concerned.[28]

Sherman's amendment, surprisingly perhaps, was seconded by nationalist James Wilson "as better expressing the general principle."[29] In this vein, he had earlier stressed that "all interference between the general and local Governments should be obviated as much as possible."[30] However, Wilson's nationalist colleague from Pennsylvania, Gouverneur Morris, took exception to the proposed amendment. He found nothing wrong in infringing "the internal police" power of the states when they were guilty of committing "tricks" affecting the "Citizens" of other states, "as in the case of paper money."[31] Mr. Sherman attempted to assuage Gouverneur Morris's concern about national authority by reading "an enumeration of powers, including the power of levying taxes on trade."[32] In response, Morris noted that the power of levying "*direct taxation*" was omitted from Sherman's enumeration. "It must have been the meaning of Mr. Sherman," said Morris, "that the Genl. Govt. should recur to quotas & requisitions, which are subversive of the idea of Govt."[33] Sherman acknowledged that provision would have to be made "for supplying the deficiency of other taxation" but, as yet, "he had not formed any" proposal. While Sherman's amendment evoked a positive response from some delegates, failure to include provision for a national power of direct taxation undermined the wider support necessary for

28 *Ibid.*, p. 25.

29 *Ibid.*, p. 26.

30 *Ibid.*, vol. 1, p. 49. See also the following remarks by Wilson: "By a Natl. Govt. he did not mean one that would swallow up the state Govts. as seemed to be wished by some gentlemen. He thought . . . that they might (not) only subsist but subsist on friendly terms with the former." *Ibid.*, p. 322. "If security is necessary to preserve the one, it is equally so to preserve the other . . . . [L]et us try to designate the powers of each, and then no danger can be apprehended nor can the general government be possessed of any ambitious views to encroach on the state rights." *Ibid.*, p. 363.

31 *Ibid.*, vol. 2, p. 26.

32 *Ibid.*

33 *Ibid.* (emphasis in original).

adoption. As a result, Sherman's proposal was rejected by a vote of 2:8.[34]

Thereupon, Gunning Bedford of Delaware sought to save the first part of Sherman's amendment which linked federal legislation with "the general interests of the Union."[35] This part of the sixth resolution, with the addition in italics, would now read:

> and moreover to legislate *in all cases for the general interests of the Union*, and also in those to which the States are separately incompetent, or in which the harmony of the United States may be interrupted by the exercise of individual legislation.

By omitting the second half of Sherman's proposal, the scope of federal power was expanded, rather than curtailed.[36] Bedford's motion was seconded by Gouverneur Morris, but prompted the following exchange.

> Mr. Randolph. This is a formidable idea indeed. It involves the power of violating all the laws and constitutions of the States, and of intermeddling with their police. The last member [part] of the sentence is {also} superfluous, being included in the first.
> Mr. Bedford. It is not more extensive or formidable than the clause as it stands; *no state* being *separately* competent to legislate for the *general interests* of the Union.[37]

Bedford's formulation of the clause was endorsed by a vote of 6:4, and in this form it was conveyed, a week later on July 24, to the Committee of Detail.[38]

34 *Ibid.*
35 *Ibid.*
36 It may seem strange that Bedford, from the small state of Delaware, should have presented a motion which tended to expand national power — the more so since he had earlier warned the larger states that denial of state equality in at least one branch of the legislature would prompt the smaller states to "find some foreign ally . . . who will take them by the hand and do them justice." *Ibid.*, vol. 1, p. 492. Bedford, however, was apparently not averse to expansion of national power so long as equality was assured. What was needed, from his perspective, was "Enlarging the federal powers not annihilating the federal system." *Ibid.*
37 *Ibid.*, pp. 26-27 (emphasis in original). (Additions in curved brackets are in original; those in square brackets are by author.)
38 *Ibid.*, pp. 85, 95. For the text of the provision as conveyed to the Committee of Detail, see *ibid.*, pp. 131-32.

The debate over the formulation of the powers of the national legislature demonstrated that a considerable segment of the delegates were concerned to define with more precision the powers to be accorded the national government and to delineate the demarcation line between national and state authority. It is noteworthy that among the delegates thus concerned were two members of the nationalist camp, James Wilson of Pennsylvania and Edmund Randolph of Virginia. Their stand assumes particular significance since both men were selected to serve in the five-member Committee of Detail which was charged with preparing the outline of a constitution on the basis of the resolutions adopted.[39] They were joined in committee by two others who had been quite outspoken in their opposition to the broad formulation of the Virginia Plan on powers: John Rutledge of South Carolina, who was to serve as chairman, and Nathaniel Gorham of Massachusetts. The fifth member was Oliver Ellsworth of Connecticut, a principal proponent of the idea of state equality in the upper chamber of the legislature.[40]

Given this constellation of the Committee of Detail, and given the fact that not only the Virginia Resolutions, but the New Jersey and Pinckney Plans were also conveyed to this Committee,[41] it is little wonder that one of its first acts was to revise the wording of the Virginia Plan and enumerate a detailed list of powers which would appertain to the national legislature. In a very early draft of that Committee (found among the papers of George Mason), the Virginia formula was completely abandoned, and in its place there appeared a rudimentary list of powers, subject to exceptions and limitations in various cases.[42] A second draft of the Committee of Detail incorporated, practically verbatim, the clause on powers to be

39 See *ibid.*, pp. 97, 106.
40 See *ibid.*, vol. 1, pp. 193, 201.
41 *Ibid.*, vol. 2, pp. 98, 106.
42 Committee of Detail, IV, *ibid.*, pp. 142-44.

found in the New Jersey Plan, as Farrand notes in an editorial comment.[43]

When the Committee of Detail completed its labor and presented its ultimate formulation to the plenum on August 6, the draft constitution contained a detailed list of federal powers closely resembling the list contained in Article 1, section 8, of the final Constitution.[44] Interestingly, when the draft constitution of the

43 Committee of Detail, VII, *ibid.*, p. 157, n. 15. The very next draft presents an enumeration of powers. *Ibid.*, pp. 167-68. It is not here suggested that the Committee of Detail replaced the Virginia Plan with the New Jersey Plan as its working document. The latter, in any case, only recommended supplementing the list of powers already enumerated in the Articles of Confederation with two further powers. But the Committee did see fit to adopt the pattern of spelling out particular powers rather than heads of powers. Thereby it accepted the recommendation of the New Jersey Plan that the scheme of the Articles be preserved, with additional powers being added to those already enumerated. In this regard, it is perhaps instructive to note what Farrand has said:

> In tracing the work of the committee [of Detail] through its various stages a number of interesting and important things are noticeable. The first of these is that the document which proved to be of the most service to the committee was the articles of confederation . . . The provisions for the powers of congress, the prohibitions placed upon state action, . . . were taken directly from the articles . . . It is not too much to say that the articles of confederation were at the basis of the new constitution.
>
> The next most useful documents were the New Jersey and Pinckney plans. These were used more . . . for the purpose of assistance in wording various sections and clauses.

Framing of Constitution, pp. 127-28.

44 Jack N. Rakove maintains that replacement of the original open-ended formula of the Virginia Plan with a finite list of powers was probably intended from the beginning. *Original Meanings: Politics and Ideas in the Making of the Constitution* (N.Y.: Knopf, 1996), pp. 84 and 178. Lance Banning, going even further, declares categorically that Madison, and the Convention generally, never entertained the thought of leaving the powers of Congress unenumerated. *Sacred Fire of Liberty*, p. 159. In this, he concurs with the conclusion of Zuckert, "Federalism and the Founding," pp. 178-80. As noted, however, this conclusion would seem not to accord with Madison's summation on the subject of powers in his letter to Jefferson, as cited below in text at n. 78. The interpretation presented above in n. 16 coincides with that reached by Irving Brant, *James Madison: Father of the Constitution 1787-1800* (Indianapolis: Bobbs-Merrill, 1950), pp. 35-36. However, Brant does not cite Madison's letter to Jefferson.

Committee of Detail was taken up for debate by the Convention, the radical change effected in defining federal powers evoked no comment. Delegates discussed the details of the provision on powers without commenting on the major change that had been instituted. Clearly, there was a consensus that revision of the clause on powers was warranted.[45] The strong sentiment voiced in the plenum for a detailed enumeration, which had failed only by a tie vote, coupled with overwhelming support therefor in the Committee of Detail, effectively settled the issue for all parties. Nationalists could feel that central power was adequate to attain all national goals, especially with the addition of the necessary and proper clause, while those concerned with state sovereignty justly

45 For a conspiratorial interpretation of the work of the Committee of Detail in this matter, see the note by John C. Hueston, "Altering the Course of the Constitutional Convention: The Role of the Committee of Detail in Establishing the Balance of State and Federal Powers," *Yale Law Journal*, vol. 100 (1990), pp. 765-83. In Hueston's words: "This note suggests that rather than simply elaborating upon the existing resolutions, the Committee actually redefined the constitutional balance of state and federal powers by enhancing the rights of states at the expense of sweeping central powers." *Ibid.*, p. 766. On the basis of his thesis, that the five members of the Committee of Detail "hijacked" the Convention's resolutions to produce a much weaker constitution than was really intended, Hueston reaches the startling conclusion that the final text of the Constitution on state powers should be regarded as only "second choice." "Scholars and judges," he claims, "should redefine intent" in light of this interpretation. The thrust of his argument is precisely the converse of that presented in this paper, that the format of the New Jersey Plan was deliberately adopted by the Committee and endorsed by the Convention out of a strong desire to preserve state sovereignty and as better and more faithfully reflecting the true wishes of the Convention on the division of powers between central and state governments. Hueston, it must be pointed out, completely fails to note that the New Jersey and Pinckney Plans were also conveyed to the Committee of Detail and presumably the Committee was asked to take them also into account in preparing a draft constitution. But above all, as Hueston himself acknowledges, the Committee's Report on powers did not evoke even a murmur of protest from a single member and was solidly confirmed by repeated votes of the Convention for a period of over six weeks. One needs no greater proof that the Committee's formulation of the provision on powers accurately reflected the consensus of the delegates at the Convention and must be regarded as the definitive expression of their will. Any other interpretation flies in the face of the freely expressed decision of the Convention.

felt that they had eliminated the threat of an all-powerful central government whose reach would extend into all spheres of state activity.

The considerations underlying the formulation of the provision on powers are reflected in a letter which Sherman and Ellsworth sent to the Governor of Connecticut upon conclusion of the Convention:

> Some additional powers are vested in congress, which was a principal object that the states had in view in appointing the convention. Those powers extend only to matters respecting the common interests of the union, and are specifically defined, so that the particular states retain their sovereignty in all other matters.[46]

This letter highlights the fundamental purpose for which the Convention assembled: to revise the distribution of powers between the state and national governments so as to substantially enhance the authority of the latter. While this was the acknowledged goal, a considerable number of delegates were obviously intent on ensuring that the federal government, with its newly expanded powers, would not interfere with, or eclipse, the authority of the state governments in their domestic affairs. Apparently, these delegates regarded the Virginia formula as a threat to state sovereignty. The format of the New Jersey Plan, which circumscribed the scope of federal authority even while it increased the number of powers to be granted, was a safer instrument than the Virginia Plan's formula for open-ended heads of power. As has been said: "Enumeration marked another moderate victory for the states' rights bloc."[47] In the view of these delegates, there was no need to become involved in, or to dominate, strictly state affairs. This conclusion emerges more starkly from a consideration of the Convention's handling of the legislative veto.

46 Sept. 26, 1787. Farrand, *Records*, vol. 3, p. 99. Pierce Butler, of South Carolina, in a letter dated Oct. 8, 1787, summed it up as follows: "The powers of the General Government are so defined as not to destroy the Sovereignty of the Individual States." *Ibid.*, p. 103.

47 Kelly and Harbison, *The American Constitution*, p. 143.

Federal Legislative Veto

Resolution 6 of the Virginia Plan, in addition to its clauses on federal power, also contained a provision for a national legislative veto. The clause ran as follows: "To negative all laws passed by the several States, contravening in the opinion of the National Legislature the articles of Union."[48] This legislative veto was derived from an even more ambitious veto scheme formulated by Madison in advance of the Convention.

In a letter to Thomas Jefferson, dated March 19, 1787, Madison referred to "the mortal diseases of the existing constitution" and suggested several key points for inclusion in the proposed new document, including national supremacy and the separation of powers.[49] At the heart of his proposals was a suggestion for a national legislative veto:

> Over & above the positive power of regulating trade and sundry other matters in which uniformity is proper, to arm the federal head with a negative *in all cases whatsoever* on the local Legislatures. Without this defensive power . . . however ample the federal powers may be made, or however Clearly their boundaries may be delineated, on paper, they will be easily and continually baffled by the Legislative sovereignties of the States. The effects of this provision would be not only to guard the national rights and interests against invasion, but also to restrain the States from thwarting and molesting each other, and even from oppressing the minority within themselves by paper money and other unrighteous measures which favor the interest of the majority.[50]

Madison's letter to George Washington of April 16, 1787 contained the following paragraph:

48 Farrand, *Records*. vol. 1, p. 21.

49 Madison, *Papers*, vol. 9, pp. 317-22.

50 *Ibid.*, p. 318 (emphasis in original). Jefferson, it should be noted, objected to the veto proposal. "It fails in an essential character, that the hole & the patch should be commensurate. But this proposes to mend a small hole by covering the whole garment." *Ibid.*, vol. 10, p. 64 (June 20, 1787). In place of a legislative veto, Jefferson suggested a federal judicial veto for controlling unconstitutional state legislation. "Would not an appeal from the state judicatures to a federal court, in all cases where the act of Confederation controuled the question, be as effectual a remedy, & exactly commensurate to the defect."

> "A negative *in all cases whatsoever* on the legislative acts of the States, as heretofore exercised by the Kingly prerogative, appears to me to be absolutely necessary, and to be the least possible encroachment on the State jurisdictions. Without this defensive power, every positive power that can be given on paper will be evaded & defeated. The States will continue to invade the national jurisdiction, to violate treaties and the law of nations & to harass each other with rival and spiteful measures dictated by mistaken views of interest. Another happy effect of this prerogative would be its controul on the internal vicissitudes of State policy; and the aggressions of interested majorities on the rights of minorities and of individuals."[51]

While the notion of a legislative veto originated with Madison, the clause as formulated in the Virginia Plan reflects a significant, if subtle, change from Madison's own version, which prescribed a vastly wider scope of operation. Madison had called for "a negative *in all cases whatsoever* on the legislative acts of the States, as heretofore exercised by the Kingly prerogative." The words emphasized by Madison and his reference to a "Kingly prerogative" indicate that Madison conceived of the veto as an absolute instrument in the hands of the national legislature with which to control the state governments.[52] Clearly enough, the Virginia delegation was not prepared to accept Madison's proposal for an absolute veto; it would go too far. As an alternative, the Virginia delegation proposed that the legislative veto extend only to such state laws as were deemed to be "contravening in the opinion of the National Legislature the articles of the Union."

This emendation of Madison's veto proposal revealed that the delegates to the Constitutional Convention, with all their resolve to tilt the balance of powers between central and state governments in

51 *Ibid.*, vol. 9, pp. 383-84. (Emphasis in original). See also Madison's letter to Randolph, April 8, 1787, *ibid.*, pp. 368-71.

52 During discussion of the legislative veto at the Convention, Madison described its operation as follows: "The negative {on the State laws} proposed, will make it [the national legislature] an essential branch of the State Legislatures." Farrand, *Records*, vol. 1, p. 447. Charles F. Hobson, the author of a pathbreaking article on the subject, has said: "Madison proposed nothing less than an organic union of the general and state governments." "The Negative on State Laws: James Madison, the Constitution, and the Crisis of Republican Government," *WMQ*, 3d ser., vol. 36 (1979), p. 219.

favor of the national government, were not intent on crippling the state governments or of interfering in their purely domestic affairs. So long as state action did not invade the prerogatives of the national government and thereby violate the Articles of the Union, there was no justification for the exercise of a national legislative veto. Underlying the Virginia formulation was the conviction that the expansion of national authority did not require the absolute denial of state sovereignty as envisaged by Madison.

Notwithstanding the setback he had suffered in the Virginia caucus over his proposal for an absolute legislative veto, Madison was not deterred from raising the matter several times in the Convention.[53] On May 31, the limited veto formula of the Virginia Plan was accepted by the Committee of the Whole without "debate or dissent."[54] A week later, on June 8, Charles Pinckney of South Carolina moved that the legislative veto extend to "all Laws which they [members of the national legislature] shd. judge to be improper."[55] "A universality of the power," he said, "was indispensably necessary to render it effectual." "The States must be kept in due subordination to the nation; that if the States were left to act of themselves . . . it wd. be impossible to defend the national prerogatives, however extensive they might be on paper; that the acts of Congress had been defeated by this means." Madison seconded Pinckney's motion.

> [A]n indefinite power to negative legislative acts of the States . . . [was] absolutely necessary to a perfect system. Experience had evinced a constant tendency in the States to encroach on the federal authority; to violate national Treaties, to infringe the rights & interests of each other; to oppress the weaker party within their respective jurisdictions. . . . Should no such precaution be engrafted, the only remedy wd. lie in an appeal to coercion. . . . The negative wd. render

53 Farrand, *Records*, vol. 1, pp. 318, 447; vol. 2, pp. 440, 589.

54 *Ibid*., vol. 1, pp. 47, 54. At the suggestion of Benjamin Franklin, the legislative veto was extended to also cover state laws violating treaties. *Ibid*.

55 *Ibid*., p. 164. In this regard, it might be noted that an outline of what has been described as the Pinckney Plan, submitted to the Convention on May 29, contained the following clause: "No Bill of the Legislature of any State shall become a law till it shall have been laid before S. & H.D. in C. assembled and received their Approbation." *Ibid*., vol. 2, p. 135, and vol. 3, p. 607.

> the use of force unnecessary. The States cd. of themselves then pass no operative act, any more than one branch of a Legislature where there are two branches, can proceed without the other . . . In a word, to recur to the illustrations borrowed from the planetary System. This prerogative of the General Govt. is the great pervading principle that must controul the centrifugal tendency of the States; which, without it, will continually fly out of their proper orbits and destroy the order & harmony of the political system.[56]

The Pinckney-Madison proposal for a comprehensive legislative veto was vigorously attacked. "The Natl. Legislature with such a power," declared Elbridge Gerry of Massachusetts, "may enslave the States. Such an idea as this will never be acceded to."[57] Gunning Bedford of Delaware voiced the fears of the smaller states:

> [He] would refer . . . to the smallness of his own State which may be injured at pleasure without redress. It was meant . . . to strip the small States of their equal right of suffrage. In this case Delaware would have about 1/90 {for its} share in the General Councils, whilst Pa. & Va. would possess 1/3 of the whole. Is there no difference of interests, no rivalship of commerce, of manufactures? Will not these large States crush the small ones whenever they stand in the way of their ambitions or interested views. This shows the impossibility of adopting such a system as that on the table . . . It seems as if Pa. & Va. by the conduct of their deputies wished to provide a system in which they would have an enormous & monstrous influence.[58]

Bedford also raised practical considerations which he considered insuperable. "Are the laws of the States to be suspended in the most urgent cases until they can be sent seven or eight hundred miles, and undergo the deliberations of a body who may be incapable of Judging them? Is the National Legislature too to sit continually in order to revise the laws of the States?"[59] Madison attempted to resolve the practical difficulties by suggesting procedures for implementing the comprehensive negative,[60] but his scheme was

56 *Ibid.*, vol. 1, pp. 164-65.
57 *Ibid.*, pp. 165-66.
58 *Ibid.*, p. 167.
59 *Ibid.*, pp. 167-68.
60 *Ibid.*, p. 168. For the purpose of affirming urgent state legislation, Madison suggested the possibility of "some emanation of the power from the Natl. Govt. into each State so far as to give a temporary assent at least."

dismissed by Mr. Pierce Butler of South Carolina "as cutting off all hope of equal justice to the distant States." "The people there," he was sure, "would not . . . [even] give it a hearing."[61] The suggestion to broaden the national legislative veto was voted down by a 3:7:1 majority.[62] The Report of the Committee of the Whole adhered to the pattern of the Virginia Plan in limiting the legislative veto to instances of unconstitutional state action.[63]

The issue of the national legislative veto was taken up again on July 17, immediately after the question of the composition of the second house was settled. The right of the national legislature to nullify state laws that, in its view, violated the constitution, was vigorously criticized.[64] Gouverneur Morris, a foremost nationalist, opposed the power "as likely to be terrible to the States, and not necessary, if sufficient Legislative authority should be given to the Genl. Government." Roger Sherman of Connecticut "thought it unnecessary, as the Courts of the States would not consider as valid any law contravening the Authority of the Union." Luther Martin of Maryland "considered the power as improper & inadmissable." "Shall all the laws of the States be sent up to the Genl. Legislature before they shall be permitted to operate?" he asked.

This criticism prompted Madison once again to expound on the essentiality of the veto "to the efficacy & security of the Genl. Govt." "A power of negativing the improper laws of the States is at once the most mild & certain means of preserving the harmony of the system." He adverted to the British example where "harmony & subordination of the various parts of the empire" were maintained thanks to "the prerogative by which means the Crown, stifles in the birth every Act of every part tending to discord or encroachment."[65]

As the debate wore on, Gouverneur Morris indicated that he was "more & more opposed to the negative." It would, he declared, "disgust all the States. A law that ought to be negatived will be set

61 *Ibid.*
62 *Ibid.*, pp. 162-63, 168.
63 *Ibid.*, pp. 225, 229.
64 *Ibid.*, vol. 2, pp. 27-28.
65 *Ibid.*

aside in the Judiciary departmt. and if that security should fail; may be repealed by a Nationl. law."[66] The opposition to the legislative veto was sufficiently strong to lead to its complete elimination from the draft constitution by a vote of 7:3.[67] The three states voting in favor of the legislative veto were Massachusetts, Virginia, and North Carolina, all large, or relatively large states. Each of the smaller states voted with the majority to eliminate the legislative veto entirely.

Not surprisingly, with the elimination of any authority qualified to umpire federal-state relations, Luther Martin of Maryland moved the adoption of a supremacy clause binding "the Judiciaries of the several States" to treat federal legislation as "the supreme law of the respective States" "any thing in the respective laws of the individual States to the contrary notwithstanding." Later, the clause was revised to include a reference to the Constitution itself, so as to make it and the laws of the United States "the supreme Law of the Land" — and not merely of the states. This clause, derived, as noted earlier, from the New Jersey Plan, was intended to substitute the court for the legislature in ensuring that national laws were not disregarded by the states (as they had been under the Articles of Confederation) and that in the event of a federal-state clash, the laws of the federal government would take precedence in its area of jurisdiction. The supremacy clause was thus the basis for the judicial review of state legislation, without which, as Justice Holmes declared, "the Union would be imperiled."[68] (In Marbury v. Madison, Chief Justice Marshall, of course, invoked this clause to justify establishing the principle of judicial review over federal legislation as well.)

Even as the Convention was drawing to a close, a last-minute attempt was made to institute some form of national legislative veto. On August 23, Pinckney moved that Congress, by a vote of two-thirds of both houses, be empowered to cancel state laws that interfered "with the general interests and harmony of the Union."

66 *Ibid.*, p. 28.

67 *Ibid.*

68 Oliver W. Holmes, "Law and the Court," *Collected Legal Papers* (N.Y.: Harcourt Brace, 1921), p. 295.

Pinckney stressed that the smaller states would not be disadvantaged by this form of the legislative veto. "The objection drawn from the predominance of the large {States} had been removed by the equality established in the Senate."[69] Wilson supported the proposal "as the key-stone wanted to compleat the wide arch of Government" being raised. "The power of self-defence had been urged as necessary for the State Governments — It was equally necessary for the General Government."[70]

Emphasizing the practical difficulties of administering such a veto, George Mason queried: "Is no road nor bridge to be established without the Sanction of the General Legislature? Is this to sit constantly in order to receive & revise the State Laws?"[71] John Rutledge, Pinckney's fellow delegate from South Carolina who had served as chairman of the Committee of Detail, was apparently outraged by the proposal. "If nothing else, this alone would damn and ought to damn the Constitution," he said, adding: "Will any State ever agree to be bound hand & foot in this manner?".[72] Ellsworth condemned the proposal as possibly implying that "the State Executives should be appointed by the Genl. Government, and have a controul over the State laws."[73] John Langdon of New Hampshire highlighted the matter at issue. It was "resolvable," he said, "into the question whether the extent of the National Constitution was to be judged of by the Genl. or the State Governments."[74] In this, he differed from Roger Sherman of Connecticut who thought the motion "unnecessary; the laws of the General Government being Supreme & paramount to the State laws."[75] Though Pinckney's proposal represented a significant concession to the smaller states by requiring a two-thirds majority in both houses, it failed, by a 5:6 vote, to be sent to committee.[76]

69 Farrand, *Records*, vol. 2, p. 390.
70 *Ibid.*, p. 391.
71 *Ibid.*, p. 390.
72 *Ibid.*, p. 391.
73 *Ibid.* Interestingly enough, Pinckney, in reply, indeed recommended that "State Executives ought to be so appointed." *Ibid.*
74 *Ibid.*
75 *Ibid.*, p. 390.
76 *Ibid.*, pp. 382, 391.

The foregoing review confirms that, while the Convention was determined to establish federal supremacy, it was equally determined to carefully confine this supremacy to the requirements of the Union. These requirements were spelled out in the Constitution in both positive and negative terms — in the enumeration of federal powers in Article 1, Section 8, and in the imposition of prohibitions on the states in Article 1, Section 10. The purpose of both provisions was to restrict federal power to the national sphere while excluding state encroachment on that sphere. Matters deemed inherently national were completely removed from state competence so as to avoid any cause for friction. Thus coinage, for example, was listed as a federal power and was also explicitly denied to the states. At the same time, the Convention deemed ongoing federal involvement in the exclusively internal affairs of the states to be neither warranted nor sanctioned. As summed up by Gouverneur Morris: "Within the State itself a majority must rule, whatever may be the mischief done among themselves."[77]

The debate had underscored the extreme divergence between Madison, who campaigned vigorously for a blanket legislative veto, and the majority, who opposed any legislative role in disallowing state laws, even those deemed manifestly unconstitutional. That task would be handled by the courts, not by the national legislature. State sovereignty was to be preserved even while the Union was strengthened.

The Convention's handling of the entire subject of national powers and a legislative veto is neatly summarized by Madison in his letter of October 24, 1787 to Jefferson:

> The second object, the due partition of power, between the General & local Governments, was perhaps of all, the most nice and difficult. A few contended for an entire abolition of the States; some for indefinite power of Legislation in the Congress, with a negative on the laws of the States: some for such a power without a negative: some for a limited power of legislation, with such a negative: the majority finally for a limited power without the negative.[78]

77 *Ibid.*, p. 439.
78 Madison, *Papers*, vol. 10, p. 209.

Madison, of course, had favored the second proposition: "indefinite power of Legislation in the Congress, with a negative on the laws of the States";[79] but the majority endorsed "limited power without the negative." In short, Madison's scheme for open-ended heads of power for the national legislature, as outlined in the Virginia Plan, was rejected in favor of a list of defined powers carefully enumerated, following the pattern of the Articles of Confederation and the New Jersey Plan. And even the qualified legislative veto of the Virginia Plan was totally abandoned. Federal powers were to be enhanced, but not at the expense of every semblance of state autonomy.

The consequences of abandoning Article 6 of the Virginia Plan in favor of the New Jersey Plan's format on powers were far-reaching and impressive. In place of an all-powerful legislature, the United States received a Congress of limited, defined powers directed strictly to the fulfillment of national needs, with no authority to intervene in state affairs on an ongoing basis or to meddle in strictly state concerns. And the states, rather than being totally submerged and subordinated components of the national government, survived as independent political entities, exercising governmental control at the local level. Perhaps most significantly, the courts emerged as the umpire of federal-state relations. A constitutional system in which Congress would have possessed practically unlimited power and a legislative veto over state legislation would not likely have included, within its compass, the practice of judicial review as we know it — whether in respect of state or federal laws. It is safe to conclude, therefore, that judicial review may be deemed a direct by-product of the replacement of the Virginia Plan's clause on powers with the format of the New Jersey Plan, coupled with the necessary introduction of the supremacy clause, as a natural concomitant of the abandonment of legislative supervision of the federal-state constitutional nexus.

79 For Madison's initial concept of the role of the states in relation to the national government, see his letter to Randolph, cited above in text at n. 2.

Senate Advice and Consent

Two topics are encompassed under this heading: appointments and treaties. Article 2, Section 2, Clause 2 of the Constitution reads:

> He [the President] shall have Power, by and with the Advice and Consent of the Senate, to make Treaties, provided two-thirds of the Senators present concur; and he shall nominate, and by and with the Advice and Consent of the Senate, shall appoint Ambassadors, other public Ministers and Consuls, Judges of the supreme Court, and all other Officers of the United States, whose Appointments are not herein otherwise provided for and which shall be established by Law; but the Congress may by Law vest the Appointment of such inferior Offices, as they think proper, in the President alone, in the Courts of Law, or in the Heads of Departments.

Several facets of this provision call for explanation: 1) why treaties and appointments require the joint operation of two branches of government, both President and Senate "in unique combination,"[80] for entry into force; 2) why the House of Representatives is denied a role with respect to both matters; and 3) why there is a difference in the size of the stipulated Senate majority, with treaties requiring a two-thirds vote and appointments a simple majority.

In order to trace the formulation of the provision at the Constitutional Convention it is first necessary to examine the relevant provision in the Articles of Confederation. Under the Articles, both functions, the treaty power and the power to appoint ambassadors, resided in "the united states in congress assembled." Appointments required a majority vote, while treaties needed the approval of nine out of the thirteen states.[81] The Virginia Plan, presented to the Convention on May 29, made no reference to either treaties or appointments, except for the appointment of judges "by the National Legislature."[82] In effect, then, both matters would

80 Louis Henkin, *Foreign Affairs and the Constitution* (N.Y.: Norton, 1975), p. 127.
81 Art. IX of the Articles of Confederation.
82 Resolution 9, Farrand, *Records*, vol. 1, p. 21.

continue to devolve on the Congress, as under the Articles of Confederation.[83]

In debate, on June 5, Madison objected to the election of judges by the whole legislature "or any numerous body." "Besides the danger of intrigue and partiality," he said, "many of the members were not judges of the requisite qualifications." Nor did he favor lodging the appointment of judges in the executive. "He rather inclined to give it to the Senatorial branch, as numerous eno' to be confided in — as not so numerous as to be governed by the motives of the other branch; and as being sufficiently stable and independent to follow their deliberative judgments."[84] On June 13, Madison's formal proposal for lodging the appointment of judges in the Senate was carried unanimously.[85] At this point, the Senate to which Madison and the Convention referred was that outlined in the Virginia Plan (essentially drafted by Madison) in which representation would be proportional to population, as in the lower house.[86]

The New Jersey Plan, first presented to the plenum on June 15, provided for the appointment of judges to the supreme court by the executive acting alone.[87] This may ring strange in a Plan devoted to

83 See Resolution 6 in Report of the Committee of the Whole on the Virginia Plan on June 13. *Ibid.*, p. 236.
In debate, Madison moved that the executive be empowered "to appoint to offices in cases not otherwise provided for." *Ibid.*, p. 67. His motion was accepted, and the provision appeared in that form in the Report of the Committee of the Whole. *Ibid.*, p. 236.

84 *Ibid.*, p. 120.

85 *Ibid.*, pp. 232-33.

86 At the time, Hamilton made a proposal that was little noticed. (There is no reference to it in Madison's minutes. It is noted only in Pierce's record.) Hamilton suggested that the executive nominate and the Senate have "the right of rejecting or approving" appointments. *Ibid.*, p. 128. When Hamilton, in a major address, presented his own Plan to the Convention on June 18, he proposed that the executive have the power to make all treaties "with the advice and approbation of the Senate"; "to have the sole appointment of the heads or chief officers of the departments of Finance, War, and Foreign Affairs"; and to nominate all other officers, including ambassadors, "subject to the approbation or rejection of the Senate." *Ibid.*, p. 292.

87 *Ibid.*, p. 244. The New Jersey Plan also empowered "the [national] Executives . . . to appoint all federal officers not otherwise provided for."

according the states, and particularly the smaller states, a greater role in the operation of the federal government. However, two things should be borne in mind. First, the New Jersey Plan endorsed a plural executive; and second, the national executive was subject to the control of state executives who could apply to Congress for his removal.[88] Consequently, a restraining feature was built into the appointment process, and there was no need for additional restraint by another branch of government. The New Jersey Plan made no reference to the adoption of treaties, and presumably under its scheme, the power to make treaties would continue to reside in the one-House, state-controlled Congress that operated under the Articles of Confederation.

On June 19, the Convention opted for the Virginia Plan in preference to the New Jersey Plan.[89] This, of course, did not put an end to small-state agitation for equality in at least one house of the national legislature.[90] The matter was only resolved with finality when the Connecticut Compromise was adopted on July 16 granting all states equality in the Senate.[91] The previously adopted formula, according to which the Senate alone made judicial appointments, was now significantly weighted in favor of the smaller states. This fact was not lost on the delegates of the larger states when the judicial appointments provision was once again taken up for debate on July 18.

Randolph was quite candid in noting the objections raised against leaving appointments in the new Senate. "It is true," he said, "that when the appt. of the Judges was vested in the 2d. branch an equality of votes had not been given to it." Nonetheless, he preferred leaving that power in the Senate rather than transferring it to the executive as other delegates desired.[92] Among the latter was James Wilson, who made a formal proposal

88 *Ibid.*
89 *Ibid.*, pp. 313, 322.
90 See, e.g., Forrest McDonald, *Novus Ordo Seclorum: The Intellectual Origins of the Constitution* (Lawrence, Kansas: University Press of Kansas, 1985), pp. 227-33; McLaughlin, *Constitutional History*, pp. 168-76.
91 Farrand, *Records*, vol. 2, pp. 14, 15.
92 *Ibid.*, p. 43.

to that effect.[93] Gunning Bedford of Delaware demurred since "it would put it in his [the executive's] power to gain over the larger States, by gratifying them with a preference of their Citizens."[94] Nathaniel Gorham of Massachusetts submitted a motion to accept the formula practiced in his own state, according to which the executive appointed with the advice and consent of the second branch of the legislature.[95] Neither the Wilson nor Gorham suggestion was accepted by the Convention.[96]

Although Madison had been instrumental in getting the Convention to lodge the appointment power in the Senate exclusively, following the change in circumstances he moved to have that formula revised.[97] His first suggestion was for appointment by the executive "with the concurrence of {1/3 at least} of the 2d. branch." "This," he said, "would unite the advantage of responsibility in the Executive with the security afforded in the 2d. branch agst. any incautious or corrupt nomination." The failure of Gorham's proposal to be accepted led Madison to move that judges be nominated by the executive, which appointments should enter into force unless "disagreed to within — days by 2/3 of the 2d. branch."[98] The negative formulation and stipulation of a high percentage for disapproval would, of course, preclude a veto by the smaller states.

Madison candidly revealed the considerations which led him to make his proposal. "As the 2d. b. was very differently constituted when the appointment of the Judges was formerly referred to it, and was now to be composed of equal votes from all the States, the principle of compromise which had prevailed in other instances required in this that their [sic] shd. be a concurrence of two authorities, in one of which the people, in the other states, should be represented. The Executive Magistrate wd be considered as a

93 *Ibid.*, pp. 37, 41.
94 *Ibid.*, p. 43.
95 *Ibid.*, pp. 38, 41, 44.
96 *Ibid.*, pp. 37, 38, 44.
97 *Ibid.*, pp. 42-43.
98 *Ibid.*, pp. 38, 44.

national officer, acting for and equally sympathising with every part of the U. States."[99]

> If the 2d branch alone should have this power, [of appointment], the Judges might be appointed by a minority of the people, tho' by a majority, of the States, which could not be justified on any principle as their proceedings were to relate to the people, rather than to the States; and as it would moreover throw the appointments entirely into the hands of ye Nthern States, a perpetual ground of jealousy & discontent would be furnished to the Southern States.[100]

Concerned with the implications of the proposal for the status of the states, Elbridge Gerry of Massachusetts objected to Madison's proposal.[101] "The appointment of the Judges like every other part of the Constitution shd. be so modeled as to give satisfaction both to the people and to the States"; but "the mode under consideration will give satisfaction to neither." He also disagreed with the suggestion that a 2/3 vote in the Senate be required to reject a nomination. Thereupon Madison revised his proposal to allow Senate disapproval by simple majority.[102] Even with this revision, however, Madison's motion failed, by a vote of 3:6.[103]

It is noteworthy that the only states favoring Madison's proposal were the three large states — Massachusetts, Pennsylvania, and Virginia. In a separate vote, with the same three large states opposed, the Convention immediately confirmed that judges were to be appointed by the Senate alone.[104] This formula on judicial appointments became part of the clause on Senate powers incorporated in the outline of a constitution prepared by the Committee of Detail. In the meantime, several delegates were becoming alarmed at the inordinate concentration of powers in the Senate. Thus, in a discussion on August 15, George Mason strongly protested the fact that the treaty power was lodged in the Senate alone. "The Senate by means of [a] treaty might alienate territory

99 *Ibid.*, pp. 80-81.
100 *ibid.*, p. 81.
101 *Ibid.*, p. 82.
102 *Ibid.*, pp. 71-72, 82.
103 *Ibid.*, pp. 72, 83.
104 *Ibid.*, pp. 72, 83.

&c. without legislative sanction . . . [It] might by treaty dismember the Union."[105]

On August 23, the Convention took up for consideration the draft provision on Senate powers which read: "The Senate of the United States shall have power to make treaties, and to appoint Ambassadors, and Judges of the supreme Court."[106] Gouverneur Morris argued against Senate appointment of officials. "He considered the body as too numerous for the purpose; as subject to cabal; and as devoid of responsibility."[107] He was supported in this stand by his colleague from Pennsylvania, James Wilson.

Madison spoke out against granting the Senate exclusive control over treaty-making. "The Senate represented the States alone," he said, "and . . . for this as well as other obvious reasons it was proper that the President should be an agent in Treaties."[108] Madison's comment reflected both a more "national" perspective on the foreign affairs power and the dissatisfaction of the larger states with the disproportionate influence the smaller states would now be wielding in the Senate. Hence his suggestion that the President, the only truly national figure in the structure of government, be brought into the picture.

Gouverneur Morris was skeptical about according the Senate any role in treaty-making but, as a minimum, he suggested that no treaty bind the United States unless "ratified by a law."[109] This meant that the House of Representatives, the repository of large-state influence, would be involved in the treaty-making process. The implications of the Morris amendment were spelled out by Mr. Dickinson of Delaware. He "concurred in the amendment, as most safe and proper, tho' he was sensible it was unfavorable to the little States; which would otherwise have an *equal* share in making Treaties."[110] Gouverneur Morris's motion, however, was rejected,

105 *Ibid.*, pp. 297-98.

106 *Ibid.*, pp. 183, 389 n. 8. The Committee of Detail had apparently, on its own, added the appointment of ambassadors to the powers of the Senate.

107 *Ibid.*, p. 389.

108 *Ibid.*, p. 392.

109 *Ibid.*

110 *Ibid.*, p. 393 (emphasis in original).

with only his own state, Pennsylvania, voting in favor.[111] Obviously, the states, and particularly the smaller states, were not disposed to share the foreign-affairs power with the lower house of the national legislature, in which the larger states would exercise predominant influence.[112]

At this point, therefore, the treaty power remained lodged in the Senate exclusively. Madison, however, had reservations regarding this arrangement and "hinted for consideration, whether a distinction might not be made between different sorts of Treaties — Allowing the President and Senate to make Treaties eventual and of Alliance for limited terms — and requiring the concurrence of the whole Legislature in other Treaties."[113] Many delegates were apparently not fully satisfied with the treaty provision as it stood, and the whole draft provision on Senate powers was therefore unanimously conveyed to the Brearley Committee on Postponed Parts.

All draft items not yet finally formulated were referred to this Committee, named after its chairman, and composed of a representative from each state.[114] Both Madison and Gouverneur Morris served on the Committee which introduced significant changes in the draft clause. For one thing, Madison's suggestion for presidential involvement in the treaty-making process was accepted, as was a presidential role in appointments. Senate approval of both treaties and appointments was stipulated, but the Senate was no longer the referent; it was the President. Both by formulation and location — in Article 2 — the powers were confirmed as essentially presidential in nature. And finally, the vote required for Senate approval for treaties was raised to two-

111 *Ibid.*, pp. 382-83, 394. However, the term "and other public ministers" was inserted after the word "ambassadors."

112 No doubt other factors, including the transient nature of House membership resulting from biannual elections, and the larger size of the body, in which secrets would be preserved with difficulty, also militated against giving the House of Representatives a role in the adoption of treaties. See, in this regard, John Jay, *Federalist* No. 64. But the debate makes clear that for the smaller states the crucial factor was the desire to retain the treaty power in the chamber in which they had secured an advantage in terms of representation.

113 Farrand, *Records*, vol. 2, p. 394.

114 *Ibid.*, pp. 473, 481.

thirds. The clause now read: "The President by and with the advice and Consent of the Senate, shall have power to make Treaties; and he shall nominate and by and with the advice and consent of the Senate shall appoint Ambassadors, and other public Ministers, Judges of the Supreme Court, and all other Officers of the U — S — , whose appointments are not otherwise herein provided for. But no Treaty shall be made without the consent of two thirds of the members present."[115] The Committee of Style and Arrangement reformulated the provision, without introducing any substantive change, into its present form in the Constitution.

Clearly, tension between the large and small states contributed significantly to the formulation of the provision on treaties and appointments. As happened in the compromise on the composition of the national legislature, both groups of states gained a measure of control and some of their desiderata; and the small-state gains were significant. The small states strove to have treaties and appointments lodged in the Senate alone, where they had gained a privileged position, while the larger states fought for the involvement of the President, representative of the national will and more beholden to the wishes of the larger states.[116] The House of Representatives was excluded from the whole process, not only

115 *Ibid.*, pp. 495, 498-99. The provision was affirmed in the Convention on September 7, with the word "consuls" being added to the appointments clause. *Ibid.*, pp. 533, 539-40.

116 Arthur Bestor, in a lengthy article, "Respective Roles of Senate and President in the Making and Abrogation of Treaties — The Original Intent of the Framers of the Constitution Historically Examined," *Washington Law Review*, vol. 55 (1979), pp. 1-135, contends that the introduction of the executive into the treaty-making process was only intended to make the President the "agent" of the Senate, not to endow him with independent, initiating, powers in the sphere of foreign relations. Jack N. Rakove takes issue with this assumption both in an article, "Solving a Constitutional Puzzle: The Treatymaking Clause as a Case Study," *Perspectives in American History*, New Series, vol. 1 (1984), pp. 233-81, and in his Pulitzer prize-winning book, *Original Meanings: Politics and Ideas in the Making of the Constitution*, pp. 240-42, 250-51, 266-67. The fact that the treatymaking power was lodged in Article 2, coupled with the comment of Gouverneur Morris in reference to treaties, that the President represented "the general guardian of the National interests," [Farrand, *Records*, vol. 2, pp. 540-41] would seem to confirm that the President was to serve as more than merely a "Senate agent" in this connection.

because it was more numerous, and therefore less guarded in relation to secret matters, but because its involvement would dilute the dominant influence which the smaller states sought to exercise through the Senate.

The remarks of Jonathan Davie in the North Carolina Ratifying Convention testify to the tenacity of the smaller states in these matters. The power of making treaties, he noted, had in all countries been placed in the executive department, and the United States constitution would also have followed this practice. The President, "being elected by the people . . . at large, will have their general interest at heart," he said. However,

> the extreme jealousy of the little states, and between the commercial states and the non-importing states, produced the necessity of giving an equality of suffrage to the Senate. The same causes made it indispensable to give to the senators, as representatives of states, the power of making, or ratifying, treaties . . . The small states would not consent to confederate without an equal voice in the formation of treaties. Without the equality, they apprehended that their interest would be neglected or sacrificed in negotiations. This difficulty could not be got over . . . [Because] of the inflexibility of the little states in this point it . . . became necessary to give them an absolute equality in making treaties . . . The necessity of their interfering in the appointment of officers resulted from the same reason . . . The small states would not agree that the House of Representatives should have a voice in the appointment to offices; and the extreme jealousy of all the states would not give it to the President alone.[117]

Explaining the roots of Senate involvement does not, however, tell the full story. Why was a special majority deemed necessary for approving treaties? The considerations which prompted the Brearley Committee to raise the vote required in the Senate to two-thirds are not readily apparent, since that Committee's deliberations were not preserved, and the Convention itself approved the revised treaty clause "with surprising unanimity and surprisingly little debate."[118] It would seem, however, that sectional interests, that other perennial factor at the Convention, influenced the delegates to raise the vote required for treaties from

117 Elliot, *State Debates*, vol. 4, pp. 119-22.
118 Farrand, *Framing of Constitution*, p. 171.

simple majority to two-thirds.[119] The size of the majority required for Senate advice and consent for treaties became caught up in one of the more famous compromise settlements of the Convention.[120]

Throughout the Convention, the adoption of navigation laws had been made dependent on a qualified majority of two-thirds in Congress.[121] This reflected southern concerns that the north might promote legislation restricting the shipment of goods to American ships, thus disadvantaging the south by making the importation of goods and the exportation of staples more expensive than if a free choice of available ships were allowed.[122] As the end of the Convention approached, north-south differences over the issue of navigation laws[123] and two other issues — the right of the south (really the deep south) to continue the importation of slaves[124] and a ban on export taxes[125] — became the subject of a compromise. In return for abolishing the two-thirds requirement for navigation laws, the north relented on the importation of slaves for a further

119 The background to the two-thirds requirement for treaties is traced in a short article by R. Earl McClendon, "Origin of the Two-Thirds Rule in Senate Action Upon Treaties," *AHR*, vol. 36 (1931), pp. 768-72. The present discussion is based largely on McClendon's note except that McClendon does not discuss navigation laws. See also above, chap. 6, "Congressional-Executive Agreements," pp. 177-87. Strangely enough, neither Bestor nor Rakove cite the McClendon article in discussing the two-thirds requirement for treaties.

120 Andrew C. McLaughlin, *The Confederation and the Constitution, 1783-1789* (N.Y.: MacMillan, 1905), pp. 84-86, 260-62; Farrand, *Framing of Constitution*, pp. 147-52; and Warren, *Making of Constitution*, pp. 579-86.

121 See Committee of Detail, Farrand, *Records*, vol. 2, pp. 169, 183.

122 See Farrand, *Framing of Constitution*, pp. 147-48. Interestingly, during the course of the debate it apparently occurred to George Mason that Senate adoption of treaties by majority vote posed as much danger to the interests of the south as did the adoption of navigation laws by Congress. There was need, therefore, to require a two-thirds vote in both cases. Farrand, *Records*, vol. 4, pp. 52-53. Mason does not seem to have submitted any formal proposal to this effect. It is ironic to note that, in the end, treaties gained the security of a special majority while navigation laws lost it. In the one case, the issue of fisheries was also involved, in the other it was not.

123 See Farrand, *Records*, vol. 2, pp. 374-75.

124 *Ibid.*, pp. 364-65, 369-74.

125 See *ibid.*, pp. 359-64.

twelve (ultimately twenty) years, and all export taxes were banned.[126] In conjunction with that compromise, the majority required for Senate advice and consent for treaties was raised to two-thirds. While navigation laws affected the southern staple states only, the treaty power bore both on the south as well as on the fishing rights of the north. Confirmation for this interpretation of the turn of events is provided by the remarks of George Mason at the Virginia Ratifying Convention:

> Mr. Chairman — With respect to commerce and navigation . . . I will give you, to the best of my recollection, the history of that affair. This business was discussed at Philadelphia for four months, during which time the subject of commerce and navigation was often under consideration; and I assert, that eight states out of twelve, for more than three months, voted for requiring two-thirds of the members present in each House to pass commercial and navigation laws. True it is, that afterwards it was carried by a majority, as it stands. If I am right, there was a great majority for requiring two-thirds of the States in this business, till a compromise took place between the Northern and Southern States; the Northern States agreeing to the temporary importation of slaves, and the Southern States conceding, in return, that navigation and commercial laws should be on the footing on which they now stand . . . The Newfoundland fisheries will require that kind of security which we are now in want of: The Eastern States therefore agreed at length, that treaties should require the consent of two-thirds of the members present in the senate.[127]

Thus, the mutual fear of both east and south regarding possible adverse effects of commercial treaties on their respective interests had prompted raising the vote required for treaties from simple majority to two-thirds.

Attempts by Madison to except peace treaties from the two-thirds requirement and permit their endorsement by simple majority were initially accepted[128] but then rejected, once it became clear to the delegates that peace treaties could serve as a means of the United States conceding shipping, fishing and other rights to foreign

126 *Ibid.*, pp. 396, 400, and see pp. 449-53.

127 Reprinted in Farrand, *Records*, vol. 3, pp. 334-35, and cited in McClendon, "Origin of Two-Thirds Rule," p. 772. See also Warren, *Making of Constitution*, p. 584, for a statement made subsequently by Mason to Jefferson summarizing his remarks at the Virginia Convention.

128 Farrand, *Records*, vol. 2, pp. 533, 540.

countries.[129] The memory of Jay's recent attempt under the Continental Congress to bargain away U.S. rights of passage on the Mississippi to the Spaniards for a period of twenty-five years in return for certain commercial rights that would benefit the north[130] spurred the southern delegates to insist that all treaties, peace treaties included, be made subject to the advice and consent of a two-thirds vote in the Senate.

When the treaty-making clause came up for discussion in the Convention on September 7 and 8, the delegates overwhelmingly rejected two proposals submitted by James Wilson, the Pennsylvania nationalist, to modify the details of the treaty provision. The first would have included the House in the treaty-making process,[131] and the second would have eliminated the two-thirds requirement.[132] Thus, the power to approve treaties remained the

129 See *ibid.*, pp. 534, 543, 544, 547, and 548-49.
Madison also moved to empower two-thirds of the Senate "to make treaties of peace without the concurrence of the President." The President, Madison argued, "would necessarily derive so much power and importance from a state of war that he might be tempted, if authorized, to impede a treaty of peace." *Ibid.*, p. 540. His proposal was seconded by Butler of South Carolina, who "was strenuous for the motion, as a necessary security against ambitious & corrupt Presidents." *Ibid.*, p. 541. The motion was rejected by a vote of 3:8. *Ibid.*, pp. 533, 541.

130 For further discussion of this episode, known as the Jay-Gardoqui negotiations, see Samuel Flagg Bemis, *Pinckney's Treaty* (Baltimore: Johns Hopkins, 1926); Bemis, *A Diplomatic History of the United States*, 5th ed. (N.Y.: Holt, Rinehart and Winston, 1965), pp. 78-80; McLaughlin, *Confederation and Constitution*, pp. 94-101; Frank Monhaghan, *John Jay: Defender of Liberty* (N.Y.: Bobbs-Merrill, 1935), pp. 255-61; Warren, *Making of Constitution*, pp. 24-30; Rakove, "Solving a Constitutional Puzzle," pp. 272-74; and Banning, *Sacred Fire of Liberty*, pp. 66-70.

131 Farrand, *Records*, vol. 2, pp. 532, 538. Wilson contended that the need for secrecy was not sufficient reason to exclude the House from sharing in the treaty-making power. "As treaties . . . are to have the operation of laws, they ought to have the sanction of laws also." In response, Sherman of Connecticut argued that "the necessity of secrecy in the case of treaties forbade a reference of them to the whole Legislature." *Ibid.*, p. 538. The vote was 1:10 with only Pennsylvania, Wilson's own state, voting in favor.

132 "Mr. Wilson thought it objectionable to require the concurrence of 2/3 which puts it in the power of a minority to controul the will of the majority." *Ibid.*, p. 540. Of course, this is precisely what these states wanted to achieve. The vote was 1:9 with one state divided. *Ibid.*, p. 549.

prerogative of the Senate, the bastion of the states, and the two-thirds requirement was sacrosanct, serving as it did to protect sectional interests.

The significance of the Mississippi episode in prompting the south to institute the two-thirds requirement is highlighted by the following account of the Convention discussions given by Hugh Williamson, delegate of North Carolina, in a letter which he subsequently wrote to Madison:

> It is said that some antifed in Maryland on the last Winter fastened on the Ear of Genl Wilkinson who was accidentally there and persuaded him that in case of a new Govt. the Navigation of the Mississippi would infallibly by given up. Your Recollection must certainly enable you to say that there is a Proviso in the new Sistem which was inserted for the express purpose of preventing a majority of the Senate or of the States which is considered as the same thing from giving up the Mississippi. It is provided that two thirds of the Members present in the senate shall be required to concur in making Treaties and if the southern states attend to their Duty, this will imply 2/3 of the States in the Union together with the President, a security rather better than the present 9 States especially as Vermont & the Province of Main may be added to the Eastern Interest and you may recollect that when a Member, Mr. Willson objected to this Proviso, saying that in all Govts. the Majority should govern it was replyed that the Navigation of the Mississippi after what had already happened in Congress was not to be risqued in the Hands of a meer Majority and the Objection was withdrawn.[133]

It might also be noted that consideration of the treaty-making clause in the state ratifying conventions evoked criticism, as Charles Warren has noted, primarily because of the ease with which treaties could be adopted and the vulnerability of critical sectional interests.[134] Several states proposed amendments to tighten the treaty-making procedure. The following draft amendment, submitted by the Virginia Ratifying Convention for adoption by

133 *Ibid.*, vol. 3, pp. 306-7. The letter, dated June 2, 1788, is also quoted in McClendon, "Origin of Two-Thirds Rule," pp. 771-72, and Warren, *Making of Constitution*, pp. 657-58.

134 *Ibid.*, pp. 658 and 773-74.

the first Congress, embraced all the specific interests noted above — commercial interests, territorial rights, fishing, and navigation of the Mississippi. It also called for a qualified majority in *both* Houses in certain instances.

> That no commercial treaty shall be ratified without the concurrence of two-thirds of the whole number of the Members of the Senate; and no treaty, ceding, contracting, restraining or suspending, the territorial rights or claims of the United States, or any of them, or their, or any of their rights or claims to fishing in the American seas, or navigating the American rivers shall be made, but in cases of the most urgent and extreme necessity, nor shall any such treaty be ratified without the concurrence of three fourths of the whole number of the Members of both Houses respectively.[135]

The considerations of the Convention in its drafting of the treaty provision is also noted by President Washington in his message to the House of Representatives in relation to the Jay Treaty.[136] Explaining his refusal to convey the background papers to the House, Washington stressed that the function of advice and consent for treaties had been vested exclusively in the Senate, since in that body large and small states had equal representation. "For, on the equal participation of those powers [of the Senate], the sovereignty and political safety of the smaller States were deemed essentially to depend."[137] A proposal to include the House in the treaty-making process was explicitly rejected by the Convention, Washington noted.

In sum, formulation of the treaty-making clause at the Constitutional Convention proceeded through three stages. With the establishment of the Senate as the repository of state power, the smaller states, intent on ensuring an equal role, restricted the treaty-making power to the Senate, the counterpart of the Congress under the Confederation. For their part, representatives of the larger states, the dissatisfied nationalists, succeeded in reserving for the

135 Elliot, *State Debates*, vol. 3, p. 660. Reproduced in Charles C. Tansill, *Documents Illustrative of the Formation of the Union of the American States* (1927), pp. 1029-30.

136 *Annals of Congress*, vol. 5, p. 760 [1789-1824].

137 *Ibid.*, p. 761.

President — the only truly national figure in government — a central role in the process. Finally, sectional interests, from both the northeast and the south, operated to raise the voting requirement from simple majority to two-thirds. The influence of each of these three groups — small states, nationalists, and sectional interests — is reflected in the composite compromise that was the final product of the Constitutional Convention in its formulation of the treaty-making power.

The Electoral College

The adoption of the electoral college clause at the Convention is a further illustration of the pervasive influence of the smaller states in the drafting of the provisions of the Constitution. For many years it was commonly held, in accordance with Charles Beard's economic interpretation of the Constitution, that the indirect method of choosing a president by means of the Electoral College was a reflection of the Founders' deep distrust of the influence of the masses in the selection of a chief executive.[138] In this sense, the College was regarded as a device invented by the Founding Fathers for insulating the choice of a president from popular pressures. Alternatively, as John Roche explained it, the College was in fact a jerry-rigged contraption devised in a last-minute compromise to enable the delegates to wind up their business and return home.[139] In fact, however, the evidence points more persuasively to the conclusion that the electoral college scheme constituted an ingenious device for satisfying state demands for equality in the selection of a President. This is borne out by tracing the manner in which the Electoral College system evolved at the Constitutional Convention.[140]

Both the Virginia and New Jersey Plans called for election of the executive by the legislature,[141] but the legislature in each case was,

138 Beard, *Economic Interpretation*, pp. 161-62.

139 John P. Roche, "The Founding Fathers: A Reform Caucus in Action," *APSR*, vol. 55 (1961), pp. 799-816, and esp. pp. 810-11.

140 For a more comprehensive analysis of this topic, see above, chap. 1.

141 Farrand, *Records*, vol. 1, pp. 20-22, 242-45.

of course, composed quite differently. As noted earlier, unlike the Virginia Plan's popularly elected congress, the New Jersey Plan's legislature would have remained, as under the Articles of Confederation, the representative body of the states, with each state entitled to one vote. However, lodging the choice of executive in the national legislature, whatever its composition, was problematic. For one thing, it violated the principle of the separation of powers which called for independent means of electing each branch of government. Secondly, there was a danger of the executive conspiring with members of the legislature to ensure his reelection. Consequently, if the choice was to be made by the legislature, the executive would have to be limited to one term of office, preferably a longer one. Thus, initially, when only the Virginia Plan lay before the delegates, the Convention resolved that the executive be elected by the legislature for a lengthy term of seven years and be ineligible for reelection.[142] But this formula was deficient because it eliminated a vital incentive for effective administration, namely, the right to stand for reelection. As Gouverneur Morris said, ineligibility "tended to destroy the great motive to good behavior, the hope of being rewarded by a re-appointment."[143] Consequently, even though the delegates returned time and again to the Virginia formula in their search for a suitable procedure for electing a chief executive, they just as often abandoned this arrangement on the grounds that it penalized a successful executive by barring his reelection.

In the course of the debate, John Dickinson of Delaware moved that the executive be removable "by the National Legislature on the request of a majority of the Legislatures of individual States." "He had no idea of abolishing the State Governments," he said, "as some gentlemen seemed inclined to do . . . He hoped that each State would retain an equal voice at least in one branch of the National Legislature."[144] Madison and Wilson opposed Dickinson's motion

142 *Ibid.*, pp. 68-69, 77-79, 81, 88.
143 *Ibid.*, vol. 2, p. 33.
144 *Ibid.*, vol. 1, p. 85.

on the ground, inter alia, that "it would leave an equality of agency in the small with the great States."[145]

This dialogue foreshadowed the critical debate that would engage the Convention for three weeks over the composition of the upper house in the legislature, ultimately resolved on July 7 with acceptance of the Connecticut Compromise.[146] But the equality granted the states in the upper chamber meant that the smaller states would now exercise a disproportionate influence in the selection of an executive. It is not surprising, therefore, that upon acceptance of the Compromise, representatives of the larger states moved that the choice of executive be moved from the legislature to the public at large. As explained by Wilson, this would "prevent in a great degree" the "intrigue & cabal" that could arise in election by the legislature.[147] Pinckney of South Carolina opposed the motion on the ground that "the most populous States by combining in favor of the same individual will be able to carry their points." Similarly, Sherman of Connecticut feared that the people "will generally vote for some man in their own State and the largest State will have the best chance for the appointment."[148] Obviously, the smaller states were not inclined to accept large-state domination of the choice of executive, any more than they had been prepared to surrender control of the legislature to those states.

Hugh Williamson of North Carolina injected a novel point in stressing that "the largest state will be sure to succede." "This will not be Virga. however. Her slaves will have no suffrage."[149] Williamson was hinting at the voting increment which the slave states presently enjoyed in the lower house as a result of the three-fifths rule. This advantage, based on the number of slaves in a state, only accrued to a state's representation in the legislature; it would have no bearing in a straight-out vote by the white populace in a

145 *Ibid.*, p. 86.
146 *Ibid.*, pp. 242-45, 549-51.
147 *Ibid.*, vol. 2, pp. 22, 29.
148 *Ibid.*, pp. 29-30.
149 *Ibid.*, p. 32.

popular election. In effect, both the small states and slave states preferred to keep the choice in the legislature where each group enjoyed an advantage in one of the two houses.

Madison objected to granting the legislature any role in the selection of an executive since it would "establish an improper connection between the departments," and thus violate the principle of the separation of powers. In his opinion, "the people at large was . . . the fittest in itself." There was, however, "one difficulty of a serious nature attending an immediate choice by the people."

> The right of suffrage was much more diffusive in the Northern than the Southern States; and the latter could have no influence in the election on the score of the Negroes. The substitution of electors obviated this difficulty and seemed on the whole to be liable to the fewest objections.[150]

The use of electors, since states would be graded from 1 to 3 electors, would attenuate the loss which the smaller states and slave states would suffer by moving the choice out of the legislature. The difference between small and large state would be no more than 1:3, rather than the actual population ratio which could be as much as 1:10.

As the work of the convention proceeded, the delegates were still in a quandary about a suitable method for electing a president. This prompted Madison to deliver a lengthy address on the subject. "There are objections agst. every mode that has been, or perhaps can be proposed. The election must be made either by some existing authority under the Natil. or State Constitutions — or by some special authority derived from the people — or by the people themselves." The legislature, he declared, was "liable to insuperable objections." Election by the people, "with all its imperfections," was the method "he liked best." He recognized, however, that there were two serious difficulties with this method. "The first arose from the disposition in the people to prefer a Citizen of their own State, and the disadvantage this wd. throw on the smaller States." The

150 *Ibid.*, pp. 34, 56-57.

second difficulty arose "from the disproportion of {qualified voters} in the N. & S. States, and the disadvantage which this mode would throw on the latter."[151]

Madison's comment highlighted the considerations which would dispose the delegates from the smaller and slave states to oppose conveying the choice to the people in direct elections. Ellsworth confirmed these considerations by stating: "The Citizens of the largest States would invariably prefer the Candidate within the State; and the largest States wd. invariably have the man."[152] It was Williamson who suggested a means of avoiding the preponderant influence of a large state in the selection process. Each person would be required to vote for three candidates, two of whom would be from states other than his own "and as probably of a small as a large one."[153] The idea appealed to Gouverneur Morris and Madison who moved an amendment to Williamson's popular-election proposal, to the effect that each person be required to vote for two candidates, one of whom was to be from a state other than his own. The outcome, Madison said, was that "the second best man in this case would probably be the first, in fact."[154] However, Williamson's proposal (as amended) was defeated by the narrow margin of 5:6.[155]

Thereupon, the Convention, at the suggestion of George Mason, restored the original formula of election by the national legislature for a term of seven years, without right of reelection.[156] Yet this was not the last word. When the convention took up for consideration the steps necessary for putting the government into operation, it became clear that the delegates were still not settled on a definite formula for the selection of an executive.[157] This unresolved issue, together with other like matters, was conveyed to the Brearley Committee on Unfinished Parts for resolution.[158]

151 *Ibid.*, pp. 107-11.
152 *Ibid.*, p. 111.
153 *Ibid.*, p. 113.
154 *Ibid.*, pp. 113-14.
155 *Ibid.*, p. 115.
156 *Ibid.*, p. 120.
157 See above, chap. 1, pp. 29-30.
158 Farrand, *Records*, vol. 2, pp. 480-81.

After four days of deliberation, the Committee presented its solution to the convention — the Electoral College.[159] It was remarkable for having combined the good points of all the proposals that had surfaced on the subject, while overcoming their deficiencies. It removed the choice from Congress and conveyed it instead to a body that, in its composition, was the exact replica of Congress. Each state received the same representation in the Electoral College as it was entitled to in Congress, so that the smaller states and slave states had no cause to object. The independence of the President was assured, and his reelection freed from congressional interference. Since the electors met but once, in their respective state capitals, there was no danger of cabal or corruption.[160] And with each elector voting for two candidates, one of whom had to be from a state other than his own, there was no fear that the larger states would overwhelm the process.[161]

The whole scheme was a reflection of concern for statal influence, as such, and, in particular, for small-state influence. As noted, the advantages which the smaller states and slave states had secured in the real Congress were now faithfully preserved in the

159 *Ibid.*, pp. 493-494, 497-498.

160 The indirect method of electing a President also overcame the objections of other delegates, including George Mason, who maintained that the "extent of the Country" precluded an informed choice by the public at large. "He conceived it would be as unnatural to refer the choice of a proper character for chief Magistrate to the people as it would to refer a trial of colours to a blind man." *Ibid.*, p. 31. Selection of a President by electors appointed by the state legislatures would provide that information which Mason felt was necessary for an informed choice. Mason, it should be noted, was one of the leading liberals at the Convention, and his comment by no means reflected opposition to the spirit of democracy. National elections, he claimed, would in fact be a denial of democracy, since the people could not be expected to be acquainted with the qualifications of the candidates. The Electoral College scheme remedied the deficiency. The popularly elected state legislatures would provide the democratic input, while the use of electors to make the selection would supply the required information.

161 The position of Vice-President resulted, of course, from the need to vote for two candidates.

congress away from home, the Electoral College. Furthermore, electors would be selected as the state legislatures prescribed. This meant that a state legislature could, if it wished, itself select the electors. And the final concessions to state influence were reflected in the contingency arrangements. In the event that no candidate received a majority in the Electoral College, the Senate — in the final version, the House of Representatives, voting as states — would make the choice from the top five. The designation of top five was deliberately designed to offer greater opportunity to a candidate from a smaller state to be selected.[162] And the requirement that voting in the House take place by state, rather than by individual Representatives, meant that the last word, and not merely the first, was reserved for the states in the selection of a chief executive for the United States.

The evolution of the electoral college system at Philadelphia revealed how tenacious the smaller states were in securing an effective role for themselves in the process to be instituted for choosing a President. They not only demanded a say in the choice but insisted on a system which would enable a candidate from a smaller state to realistically compete for the office of President. The Electoral College was assuredly an ingenious device for satisfying state demands for equality in the selection of a President.

States' Interests and their Constitutional Imprint Redux

The preceding analysis of four critical issues at the Constitutional Convention demonstrates the degree to which the three groups — the smaller states, the slave states, and those intent generally on securing states' interests at Philadelphia — contributed directly to the formulation of key parts of the Constitution. In the twin matters of powers and representation, pro-state forces played a major role in the drafting of the various provisions. The enumeration of federal

162 When George Mason moved that the choice be made from the top three rather than the top five, the smaller states objected, and Sherman said he "would sooner give up the plan." *Ibid.*, p. 514.

powers, the elimination of a national legislative veto, the advice and consent of the Senate to treaties and appointments, and the creation of the Electoral College — all reflected the determination of states-minded delegates to ensure a role for the states in the operation of the national government.

These delegates opposed every attempt to engulf the states in a tidal wave of national authority. Thus they worked to eliminate the legislative veto and insisted that the powers of Congress be defined and enumerated. These steps helped preserve state sovereignty but were deemed inadequate by the smaller states and their allies, who demanded a voice also in the actual running of the national government. This they attained through lodgement of the appointment and treaty powers in the Senate, the repository of state influence in the national legislature. Furthermore, the procedure for choosing a chief executive was designed to accord the smaller states and the slave states a disproportionate say in the selection process and to enhance the prospect that one of their own candidates would succeed in being chosen.

The emphasis on state interests in the formulation of the provisions of the Constitution highlighted the truism underlying the Tenth Amendment — that "all is retained which has not been surrendered" — even before the Amendment was adopted.[163] Additionally, a most important by-product of the states' struggle for equality was the appointment of the court as the designated umpire of federal-state differences in interpreting and applying the Constitution. This, in turn, led to the evolution of judicial review, whereby the courts assumed the power to declare even the actions of co-ordinate branches of the federal government unconstitutional.

Given the pervasiveness of state demands at Philadelphia, it is quite clear that Pinckney's assertion that conceding state equality in the Senate would put an end to small-state discontent was quite inaccurate.[164] In fact, every provision became a fresh battleground for establishing a statal interest, and therewith the interests particularly of the smaller states, in the functioning of the federal

163 See *United States v. Darby*, 312 U.S. 100, 124 (1941).
164 See text accompanying note 7, above.

government. The Virginia Plan, it is true, furnished the basic blueprint upon which every change and every revision was recorded, but the contribution of states-minded delegates to the ultimate shape of the Constitution was far from negligible. As Senator Jonathan Dayton, who had served in the Constitutional Convention as a delegate from New Jersey, subsequently said, with perhaps a slight measure of exaggeration: "Look through that instrument from beginning to end, and you will not find an article which is not founded on the presumption of a clashing of interests."[165]

165 Farrand, *Records*, vol. 3, p. 400.

Select Bibliography: Charles Beard and the Constitution

Books and Pamphlets

Abraham, Henry J. *Justices, Presidents and Senators*. Lanham, Md.: Rownan & Littlefield, 1999.

Ames, Herman V. *The Proposed Amendments to the Constitution of the United States during the First Century of Its History*. Washington, D.C.: American Historical Association, 1897.

Bailyn, Bernard. *The Ideological Origins of the American Revolution*. Cambridge, Mass.: Harvard Univ. Press, 1967, 1992.

——, ed. *The Debate on the Constitution: Federalist and Antifederalist Speeches, Articles, and Letters during the Struggle over Ratification*. 2 vols. N.Y.: Library of America, 1999.

Bancroft, George. *History of the Formation of the Constitution of the United States*. 2 vols. N.Y.: Appleton, 1882.

Banning, Lance. *The Sacred Fire of Liberty: James Madison and the Founding of the Federal Republic*. Ithaca, N.Y.: Cornell Univ. Press, 1995.

Beale, Howard K., ed. *Charles A. Beard: An Appraisal*. Lexington, Ky.: Univ. of Kentucky Press, 1954.

Beard, Charles. *The Supreme Court and the Constitution*. N.Y.: Macmillan, 1912.

——. *An Economic Interpretation of the Constitution of the United States*. N.Y.: Macmillan, 1913, 1935.

——. *The Economic Origins of Jeffersonian Democracy*. N.Y.: Macmillan, 1915.

——. *The Economic Basis of Politics*. N.Y.: Knopf, 1922

Beeman, Richard, Botein, Stephen, and Carter, Edward C. II., eds. *Beyond Confederation: Origins of the Constitution and American National Identity*. Chapel Hill, N.C.: Univ. of North Carolina Press, 1987.

Belz, Herman, Hoffman, Ronald, and Albert, Peter J., eds. *To Form a More Perfect Union: The Critical Ideas of the Constitution*. Charlottesville, Va.: Univ. of Virginia Press, 1991.

Benson, Lee. *Turner and Beard: American Historical Writing Reconsidered.* N.Y.: Free Press, 1960.

Bernstein, Richard B. with Rice, Kym S. *Are We to be a Nation? The Constitutional Convention of 1787.* Cambridge, Mass.: Harvard Univ. Press, 1987.

Billias, George Athan. *Elbridge Gerry: Founding Father and Republican Statesman.* N.Y.: McGraw-Hill, 1976.

Blinkoff, Maurice. *The Influence of Charles A. Beard upon American Historiography.* Univ. of Buffalo Studies 12, Monographs in History, vol. 4 (1936).

Bowen, Catherine Drinker. *Miracle at Philadelphia: The Story of the Constitutional Convention May to September 1787.* Boston: Little Brown, 1966.

Brant, Irving. *James Madison: Father of the Constitution 1787-1800.* Indianapolis: Bobbs-Merrill, 1950.

Brown, Robert E. *Charles Beard and the Constitution: A Critical Analysis of an Economic Interpretation of the Constitution.* Princeton: Princeton Univ. Press, 1956.

Burns, James MacGregor. *The Deadlock of Democracy.* Englewood Cliffs, N.J.: Prentice-Hall, 1963.

Crosskey, William W. *Politics and the Constitution.* 2 vols. Chicago: Univ. of Chicago Press, 1953.

Dahl, Robert A. *A Preface to Democratic Theory.* Chicago: Univ. of Chicago Press, 1956.

——. *Pluralist Democracy in the United States: Conflict and Consent.* Chicago: Rand McNally, 1967.

Eidelberg, Paul. *The Philosophy of the American Constitution.* N.Y.: Free Press, 1968.

Elliot, Jonathan, ed. *The Debates in the Several State Conventions on the Adoption of the Federal Constitution.* 5 vols. Philadelphia: Lippincott, 1881.

Farrand, Max, ed. *The Records of the Constitutional Convention of 1787.* 4 vols., rev. ed. New Haven: Yale Univ. Press, 1937.

——. *The Framing of the Constitution of the United States.* New Haven: Yale Univ. Press, 1913.

Ferguson, E. James. *The Power of the Purse: A History of American Public Finance.* Chapel Hill, N.C.: Univ. of North Carolina Press, 1961.

Fisher, Louis. *President and Congress: Power and Policy.* N.Y.: Free Press, 1972.

Fiske, John. *The Critical Period of American History, 1783-1789.* Boston: Houghton Mifflin, 1899.

Goldwin, Robert A., ed. *A Nation of States.* Chicago: Rand McNally, 1963.

Goldwin, Robert A. and Schambra, William A. eds. *How Democratic is the Constitution?* Washington, D.C.: American Enterprise Institute, 1980.

——. eds. *How Federal is the Constitution?* Washington, D.C.: American Enterprise Institute, 1982.

Greene, Jack P., ed. *The Reinterpretation of the American Revolution, 1763-1789*. N.Y.: Harper & Row, 1968.

Gummere, Richard M. *The American Colonial Mind and the Classical Tradition: Essays in Comparative Culture*. Cambridge, Mass.: Harvard Univ. Press, 1963.

Handlin, Oscar and Handlin, Lilian. *Liberty in America*. vol. 2. N.Y.: Harper & Row, 1989.

Henkin, Louis. *Foreign Affairs and the Constitution*. N.Y.: Norton, 1975.

Hofstadter, Richard. *The Progressive Historians: Turner, Beard, Parrington*. N.Y.: Knopf, 1968.

Howard, A. E. Dick. *The United States Constitution: Roots, Rights and Responsibilities*. Washington, D.C.: Smithsonian, 1990

Jensen, Merrill. *The New Nation: A History of the United States During the Confederation, 1781-1789*. N.Y.: Knopf, 1950.

Jensen, Merrill, Kaminski, John P., and Saladino, Gaspare J., eds. *Documentary History of the Ratification of the Constitution*. 18 vols.– Madison, Wisc.: State Historical Society of Wisconsin, 1976 –.

Kammen, Michael. *A Machine That Would Go of Itself: The Constitution in American Culture*. N.Y.: Random House, 1986.

Kelly, Alfred H., and Harbison, Winfred A. *The American Constitution: Its Origins and Development*. 4th ed. N.Y.: Norton, 1970.

Kelly, Alfred H., Harbison, Winfred A., and Belz, Herman. *The American Constitution: Its Origins and Development*. 6th ed. N.Y.: Norton, 1983.

Kenyon, Cecelia, ed. *The Antifederalist*. Indianapolis: Bobbs-Merrill, 1966.

Lerner, Max. *Ideas Are Weapons: The History and Uses of Ideas*. N.Y.: Viking, 1939.

Levy, Leonard W., ed. *Essays on the Making of the Constitution*. N.Y.: Oxford Univ. Press, 1969.

Levy, Leonard W., and Mahoney, Dennis J., eds. *The Framing and Ratification of the Constitution*. N.Y.: Macmillan, 1987.

McDonald, Forrest. *We the People: The Economic Origins of the Constitution*. Chicago: Univ. of Chicago Press, 1958.

——. *Novus Ordo Seclorum: The Intellectual Origins of the Constitution*. Lawrence, Kansas: Univ. Press of Kansas, 1985.

McLaughlin, Andrew C. *The Confederation and the Constitution, 1783-1789*. N.Y.: Macmillan, 1905.

——. *A Constitutional History of the United States*. N.Y.: Appleton-Century-Crofts, 1935.

McCaughey, Elizabeth P. *Government by Choice: Inventing the United States Constitution*. N.Y.: Basic Books, 1987.

Madison, James. *The Papers of James Madison*, Robert Rutland *et al.*, eds. 17 vols.– Chicago: Univ. of Chicago Press, 1975–.

Main, Jackson Turner. *The Antifederalist: Critics of the Constitution, 1781-1788.* Chapel Hill, N.C.: Univ. of North Carolina Press, 1961.

Marx, Karl and Engels, Friedrich. *Manifesto of the Communist Party*. N.Y.: International Publishers, 1948.

Mason, Alpheus T. *The States Rights Debate: Antifederalism and the Constitution.* Englewood Cliffs, N.J.: Prentice-Hall, 1964.

Morgan, Edmund S. *The Birth of the Republic, 1763-89*. Chicago: Univ. of Chicago Press, 1956.

——. *Inventing the People: The Rise of Popular Sovereignty in England and America.* N.Y.: Norton, 1988.

Morris, Richard B. *The Forging of the Union, 1781-1789*. N.Y.: Harper & Row, 1987.

Murphy, William P. *The Triumph of Nationalism,: State Sovereignty, the Founding Fathers, and the Making of the Constitution*. Chicago: Univ. of Chicago Press, 1967.

Nedelsky, Jennifer. *Private Property and the Limits of American Constitutionalism: The Madisonian Framework and Its Legacy*. Chicago: Univ. of Chicago Press, 1990.

Nore, Ellen. *Charles A. Beard*. Carbondale, Ill: Southern Illinois Univ. Press, 1983.

Poore, Benjamin, ed. *The Federal and State Constitutions, Colonial Charters and other Organic Laws of the United States*. 2 vols. Washington, D.C.: Govt. Printing Office, 1870.

Rakove, Jack N. *The Beginnings of National Politics: An Interpretive History of the Continental Congress*. Baltimore: Johns Hopkins Univ. Press, 1979.

——. *Original Meanings: Politics and Ideas in the Making of the Constitution*. N.Y.: Knopf, 1996.

Rossiter, Clinton. *1787: The Grand Convention*. N.Y.: Macmillan, 1966.

Rutland, Robert A. *The Ordeal of the Constitution: The Antifederalists and the Ratification Struggle of 1787-1788*. Norman, Okla.: Univ. of Oklahoma Press, 1966.

Schattschneider, E. E. *Party Government*. N.Y.: Rinehart, 1942.

Schuyler, Robert L. *The Constitution of the United States*. N.Y.: Macmillan, 1923.

Seligman, Edwin. *The Economic Interpretation of History*. N.Y.: Columbia Univ. Press, 1902.

Slonim, Shlomo, ed. *The Constitutional Bases of Political and Social Change in the United States*. N.Y.: Praeger, 1990.

Smith, J. Allen. *The Spirit of American Government: A Study of the Constitution: Its Origin, Influence and Relation to Democracy*. N.Y.: Macmillan, 1907.

Storing, Herbert J., ed. *The Complete Anti-Federalist*. 7 vols. Chicago: Univ. of Chicago Press, 1981.

Tansill, Charles C., ed. *Documents Illustrative of the Formation of the Union of the American States*. Washington, D.C.: Govt. Printing Office, 1927.

Thach, Charles C. *The Creation of the Presidency, 1775-1789: A Study in Constitutional History*. Baltimore: Johns Hopkins Univ. Press, 1923.

Tomlins, Christopher L. *Law, Labor and Ideology in the Early American Republic*. N.Y.: Cambridge Univ. Press, 1993.

Van Doren, Carl. *The Great Rehearsal: The Story of he Making and Ratifying of the Constitution of the United States*. N.Y.: Viking Press, 1948.

Warren, Charles. *The Supreme Court in United States History*. 2 vols., rev. ed. Boston: Little Brown, 1926.

——. *Making of the Constitution*. Boston: Little Brown, 1928.

Washington, George. *The Writings of George Washington*. John C. Fitzpatrick, ed. 39 vols. Washington, D.C.: Govt. Printing Office, 1931-1944.

White, Morton G. *Social Thought in America: The Revolt Against Formalism*. N.Y.: Viking, 1949.

Wood, Gordon S. *The Creation of the American Republic, 1776-1787*. Chapel Hill: Univ. of North Carolina Press, 1969.

——. *The Making of the Constitution*. Waco, Texas: Baylor Univ. Press, 1987.

——. *The Radicalism of the American Revolution*. N.Y.: Knopf, 1992.

Wright, Benjamin F. *Consensus and Continuity, 1776-1787*. Boston: Boston Univ. Press, 1958.

Articles

Adair, Douglass. "The Tenth Federalist Revisited," *WMQ*, 3d ser., vol. 8 (1951), pp. 48-67.

——. "That Politics May be Reduced to a Science: David Hume, James Madison and the Tenth *Federalist*," *Huntington Library Quarterly*, vol. 20 (1957), pp. 343-60.

——. "Experience Must be Our Only Guide: History, Democratic Theory, and the United States Constitution." In Ray Allen Billington, *The Reinterpretation of Early American History*. N.Y.: Norton, 1968, pp. 129-50.

Amar, Akhil Reed. "Of Sovereignty and Federalism," *Yale Law Journal*, vol. 96 (1987), pp. 1425-1520.

Berns, Walter. "Does the Constitution 'Secure These Rights'?," in Goldwin and Schambra, *How Democratic is the Constitution?*, pp. 59-78.

Appleby, Joyce. "The American Heritage: The Heirs and the Disinherited," *JAH*, vol. 74 (1987), pp. 798-813.

Belz, Herman. "Constitutionalism and the American Founding." In Levy and Mahoney, *The Framing and Ratification of the Constitution*, pp. 333-54.

Bloch, Ruth H. "The Constitution and Culture," *WMQ*, 3d. ser., vol. 44 (1987), pp. 550-55.

Commager, Henry S. "The Constitution: Was It an Economic Document?" *American Heritage*, vol. 10 (1958), pp. 58-61, 100-3.

Corwin, Edward S. "An Answer to the Economic Interpretation," *History Teachers Magazine*, vol. 5 (1914), pp. 65 ff.

Countryman, Edward. "Of Republicanism, Capitalism, and the 'American Mind,'" *WMQ*, 3d ser., vol. 44 (1987), pp. 556-62.

Diamond, Martin. "What the Framers Meant by Federalism." In Goldwin, *A Nation of States*, pp. 24-41.

Diamond, Ann Stuart. "Decent, Even Though Democratic." In Goldwin and Schambra, *How Democratic is the Constitution?*, pp. 18-38.

Diggins, John Patrick. "Power and Authority in American History: The Case of Charles A. Beard and His Critics," *AHR*, vol. 86 (1981), pp. 701-30.

——. "Between Bailyn and Beard: The Perspectives of Gordon S. Wood," *WMQ*, 3d ser., vol. 44 (1987), pp. 563-68.

Dry, Murray P. "The Case Against Ratification: Anti-Federalist Constitutional Thought." In Levy and Mahoney, *The Framing and Ratification of the Constitution*, pp. 271-91.

Elazar, Daniel. "Our Thoroughly Federal Constitution." In Goldwin and Schambra, eds., *How Federal Is the Constitution?* pp. 38-66.

Elkins, Stanley and McKitrick, Eric. "The Founding Fathers: Young Men of the Revolution," *PSQ*, vol. 76 (1961), pp. 181-216.

Farrand, Max. "Compromises of the Constitution," *AHR*, vol. 9 (1904), pp. 470-89.

Hobson, Charles F. "The Negative on State Laws: James Madison, the Constitution, and the Crisis of Republican Government," *WMQ*, 3d ser., vol. 36 (1979), pp. 215-35.

Howe, John. "Gordon S. Wood and the Analysis of Political Culture in the American Revolutionary Era," *ibid.*, vol. 44 (1987), pp. 569-75.

Hueston, John C. "Altering the Course of the Constitutional Convention: The Role of the Committee of Detail in Establishing the Balance of State and Federal Powers," *Yale Law Journal*, vol. 100 (1990), pp. 765-83.

Hutson, James H. "Robert Yates' Notes on the Constitutional Convention of 1787: Citizen Genet's Edition," *Quarterly Journal of the Library of Congress*, vol. 35 (1978), pp. 173-82.

——. "Country, Court and Constitution: Antifederalism and the Historians," *WMQ*, 3d ser., vol. 38 (1981), pp. 337-68.

——. "Riddles of the Federal Constitutional Convention," *WMQ*, 3d ser., vol. 44 (1987), pp. 411-23.

——. "The Constitution: An Economic Document?" In Levy and Mahoney, *The Framing and Ratification of the Constitution*, pp. 259-70.

Kenyon, Cecelia M. "Men of Little Faith: The Anti-Federalists on the Nature of Representative Government," *WMQ*, 3d ser., vol. 12 (1955), pp. 3-43.

——. "An Economic Interpretation of the Constitution After Fifty Years," *Centennial Review*, vol. 7 (1963), pp. 327-52.

Ketcham, Ralph. "Publius: Sustaining the Republican Principle," *WMQ*, 3d. ser., vol. 44 (1987), pp. 576-82.

Kramnick, Isaac. "The 'Great National Discussion': The Discourse in Politics in 1787," *ibid.*, vol. 45 (1988), pp. 3-32.

Kristol, Irving. "American History and the Democratic Idea," *American Scholar*, vol. 39 (1969-70), pp. 89-104.

Lutz, Donald S. "Bernard Bailyn, Gordon S. Wood, and Whig Political Theory," *Political Science Reviewer*, vol. 7 (1977), pp. 111-42.

——. "The First American Constitutions." In Levy and Mahoney, *The Framing and Ratification of the Constitution*, pp. 69-81.

McCorkle, Pope. "The Historian as Intellectual: Charles Beard and the Constitution Reconsidered," *American Journal of Legal History*, vol. 28 (1951-52), pp. 314-63.

McClendon, R. Earl. "Origin of the Two-Thirds Rule in Senate Action Upon Treaties," *AHR*, vol. 36 (1931), pp. 768-72.

McDonald, Forrest. "Rebuttal to Jackson Turner Main's Critical Review of *We the People*," *WMQ*, 3d. ser., vol. 17 (1961), pp. 102-10.

——. "The Anti-Federalists, 1781-1789," *Wisconsin Magazine of History*, 1963, pp. 46, 206-14.

Maier, Pauline. "A Pearl in a Gnarled Shell: Gordon S. Wood's *The Creation of the American Republic* Reconsidered," *WMQ*, 3d. ser., vol. 44 (1987), pp. 583-90.

Main, Jackson Turner. "Charles A. Beard and the Constitution: A Critical Review of Forrest McDonald's, *We the People*," *ibid.*, vol. 17 (1961), pp. 86-110;

Murrin, John M. "Gordon S. Wood and the Search for Liberal America," *ibid.*, vol. 44 (1987), pp. 597-601.

Nash, Gary B. "Also There at the Creation: Going Beyond Gordon S. Wood," *ibid.*, pp. 602-11.

Nelson, William E. "Reason and Compromise in the Establishment of the Federal Constitution, 1787-1801," *ibid.*, pp. 458-484.

Onuf, Peter S. "State Politics and the Ideological Transformation: Gordon S. Wood's Republican Revolution," *ibid.*, pp. 612-16.

——. "Reflections on the Founding: Constitutional Historiography in Bicentennial Perspective," *ibid.*, vol. 46 (1989), pp. 341-75.

Parenti, Michael. "The Constitution as an Elitist Document." In Goldwin and Schambra, *How Democratic is the Constitution?*, pp. 39-58.

Pole, J. R. "Historians and the Problem of Early American Democracy," *AHR*, vol. 67 (1962), pp. 626-46.

Rakove, Jack N. "The Great Compromise: Ideas, Interests, and the Politics of Constitution Making," *WMQ*, 3d. ser., vol. 44 (1987), pp. 424-57.

——. "Gordon S. Wood,'The Republican Synthesis,'and the Path Not Taken," *ibid.*, pp. 617-22.

Roche, John P. "The Founding Fathers: A Reform Caucus in Action," *APSR*, vol. 55 (1961), pp. 799-816.

Rogow, Arnold A. "The Federal Convention: Madison and Yates," *AHR*, vol. 60 (1954-55), pp. 323-35.

Schmitt, Gary J. and Webking, Robert H. "Revolutionaries, Antifederalists, and Federalists: Comments on Gordon Wood's Understanding of the American Founding," *Political Science Reviewer*, vol. 9 (1979), pp. 195-229.

Schuyler, Robert L. "Forrest McDonald's Critique of the Beard Thesis," *Journal of Southern History*, vol. 28 (1961), pp. 73-80.

Thomas, Robert E. "A Reappraisal of Charles A. Beard's *An Economic Interpretation of the Constitution of the United States*," *AHR*, vol. 57 (1951-52), pp. 370-75.

Tushnet, Mark V. "The Constitution as an Economic Document," *George Washington Law Review*, vol. 56 (1987), pp. 106-13.

Wills, Gary. "Taking Ourselves out of a Fight," *WMQ*, 3d. ser., vol. 44 (1987), pp. 623-27.

Wolfe, Christopher. "On Understanding the Constitutional Convention of 1787," *Journal of Politics*, vol. 39 (1977), pp. 97-118.

Wood, Gordon S. "Democracy and the Constitution." In Goldwin and Schambra, *How Democratic is the Constitution?*, pp. 1-17.

——. "Interests and Disinterestedness in the Making of the Constitution." In Richard Beeman, *et al.*, *Beyond Confederation*, pp. 69-109.

——. "Ideology and the Origins of Liberal America," *WMQ*, 3d. ser., vol. 44 (1987), pp. 628-40.

——. "The Founding Fathers and the Constitution as a Vehicle for Change." In Slonim, *Constitutional Bases*, pp. 15-22.

Young, Alfred F. "Conservatives, the Constitution, and the 'Spirit of Accommodation.'" In Goldwin and Schambra, *How Democratic is the Constitution?*, pp. 117-47.

Zuckerman, Michael. "Charles Beard and the Constitution: The Uses of Enchantment," *George Washington Law Review*, vol. 56 (1987), pp. 81-105.

Zuckert, Michael P. "Federalism and the Founding," *Review of Politics*, vol. 48 (1986), pp. 166-210.

Index

Major Concepts in Politics and Political Theory

This series invites book manuscripts and proposals on major concepts in politics and political theory—justice, equality, virtue, rights, citizenship, power, sovereignty, property, liberty, etc.—in prominent traditions, periods, and thinkers.

Send manuscripts or proposals, with author's vitae to:

Garrett Ward Sheldon
General Editor
Clinch Valley College
of the University of Virginia
College Avenue
Wise, VA 24293

To order other books in this series, please contact our Customer Service Department:

(800) 770-LANG (within the U.S.)
(212) 647-7706 (outside the U.S.)
(212) 647-7707 FAX

Or browse online by series at:

www.peterlang.com